Second Edition

Travel Sales and Customer Service

Roberta Schwartz, CTC
Debra J. MacNeill, CTC
and the Staff of the
Institute of Certified Travel Agents

Institute of Certified Travel Agents

Brief Contents

Contents

Contents

CUNARD
LINE LIMITED

A Letter from ICTA's Chairman

Dear Future Travel Professional,

First, let me congratulate you on your sound decision to build career opportunities for yourself through education. As you study this new edition of *Travel Sales and Customer Service,* I am confident you will learn many skills and concepts that will help you on the path to a successful and fulfilling travel industry career.

Travel Sales and Customer Service, second edition, is not an abstract, difficult to comprehend textbook. It is a practical and easy-to-follow learning tool that will show you clearly and simply how to sell travel. Today, sales and customer service skills are more highly valued than ever in all segments of this important and intriguing international industry.

In addition to textbooks designed for use in college and school travel and tourism courses, ICTA also offers continuing professional education opportunities that will be valuable to you in the future. These include the Destination Specialist courses and ICTA's certification process offering two levels of recognition for experienced travel professionals, the Certified Travel Associate (CTA), and the Certified Travel Counselor (CTC).

Over the years ICTA has been very important in my professional career. I received my CTC designation in 1982. Today, I credit ICTA with helping me forge a career path and a focus for my professional life.

Again, congratulations on your wise decision to invest in education. I wish you much success in your travel industry career.

Sincerely,

Larry Pimentel, CTC
Chairman
Institute of Certified Travel Agents

Larry Pimentel, CTC
President and CEO

CORPORATE OFFICES
Miami, Florida
San Francisco, California

UNITED KINGDOM
London
Southampton

GERMANY
Hamburg

ASIA/PACIFIC
Sydney

NORWAY
Oslo

6100 BLUE LAGOON DRIVE • SUITE 400 • MIAMI, FLORIDA 33126
☎ (305) 463-3000 • 📠 (305) 463-3010 • WEBSITES: www.cunardline.com • www.seabourn.com

SEABOURN — **CUNARD**

Preface

In response to the crucial need for travel professionals to have strong sales and customer service skills, the Institute of Certified Travel Agents (ICTA)—the travel industry's only organization devoted exclusively to education—published the first edition of *Travel Sales and Customer Service* nearly five years ago. We are confident you will find this second edition to be even more authoritative, thorough, practical, and technologically current than the first edition.

Purpose and Method

This book is designed to help travel and tourism students prepare for a successful career selling travel. Each chapter introduces students to issues confronting salespeople in the travel industry—from common misperceptions about selling to strategies for managing time to on-line selling. Through the book's nine chapters, we present the key skills that salespeople need in order to be successful.

These necessary skills involve more than the ability to handle specific sales situations. In an increasingly competitive marketplace, travel professionals also need an understanding of the broader sales environment. Thus, we have incorporated coverage of basic marketing principles throughout the text, and we discuss customer service as an integral part of the selling process. For example, Chapter 1 introduces the four *P*s of the marketing mix (product, place, price, and promotion); Chapter 2 discusses ways of segmenting the travel market; Chapter 7 is devoted to customer service; and every chapter includes a case related to service. In essence, this book presents selling and service within the context of the total marketing effort.

Abstract knowledge alone, of course, will not create successful travel sellers. To help students apply the concepts and master the techniques discussed, we include numerous sample sales dialogues, examples and cases within the body of the text, and in each chapter a boxed "Selling through Service" case that provides a window into the everyday challenges of serving travel buyers. In Chapters 2-6, these boxed cases take students step by step through the problem-solving process. Furthermore, the Chapter ending Wrap-Ups provide numerous exercises and worksheets that encourage students to practice techniques and develop their selling and customer service skills.

New Coverage and Features

To keep pace with the dynamic travel industry, the text has been thoroughly updated throughout. For example, home-based offices, service fees, and selling over the Web are all discussed. It features new tables and figures, a simplified organization, and new coverage of many key topics, including careers in selling travel and how to

- Handle objections.
- Close a sale.
- Use the tools of the modern office—from voice mail to e-mail.
- Maintain professionalism—in terms of dress, etiquette, and dealing with ethical issues.

Chapter 6, for example, provides expanded coverage of how to sell over the phone, as well as new coverage of the Web and other computer technology. Chapter 9 offers a new discussion of current trends in the travel industry.

In addition, the book's features have been refined. The objectives that open each chapter are now numbered. More sample sales dialogues and role-playing exercises provide students the opportunity to apply the concepts and techniques presented throughout the text.

Organization

The text has been developed and organized with the needs of both the student and the instructor firmly in mind. The material can be covered within the time constraints of various course configurations.

The book begins with a brief overview of basic marketing concepts and an introduction to steps in selling and problem solving; it ends with guidelines to help students develop a plan for continuing their professional development. Each of the book's nine chapters provides students with an opportunity to learn and to practice skills that will enhance their sales proficiency.

- In Part One, Getting Ready for the Sale, the chapters help students to understand the role of the salesperson, to appreciate what motivates buyers, and to learn how to keep informed about travel products.
- Part Two, The Selling Process, examines sales situations in depth. These chapters take students through the sales cycle step by step, describing techniques for getting and giving information and exploring the challenges of using the phone, the Web, and other technology in selling.
- In Part Three, Strategies for Sales and Marketing Success, the chapters go beyond the presentation of specific selling skills to examine broader topics that concern travel professionals. These chapters examine the relationship between selling and customer service; review the essential elements of professionalism, including dealing with stress and ethical issues; and how travel sellers can continue their professional development and thrive in the twenty-first century.

Learning Aids

An extensive set of features is provided to help students master concepts and apply them cre-

atively. Because learning is often facilitated by previewing material, each chapter begins with a numbered list of objectives and a brief preview of the chapter. Within the chapter, major topics are indicated by the headings, and key terms are highlighted in boldface italic when they are introduced. (These terms are then listed in the Chapter Wrap-Up and included in the Glossary.)

Students should also find learning easier if they review and rehearse material periodically by using the interim summaries. These summaries take two forms: the Time Out exercises and the Tips boxes, which review key points.

In addition, the Chapter Wrap-Up at the end of each chapter offers a built-in study guide to the chapter. First, the Chapter Highlights section summarizes each chapter through a brief numbered review correlated to the numbered chapter-opening objectives. New terms are then listed. Next, Review Exercises reinforce the objectives and move from reviewing concepts to applying them. These exercises include

- The Check-Up section, which is a brief set of true-false questions that allows students to check their mastery of key concepts.
- Discussion Questions, which ask students not only to demonstrate their knowledge of concepts discussed in the chapter but also to develop their own strategies applying that knowledge.
- Questions related to the Selling through Service case.
- Role-playing exercises.

Thus, each Chapter Wrap-Up provides opportunities to review facts, apply concepts, and practice skills, both individually and in groups.

The Instructor's Resource Manual

Instructors can use the Instructor's Resource Manual accompanying this text to help plan effective lectures and reinforce teaching strategy. This teaching aid provides an overview of the text, concrete teaching suggestions and sample syllabi, a text outline, answers to text exercises that do not appear in the text, and transparency masters. The Manual also includes supplementary exercises to expand classroom discussion.

Acknowledgements

We gratefully acknowledge the following educators and industry executives who provided detailed evaluations of the draft manuscript for the second edition of *Travel Sales and Customer Service*. Their assistance was invaluable.

Christopher DeSessa, CTC—Johnson and Wales University
Mimi Gough—Casco Bay College
Beth O'Donnell, CTC—Edmonds Community College
Mary Beth Walsh, CTC—Moraine Valley Community College
Barbara A. Will, CTC—Rasmussen College
Scott Ahlsmith, CTC—TRAMS
David Tossell, CTC—API Travel Consultants

Additionally, we thank the many educators who offered constructive suggestions which helped us plan the first edition of the text and also those who assisted with the development of the second edition.

Toby Bell—International Business College
Nancy Birkett, CTC—American Institute of Commerce
Ruth Delach, CTC—The Boyd School
B.J. Flaherty, CTC—AIC Junior College
Robert Gandolfo—MTI College
Renee Jedlicka—Iowa Lakes Community College
Nancy Kist, CTC—The Boyd School
Clare Lagiewski—Champlain College
John Lindsay, CTC—Highline Community College
Pat Merrill, CTC—Salt Lake Community College
Joan Minnich—International Air Academy
Sandra Robeson—Heritage College
Conee Sousa—Kinyon-Campbell Business School
Susan VanWinkle—Milwaukee Area Technical College

About ICTA

The Institute of Certified Travel Agents (ICTA) is an international nonprofit organization that provides educational services, textbooks, and learning materials for students and travel industry members at all career stages. Founded in 1964 to enhance the quality of professional practice in the travel industry, ICTA's goal is to encourage the pursuit of excellence through education. Though ICTA has expanded since 1964, our mission—professionalism through education—remains the same.

We invite you to contact us to learn more about the Institute's publications and programs.

Institute of Certified Travel Agents
148 Linden Street
P.O. Box 812059
Wellesley, MA 02482-0012
Telephone: 781-237-0280
Fax: 781-237-3860
Web site: www.icta.com

Getting Ready for the Sale

Sales and Service in the Travel Industry

Objectives

After reading this chapter, you should be able to

1. Identify five key decisions involved in marketing travel.
2. Outline the eight steps of the sales cycle.
3. Describe the role of the salesperson in the travel industry.
4. Explain two key ways in which selling travel differs from other types of selling.
5. Outline the role of service in the sales process.
6. Name seven steps to take to solve a problem.

Preview

Today's travel industry is very competitive. To attract and keep customers, travel businesses need good salespeople. In other words, they need people who can identify and respond to the needs of customers and provide them with good service.

In this chapter we provide an overview of the job of travel sellers. We discuss how and why people sell travel; then we outline the many jobs available in travel selling. Finally, we examine the important role of service in travel sales. You will see that selling can be a challenging and frustrating but also very rewarding career.

Selling Travel: An Overview

You are planning to travel for a weekend to attend a cousin's wedding in St. Louis, or to look for a job in San Francisco. Or perhaps you want to take a month off for a trek in Nepal or a cruise of the Greek islands. How do you buy your trip?

Anyone who wants to travel has basically two choices. Travelers can buy directly from **suppliers,** which are businesses that own and control the product they are selling, such as airlines or hotels. Or travelers can buy their travel arrangements from **intermediaries,** such as tour operators or travel agencies, which act as links between suppliers and travelers. These are the two **distribution channels** for travel, the ways in which travel products reach consumers, as Figure 1.1 shows.

In each of these distribution channels, competition rules. Travel businesses cannot afford simply to wait for customers to come to them. Instead, they aggressively reach out to attract buyers, a process known as marketing. Selling is at the heart of this process.

Marketing Travel

When a hotel decides to install coffee makers and hair dryers in its rooms, it is engaged in marketing. When a travel agency decides to hire two new travel counselors who are experts in exotic trips, it has made a marketing decision. And when an airline slashes prices for flights to Orlando, that is marketing, too. **Marketing** consists of decisions and actions aimed at shaping consumers' preferences in order to make a match between a product or service and consumers' choices.

Identifying the consumers to be influenced is one important step in the marketing process. Out of all the potential travelers, travel businesses select **target markets,** which are the specific groups they aim to reach. One hotel, for example, might select middle-income families as its target market; another might target businesspeople. One travel agency might include people of every age and income in its target market; another might target only people who can afford long and luxurious trips.

Whatever the target market, a travel business also needs a marketing plan for reaching that market. At the heart of the plan are decisions about four elements, often called the *four Ps:*

1. *The product.* Exactly what is to be sold? For example, if you run a travel agency, will you sell luxury cruises? What about bargain trips to Atlantic City? Will you sell rail tickets or bus tickets? Will you offer all of these possibilities, or will you specialize in certain types of travel or certain destinations?
2. *The place.* Where will the product be sold?

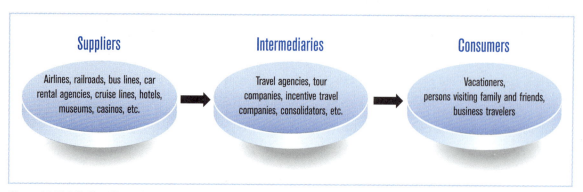

Figure 1.1 Distribution Channels for Travel
Travel products reach consumers through either a direct or an indirect distribution channel. In the direct channel, travel products go from the supplier, who owns and controls the product, directly to the consumer. In the indirect channel, travel products go from the supplier through an intermediary, such as a travel agency, that sells the product to the consumer.

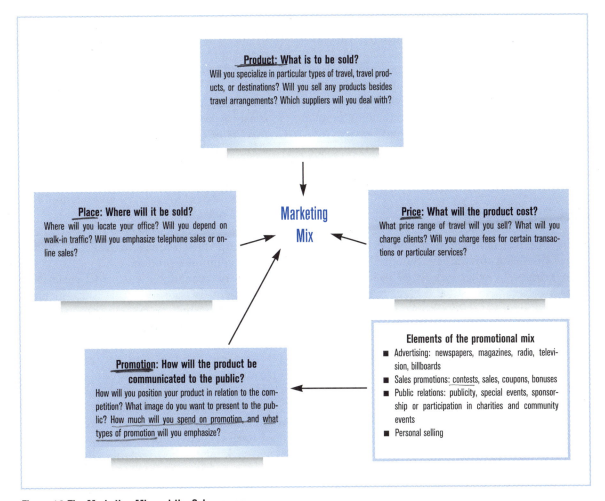

Figure 1.2 The Marketing Mix and the Salesperson
Salespeople play a critical role in marketing. They are one element of the promotional mix, which in turn is one of the four *P*s that make up the marketing mix. Shown here are just a few of the questions that a company might consider for each element of the marketing mix in order to come up with a marketing plan.

Will you have a storefront at a mall or in a business district? Will you plan to make most of your sales over the phone, or will you rely on people stopping by the office? Will you sell over the **Internet,** the worldwide network of computer networks and computer services?

3. *The price.* What will the product cost? Will you specialize in low-cost or luxurious offerings? What fees, if any, will you charge for transactions that earn a commission from suppliers? Will you charge a service fee for consultations?

4. *The promotion.* How will the product be communicated to the public? As Figure 1.2

shows, promotion involves some mix of four elements: advertising; sales promotions, such as frequent-flyer programs and contests; public relations, such as press releases about contributions to charity; and personal selling. **Personal selling** means making a sale through person-to-person contact; we usually refer to it simply as "selling."

These four aspects of marketing make up the **marketing mix.** A successful player in the travel industry is likely to have a detailed plan that takes into account each element of the mix. Our interest focuses on one element: personal selling and the role of the salesperson.

In travel, as in any industry, the job of the **salesperson** is to identify the needs of clients and to meet those needs. Thus, becoming a good salesperson means acquiring two tools. First, you need to gain knowledge about clients and about the travel product. Second, you must become skillful at getting information from clients and giving information and service to them. If you can carry out these tasks, you can make a sale.

The Sales Cycle

Every sale is a little different from every other one. Underlying this variety, though, is a common *process*. In other words, all selling situations involve a set of steps.

As an analogy, think about making dinner. When you want to cook dinner, you go through a series of steps. First, you need to plan your menu. Next, you see if you have the necessary ingredients to prepare the meal. Once you have gathered the ingredients, you must mix them together in the right order and amount and in the right way to get the dish to taste the way you want. Thus, cooking is a *process,* a series of steps that you take in order to achieve the desired outcome—a good meal.

Selling, too, is a process, and it requires steps like the following:

1. *Identify customers.* This step has two parts: finding new potential customers and determining whether they are not just "shoppers," but "buyers." In other words, are they seriously interested in buying travel arrangements now, are they able to pay for those arrangements, and are they in a position to make the decision to buy?
2. *Establish rapport.* In other words, you form a link with the client so that the client is comfortable with you and trusts you. Being friendly and concerned is the foundation for this step.
3. *Find out what the client needs.* Who is traveling? When? Where? Why? What does the client expect from the trip?
4. *Figure out what product fits the client's needs.* At this stage, you restate the customer's needs to be sure you have under-

stood them, and you apply your knowledge of travel arrangements to find the product that will meet those needs.
5. *Present your recommendations to the client.* Both knowledge of the travel product and the ability to communicate your ideas persuasively are needed for success at this stage.
6. *Deal with obstacles.* If the client objects to your recommendations, you must address those objections. Sometimes, you simply clarify your recommendation. At other times, you go back to step 3 and clarify your client's needs.
7. *Motivate the client to action.* In other words, you lead the customer to make a commitment to buy the product.
8. *Follow up.* After the sale is made, ensure that the client is satisfied. This step includes everything from processing paperwork to checking that the product is delivered as promised, dealing with anything that goes wrong on the trip, and seeking feedback from the client after the trip.

These eight steps make up the **sales cycle of success.** Why do we call it a "cycle"? Ideally, the process keeps repeating: your customers come back after the first sale, and you go through the steps again. Also, in any interaction with a client, you might go through some steps in the cycle several times. If the purpose of one step has not been achieved, you move back and repeat the step before going on to the next one. At other times, one of the steps may be unnecessary. For example, the client might have no objections to your recommendation, eliminating step 6.

In other words, selling is not like climbing a ladder, in which the best path to the top always follows the same sequence of steps. Instead, selling comes closer to resembling a trip up a mountain. It helps to have a map, much like our eight steps. But once you know the territory, sometimes the best trip means taking a shortcut; at other times, it's worth taking a detour or retracing your steps.

In Chapters 4–6 we discuss the sales cycle in detail, describing the goals and difficulties of each step. By learning how to work through these steps, you can become a successful salesperson.

Tips

The Sales Cycle of Success

To be successful at selling, think of selling as a process that includes eight steps:

1. Identify customers.
2. Establish rapport.
3. Determine the client's needs.
4. Select the product that fits those needs.
5. Present recommendations.
6. Deal with obstacles.
7. Motivate the client to action.
8. Follow up to ensure after-sale satisfaction.

Some Ups and Downs of Selling

Some people enjoy cooking. They like to plan a menu, choose recipes, and experiment with ingredients. Others think cooking is a boring chore and avoid it whenever possible. Similarly, not everyone likes to sell. But there is a major difference between cooking and selling. If you don't want to cook, you may be able to get someone else in the family to do it, or go out to eat, or pop a frozen dinner in the microwave. But virtually everyone in the travel industry engages in some part of the selling process, at some point in his or her career. For example, flight attendants are not full-time salespeople, but they can succeed or fail in "selling" their airline depending on the service they offer and how they respond to travelers' questions and problems. Whether or not you like to sell, you need to know how to sell.

The rewards of selling travel are many. Whether a client is looking for an exotic safari in Africa or a relaxing weekend at a beach resort, helping clients realize their dreams can be deeply satisfying. And of course the products—destinations around the world—can be fascinating to experience or just to learn about.

If selling is so rewarding, why do many people claim that they do not want to sell? Often, their feeling grows out of misperceptions about the job of selling. They might believe one of several myths about selling.

One myth holds that selling is boring and repetitive. In fact, the variety involved in travel selling far outweighs the repetition. Every sales situation is a little different: each customer has different needs and expectations, and how you meet those needs must also vary. This variety makes selling a challenging and sometimes frustrating job, but also an exhilarating one.

A second myth says that selling is manipulative. Some people believe that the goal of selling is to trick people into buying. Certainly, there are manipulative salespeople, but in the long run they are not likely to succeed. The goal of selling should be *not* to get people to do things they don't want to do, but to help them find the product or service that will meet a specific need. The best salespeople are the ones to whom clients keep coming back, and clients will return only if salespeople are helpful.

According to yet another myth, selling is a low-level job. Some people believe that selling is an unprofessional task that people do until they find something better. It is true that many organizations start people out in sales positions. But it is also true that if you are a skillful salesperson, selling travel can be a full-time, long-term, very rewarding career.

Furthermore, people who move into managerial roles often find that selling is still an important part of their jobs. Professionals—doctors, lawyers, accountants—also sell. They look for new customers or patients, talk to potential clients, and do other tasks that salespeople do. In some of these professions, selling is referred to as "building a practice." But it is selling just the same.

In fact, selling is something that you are very likely to be doing, one way or another, forever. You might be selling for a business, or to raise money for the arts, or to run a PTA benefit, or to build a legal or accounting practice. Developing sales skills will serve you well in a variety of ways throughout your life.

Time Out

Check your understanding of the discussion so far by filling in the blanks.

1. The most often used distribution channel in the travel industry goes from the supplier (such as an airline) to

   _____ .

2. The four *Ps* that make up the marketing mix are

   _____

   _____

   _____

   _____ .

3. The fourth *P,* promotion, may include advertising, sales promotions, public relations, and

   _____ .

4. The job of the salesperson is to

   _____

   _____

   _____

   _____ .

Careers in Selling Travel

For people who have acquired the knowledge and the skill to be effective sellers, the travel industry offers many opportunities. Skilled salespeople are needed by suppliers, by travel agencies, and by other intermediaries.

Selling by Suppliers

Suppliers such as airlines, hotels, car rental agencies, cruise lines, and attractions such as Disney World all hire people who sell full-time. Some of these salespeople sell directly to travel-ers. For example, airlines hire reservations agents who handle requests for tickets as well as questions about schedules, fares, and other aspects of the airline's service. Similarly, hotels hire reservationists and front-desk clerks who deal directly with travelers, making reservations and handling guests' questions and problems.

Other salespeople for suppliers sell to intermediaries such as travel agencies and tour operators; these salespeople are usually called *sales representatives*. For example, the cruise lines have sales representatives who sell their cruises to travel agencies in a specified territory. As part of their job, these sales representatives visit travel agencies, offering information about new ships and policies as well as ideas about how to sell the cruises. Similarly, sales representatives for hotels solicit business by visiting travel agencies, tour operators, and groups that hold conventions.

To succeed, a supplier's sales representative must be able to identify and meet the needs of travel agencies. A hotel's sales representative, for example, might offer a travel agency a special rate for its rooms or extra amenities for the agency's clients; or the sales representative might suggest an ad campaign that promotes both the hotel and the travel agency. Often, the salespeople for suppliers aim to form **preferred supplier relationships,** in which travel agencies commit themselves to maximize their use of the supplier; the supplier in turn may offer the agencies an **override,** which is an extra payment for a high volume of sales.

Selling by Travel Agencies

Transportation by land, sea, or air; accommodations in hotels, motels, resorts, bed-and-breakfasts; tickets to plays and concerts; photographic safaris and white-water rafting trips—all these services and more are sold by travel agencies. The agencies do not own or provide the services themselves, but they act as brokers between the suppliers and the traveler.

In the United States, almost all cruises, most tours, eight out of ten airline tickets, and a big chunk of hotel and car rentals are sold for suppliers by travel agencies, as Figure 1.3 illustrates. Travel agencies have captured such a large share of the travel market because travelers became convinced that travel agencies could provide valuable services.

The Changing Travel Agency. During the 1980s, just getting airline tickets for travelers was an important service, one that brought travelers to travel agencies and generated most of the agencies' income. Then in the 1990s drastic changes came to the travel industry in general and travel agencies in particular. The airlines altered the commissions paid to travel agencies for selling airline tickets, making it more difficult for agen-

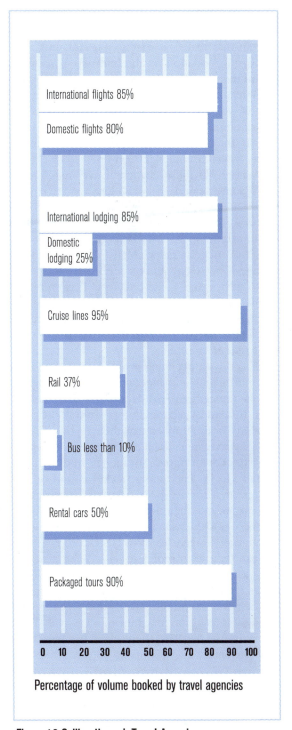

International flights 85%
Domestic flights 80%
International lodging 85%
Domestic lodging 25%
Cruise lines 95%
Rail 37%
Bus less than 10%
Rental cars 50%
Packaged tours 90%

0　10　20　30　40　50　60　70　80　90　100

Percentage of volume booked by travel agencies

Figure 1.3 Selling through Travel Agencies
When American travelers want a bus ticket or a train ticket or a domestic hotel room for the night, they are likely to buy these products directly from suppliers. But for cruises, tours, and airline tickets, they are likely to go to travel agencies, as these numbers show.
Source: Data from *Travel Industry World Yearbook—The Big Picture, 1996–97, Vol. 40,* p. 147.

cies to profit from these sales. Meanwhile, many people learned to use the **World Wide Web,** the system that makes it easy to present, link, and retrieve information on the Internet. Consumers found that they could uncover a wealth of information about airlines, hotels, and other suppliers, as well as about destinations, **on-line,** using their computer to connect with distant computers. If they chose, they could even purchase many travel arrangements on-line.

Where did these changes leave travel agencies? Some feared that travelers would bypass travel agencies, buying directly from airlines and other suppliers. Travel agencies saw that they could not prosper if they were simply order-takers and ticket-writers. Many increased their emphasis on selling and on service, on their ability to advise and guide travelers. This emphasis is reflected in the fact that, these days, those selling travel for travel agencies are often called **travel counselors** or **travel consultants** rather than **travel agents.**

Faced with declining profits from airline tickets and increased competition from other travel sellers, travel agencies adapted in other ways as well. Instead of relying almost entirely on commissions from suppliers for their income, many agencies began charging new fees for certain services. For example, an agency might charge clients $10 for each airline ticket issued or $50 for research for a trip. In addition, many agencies improved their service by adopting new technologies themselves. Like other businesses, many travel agencies now use computers to publish their own professional-looking newsletters, to keep track of their customers' preferences, and to handle their finances. They speed up their communications with suppliers and customers by using fax machines and e-mail. They not only use the Web themselves but also help guide clients who want to go to travel sites on the Web.

In recent years some travel agencies have also changed their workforce and the services they offer. Some have specialized in response to economic pressures. Instead of trying to be a "supermarket" of travel services, offering just about every type of travel service anyone could want, some have become "boutiques"—experts at offering particular types of travel or serving particular types of customers. One result of

these changes is increased variety in the jobs of those selling travel for travel agencies.

The Many Jobs of Travel Counselors. In today's travel agencies, travel counselors might serve the agency's existing clientele, or they might be **outside sales agents,** which means they are responsible for bringing new clients to the agency. Travel counselors might work in a travel agency office, but they might also work part or all of the time out of their own homes. They might work as employees of the travel agency, or they might work as **independent contractors,** people who are self-employed and work under contract to the company.

To offer expert service, travel agencies need travel counselors who can be specialists. Some agencies have long specialized in providing travel arrangements to businesses. They have *corporate account managers* who act as the liaison between the travel agency and the client, which in this case is the business paying for the travel, not the individual traveler. The account manager might negotiate airline, hotel, and car rental discounts for the business; provide reports on travel expenses; and help the company develop, monitor, and enforce policies regarding business travel. Meanwhile, the *corporate travel counselor* communicates with the individual business travelers (or with their secretaries or the company's travel arranger) and books the travelers' transportation and lodging.

Leisure travelers—people traveling on vacation—are likely to be looking for a different type of service, as Figure 1.4 illustrates. *Leisure travel counselors* help clients select travel arrangements; they research destinations and travel products, make recommendations, help clients obtain the best value for their travel dollar, and make bookings. If people are trying to figure out where they can go for a week in the sun on a limited budget, they could spend a lot of time talking to the salespeople for various suppliers and making their own comparisons and calculations. Or they could get help quickly and easily by talking to a leisure travel counselor.

Specialization goes well beyond the division between corporate and leisure travel counselors, however. Today's travel counselors might become experts in arranging travel to a certain region—such as the Caribbean or Mediter-

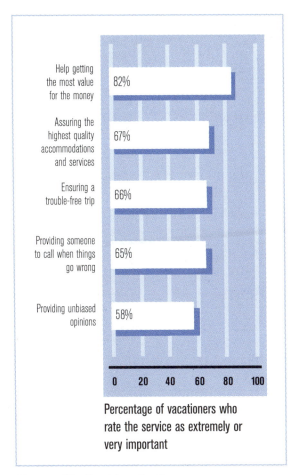

Figure 1.4 Why Travel Agencies Prosper
What is it that travel agencies offer that consumers want? A 1996 survey asked vacation travelers who currently use travel agencies to indicate whether a particular service was important to them. Itinerary planning, making reservations, and ticketing all ranked lower than the services shown here.
Source: Data from Traveline Surveys, 1996, as reported in *Travel Counselor*, October 1996, p. 18.

ranean—or travel for people with special interests—such as trips for cultural enrichment or adventure, for shopping or golf, birdwatching or mountain climbing, or scores of other possibilities. Among today's most important specializations are

■ *Cruises.* There are agencies that sell only cruises as well as departments devoted to cruise sales within agencies.
■ *Meetings and conventions.* Professional associations, corporations, trade groups, and organizations of every kind hold meetings,

conventions, and other special events. Meeting and convention planners organize these events; they act as intermediaries between suppliers and the sponsors of the event.
■ *Incentive travel.* Many businesses now use travel as part of their efforts to motivate employees or customers. For example, a company might offer a special trip as a reward for all salespeople who exceed a certain level of sales in a year. Arranging such incentive travel requires expertise not only in selling travel but also in designing motivational programs.

Selling by Other Intermediaries

Besides travel agencies, several other types of intermediaries offer opportunities for careers in selling travel. For example, there are companies devoted to planning meetings and conventions as well as incentive travel companies. Other examples include

■ **Consolidators,** who buy unsold travel products in bulk from suppliers to be sold at a discount to travel agencies or directly to the public. Airline consolidators often advertise in tiny newspaper ads that list cities with fares but no airline names.
■ **Tour operators,** who package several travel products together—such as transportation, accommodations, meals, and so on. They often buy the components of the tour (such as hotel rooms and car rentals) from suppliers in large quantities. As a result, tour operators can offer the vacation at a large discount. Special units of airlines and travel agencies, as well as tour companies, act as tour operators.

People with selling skills are also needed by local tourist bureaus, city convention centers, state tourism bureaus, and national tourist offices (NTOs). These and other *destination marketing organizations* "sell" destinations, trying to attract tourists. A *convention sales manager,* for example, works to persuade businesses and other organizations to hold their conventions at a particular convention center.

Time Out

Check your understanding of the discussion so far by filling in the blanks.

1. When a travel agency is committed to maximizing its use of a particular supplier, that supplier is called a

    _____

    _____.

2. Travel counselors who are self-employed and work under contract to an agency are known as

    _____

    _____.

3. A _____

    _____

    acts as the liaison between a travel agency and a business buying travel arrangements.

4. Travel counselors may specialize in selling

    _____

    _____

    _____

    _____.

Service and Selling

So far, we have said little about a key aspect of the selling process: *service*. It refers not just to what a customer is given with a sale but also to how a client is treated. Is the client's phone call left unreturned? Is the client greeted with a smile? When a problem comes up, is the client made to feel guilty for complaining?

Admittedly, people can be a nuisance. A travel counselor from King James Travel in Ohio told *Travel Life* (March/April 1992, p. 15) that one cruise client wanted reservations "to water-ski behind the ship." A travel counselor from Illinois recalled a client who called from the airport to ask for help "in locating the aircraft so that he could board in advance for the purpose of smelling it." And what would you

say to the client who insisted that her travel counselor "find out the interior colors of the plane on which she was to fly so that she could coordinate them with her hair, nails, and wardrobe"?

Good service, though, is the key to keeping customers, and keeping customers is often easier than finding new ones. How many people must you reach by telephone calls or direct mail or advertising in order to get just one new customer? The process can be very expensive. In fact, many businesspeople believe it costs five times as much to win a new customer as to keep an old one. Thus, over the last few years, all types of organizations have given renewed emphasis to customer service.

The Salesperson and the Customer

The salesperson's role is especially important in giving service, because salespeople are often the key contact between customers and an organization. It is the salesperson who is most likely to form a personal relationship with customers and to describe the service that is promised. To a great extent, the customer's impression of the salesperson creates his or her image of the organization.

By themselves, though, salespeople cannot completely control the service that customers receive. Even if salespeople do their job well, bad service can occur because of the organization. The phones might not work well. Company policies might be too strict. Forms might be confusing. All of these characteristics influence how customers perceive the service they receive.

Giving good service can be especially challenging during the last step of the selling process—the follow-up to ensure after-sale satisfaction. Many things can go wrong after the sale. Was a reservation erased from a computer? Was a suitcase lost? Did the traveler misunderstand the description of a room? (For another example, see the Selling through Service case below.) To conclude this introductory look at sales and service, we outline the sources of problems in the travel industry and a method for solving these problems.

Why So Many Problems?

In the travel business, it is easy to have lots of problems. Why? Three characteristics of the travel industry underlie many of the difficulties.

Selling through Service

Trouble in Paradise

What a treat this has been. You are working as the on-site coordinator during the holiday season in the Caribbean. Because your agency sends so many people to three Caribbean islands during school breaks, several agents are sent to each island to help deal with any problems. Normally, problems are few.

Now it turns out that two of your clients have been so obnoxious that they have been asked to leave their hotel. The problem started when the clients claimed that their room was filthy. They complained, at length, in the lobby. They made such a fuss that the manager told them they had 24 hours to check out. Now your clients want you to find them a new place to stay. This is a big problem. The island is packed, bursting at the seams.

You are on your way to the hotel to meet with the couple. As you ride along, you are trying to sort out what to do. If they could just stay put, things would be simple. But will the hotel take them back? Anyway, you didn't do anything wrong. If they got themselves evicted, isn't that their problem? Maybe you should tell them they will have to go home early. After all, where does customer service start and stop?

∎ ∎ ∎

Unfortunately for you, the answer is that customer service virtually never stops. To see why, imagine that you are not the travel counselor in this scenario, but the customer. What would you say if your travel counselor told you your vacation was over? What would you say about the travel agency to your friends back home?

If you were the travel counselor in this situation, what would you do? For help in solving this and other problems, see the section "Solving Problems: A Method."

First, the travel business is *transaction oriented*. During any one year a salesperson will perform hundreds or even thousands of transactions—counseling customers; making air, hotel, and car rental reservations; recommending cruise ships and destinations.

As an example, suppose you are an agent for an average commercial travel agency, one that deals only with travel arrangements for businesses. You will handle about 3,000 transactions yearly. (An agent selling only leisure travel might handle a third as many transactions.) Now let's assume that you are one of twenty full-time reservationists in the agency. And let's say that most of the time everything goes right but that about one-half of one percent of the time, something does not work. That does not seem like much. But with this error rate, the agency would have at least one problem to deal with every working day of the year, almost three hundred every year. Thus, even a low error rate can lead to lots of problems and create a reputation for bad service.

Furthermore, each transaction in the travel business may involve several people. This is the second characteristic of the business that creates many problems. Each person involved in the transaction might have slightly different ideas about what is happening. One person might make the arrangements for a vacation, but very often two or more people take the trip. Each person probably has ideas about what the trip should be like, but the travel counselor might be in touch with only one of these people. If your family goes on vacation to Walt Disney World, one person probably makes the arrangements—but all of you are likely to have your own hopes and expectations for the trip.

Finally, travel involves intangibles as well as tangibles. If you sell pencils, almost everything about your product is *tangible*—it can be seen, touched, measured. As a result, there is little room for disagreement about what was promised in the sale or what was received. Travel products do involve some tangibles. A sale either promises food on a plane trip or it doesn't, for example; it might call for a room with a single bed or a double bed, with breakfast included or not. But every travel arrangement also involves feelings, expectations, and other intangibles.

As an example, suppose you send a couple a brochure for a hotel promising luxurious accommodations. They like the rooms shown in the brochure and are happy with the hotel when they check in, but ultimately they are disappointed and want to change hotels. Why? The photograph was an accurate picture of the room, but somehow the room did not "feel" the way they expected. An intangible aspect of the arrangement has gone wrong. Intangibles open the way for ambiguities, miscommunications, and disappointments—in short, for problems galore.

Solving Problems: A Method

Mrs. Bennett comes to your desk demanding a refund because, she says, her tour bus never stopped at the monuments she expected to see. Mr. Rodriguez calls with a frantic plea for help, stranded after losing his wallet. Mr. and Mrs. Smith need a new flight to Florida to meet their cruise ship because the airline they were booked on just went out of business.

In tough situations like these, the characteristics you need most are patience, a soothing voice, a nondefensive attitude, and a willingness to go the extra step to satisfy people's needs. These qualities open the path to a solution. But to reach the solution, you also need skills.

In particular, solving your customers' problems requires the ability to listen, to uncover their needs, and to develop a plan that meets those needs. In fact, like selling, problem solving can be seen as a process. To deal with a problem effectively, you should follow seven steps, as shown in Figure 1.5.

1. *Acknowledge the problem.* You cannot work with a problem until you acknowledge that one exists. The first step in problem resolution is to say, "Yes, there is a problem."
2. *Collect the facts.* This is not always easy. Customers can be difficult. They can say things you know are not true. For example, they might say that you did not make a reservation when you know you did. You need to unearth the facts as the customer and others see them, not just as you see them.
3. *Take responsibility.* Whether you created the problem or not, consider it your job to be sure that a solution is found.

4. *Select a strategy*. Decide what to do. There are three basic strategies: just do what the client wants; find an alternative way to reach the client's goal; or redefine the client's goal and meet that new goal. In later chapters we discuss these strategies in more detail.

5. *Test the proposed solution*. Check with the customer that your plan for solving the problem is acceptable. Very often, when you say what you are going to do, new problems arise. In this case, you need to go back to step 2, collecting facts.

6. *Resolve the problem*. Take the action you promised and confirm that the desired result has taken place.

7. *Follow up*. Make sure that the customer was satisfied. Sending a follow-up letter of apology is often worthwhile.

In the chapters to come, the Selling through Service boxes describe how to apply these steps to problems. By developing your problem-solving skills, you will take a large step toward improving your ability to give top-quality service.

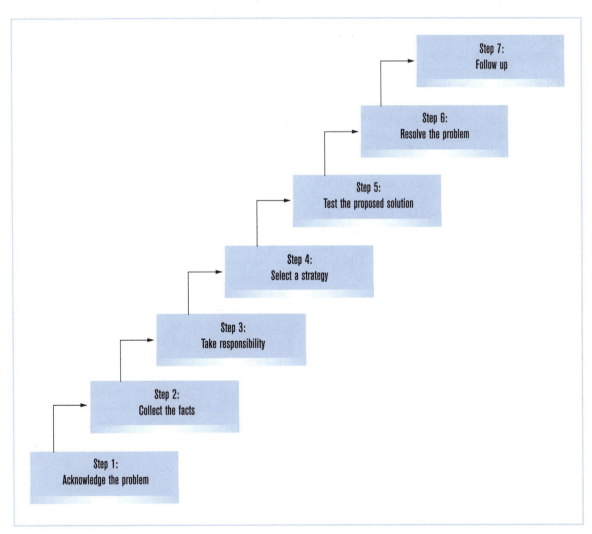

Figure 1.5 A Method for Solving Problems
When you are faced with a problem, following these seven steps should lead you to an effective response. We explain these steps in more detail in the Selling through Service cases in Chapters 2–6.

Chapter Wrap-Up

Chapter Highlights

Many jobs in the travel industry involve selling to one degree or another. Learning the principles of successful selling will benefit anyone interested in a career in travel. Here is a review of the objectives with which we began this chapter.

1. **Identify five key decisions involved in marketing travel.** A business that sells travel needs to identify its target market and make decisions about the four *Ps:* the product, the price, the place, and the promotion. These decisions make up the marketing mix.

2. **Outline the eight steps of the sales cycle.** Selling is a process that can be described in terms of eight steps: identifying customers, establishing rapport, determining client needs, selecting a product that fits the client's needs, presenting recommendations, dealing with obstacles, motivating to action, and following up to ensure after-sales satisfaction. Sometimes steps must be repeated, and sometimes steps can be skipped. Ideally, the salesperson keeps repeating this cycle because the customer keeps coming back for additional purchases.

3. **Describe the role of the salesperson in the travel industry.** Personal selling is a key part of the marketing effort. It is one element of promotion, the fourth *P* in the marketing mix. Although many travel suppliers sell directly to consumers, most travel sales go through intermediaries such as travel agencies. Some sales go through tour operators, meeting and convention planners, incentive travel companies, or consolidators. Whether the salesperson works for a supplier or for an intermediary, however, the job of selling is to identify and meet the needs of the client. Common misperceptions of selling hold that it is a boring, manipulative, and low-level task. Selling can indeed be frustrating, but it is a complex job that can be very rewarding.

4. **Explain two key ways in which selling travel differs from other types of selling.** Unlike many types of selling, travel selling involves many transactions and deals to a great extent with intangibles. Both characteristics open the way for errors and misunderstandings in dealing with customers. Furthermore, each of the transactions often involves several people.

5. **Outline the role of service in the sales process.** *Service* refers in part to how customers are treated. Because salespeople often provide the main contact between customers and an organization, the service they give is especially important. Giving good service is a key to keeping customers; thus, it is one requirement for success as a salesperson.

6. **Name seven steps to take to solve a problem.** First, acknowledge the problem. Then collect the facts, take responsibility for solving the problem, select a strategy for solving it, and check this proposed solution with the customer. After taking these steps, you resolve the problem. Finally, follow up to ensure that the customer was satisfied.

New Terms. The terms that follow were introduced in this chapter. If you do not recall their definitions, see the Glossary, which begins on page 237.

consolidators	preferred supplier
distribution channels	relationship
four *Ps*	sales cycle
independent contractors	of success
intermediaries	salesperson
Internet	suppliers
marketing	target market
marketing mix	tour operators
on-line	travel agent
outside sales agent	travel consultant
override	travel counselor
personal selling	World Wide Web

Review Exercises

Check-Up

Give yourself a quick test of your memory of a few basic points. Read each of the following statements and indicate whether it is true (T) or false (F). See the answers below the statements.

T   F   1. Most sales in the travel industry are made from suppliers directly to the public.

T   F   2. Selling is a process, or a series of steps that leads to a desired outcome.

T   F   3. Selling is a task for entry-level workers, not professionals.

T   F   4. Determining the buyer's budget is the first step in selling.

T   F   5. In the last step of the sales cycle, the buyer makes the purchase.

T   F   6. Service is an integral part of the sales process.

T   F   7. Successful salespeople develop their skills over time.

Answers: 1. F, 2. T, 3. F, 4. F, 5. F, 6. T, 7. T

Discussion Questions

1. **Understanding Selling.** What are some similarities between the job of a sales representative for a cruise line and the job of a leisure travel counselor?

    _____

    _____

    _____

    _____

2. **Service and Selling: Why So Many Problems?** Selling travel is unlike many other types of selling because (1) it is transaction oriented and (2) the product is, to a great extent, intangible. What are some of the challenges that result from these two characteristics?

    _____

    _____

    _____

    _____

3. **Handling Problems.** When customers have problems, what characteristics and skills should the salesperson bring to the situation?

_____

_____

_____

_____

_____

4. **Thinking about Selling: A Self-Assessment.** Successful salespeople are made, not born; you can learn to sell by developing certain skills. Still, people with certain characteristics are more likely than others to enjoy selling and to find it easy to learn the necessary skills.

a. Based on what you have learned about selling in this chapter, name at least two characteristics that you believe describe most successful salespeople.

_____

_____

_____

_____

b. Turn to Worksheet 1.1, page 21, to evaluate your own skills and attitudes.

A Case in Question

Consider again the case "Trouble in Paradise," page 13.

1. We described three characteristics of the travel business that contribute to the frequency of problems. Which of these characteristics is evident in this case?

_____

_____

_____

_____

_____

2. Is there anything the travel counselor in this case could have done to avoid the problem with her clients?

_____

_____

_____

_____

3. What are three possible solutions to the problem, and what are the pros and cons of each solution?

_____

_____

_____

_____

An Exercise in Selling: Dealing with Trouble in Paradise

Review the "Trouble in Paradise" case on page 13 and the steps for solving problems discussed on page 14. Now assume that the travel counselor has arrived at the hotel and has been directed to the manager's office, where one of the obnoxious clients is arguing again with the manager. Break into groups of four. One person takes the role of the travel counselor; a second acts as the client; a third acts as the hotel manager; and the fourth is the observer. Here is a description of the roles:

■ *Travel counselor.* Go through the first three steps of the problem-resolution process. To acknowledge the problem (step 1), what should you say or do? To collect the facts (step 2), what should you say or do? To take responsibility (step 3), what should you say or do?

■ *Client.* Stop arguing with the manager now that your travel counselor has arrived. Try for realism. Even though you are obnoxious, you want the counselor to help you.

■ *Manager.* You are angry. But you would like to be able to maintain good relations with the travel agency. Act accordingly.

■ *Observer.* Fill out Worksheet 1.2 on page 23.

After the "travel counselor" has taken the first three steps in problem solving, discuss the observer's ratings. If you acted as the "counselor," don't be discouraged if your ratings were low. In the coming chapters we explain techniques that should help you handle situations like this one.

Worksheet 1.1

Self-Assessment

Here is a self-assessment that should help you think about the extent to which you have some of the skills, traits, attitudes, and abilities that make it easier to learn to be a successful salesperson. Read each statement and circle the response that best describes your feeling about it according to the following scale:

5 = definitely agree
4 = sometimes agree
3 = uncertain
2 = sometimes disagree
1 = definitely disagree

There are no right or wrong answers.

	5	4	3	2	1
1. I like working with people.	5	4	3	2	1
2. I listen to what people have to say.	5	4	3	2	1
3. I am patient with others.	5	4	3	2	1
4. I would choose selling as a career.	5	4	3	2	1
5. I think selling is fun.	5	4	3	2	1
6. I want to be more than just a salesperson.	5	4	3	2	1
7. I think selling is a professional career.	5	4	3	2	1
8. Finding out what people need and want is fun.	5	4	3	2	1
9. I like to ask people questions.	5	4	3	2	1
10. I follow through on promises.	5	4	3	2	1
11. I am well organized.	5	4	3	2	1
12. I am good at explaining what I mean to others.	5	4	3	2	1
13. I am self-confident.	5	4	3	2	1

Sales and Service in the Travel Industry

14. I am polite to others.	5	4	3	2	1
15. I enjoy helping other people.	5	4	3	2	1
16. Selling travel is challenging.	5	4	3	2	1
17. I am not easily frustrated.	5	4	3	2	1
18. I am persistent when I have to be.	5	4	3	2	1
19. I think quickly on my feet.	5	4	3	2	1
20. I would enjoy helping people with their travel plans.	5	4	3	2	1

Add the points for each response and record your total.

Total score: _____

If your score is:	Then
0–20	You are going to have to work a little harder than some to acquire the skills and attitudes needed to succeed in sales.
21–40	Either your skills or your attitude about selling will make it difficult for you to enjoy selling travel. You will need to improve specific skills in order to succeed in sales.
41–60	You are predisposed toward a career in travel sales and service, but the attitudes and skills that contribute to success in selling are not easy for you.
61–80	Your attitudes and your skills make selling a good fit for you. You will have little difficulty succeeding as a salesperson if you work to improve your skills.
81–100	You are very predisposed toward selling. Acquiring the necessary skills to be a successful salesperson should be easier for you than others.

Worksheet 1.2

Name _____ Date _____

Dealing with Trouble in Paradise

As the observer for the "Trouble in Paradise" exercise, you should fill out this form to evaluate the "travel counselor's" performance. You may want to duplicate the form before writing on it.

	Good	Fair	Poor
Acknowledging the problem Did the counselor communicate concern for the client's problem?	❑	❑	❑
Collecting facts Did the counselor learn how the client views the problem?	❑	❑	❑
Did the counselor learn how the manager views the problem?	❑	❑	❑
Taking responsibility Did the counselor give the sense that he or she was ready to take control of the situation and resolve the conflict?	❑	❑	❑

Comments and suggestions for improvement:

_____

_____

_____

_____

_____

_____

_____

_____

Understanding the Travel Buyer

Objectives

After reading this chapter, you should be able to

1. Describe the types of needs that motivate buyers.
2. Explain three ways of classifying potential buyers.
3. Identify five types of travel buyers.
4. Outline key needs of different types of travel buyers.

Preview

Up to this point, we have been discussing selling and its place in the travel industry—who does it, how they do it, and why. Here, we look at selling from the buyer's point of view. In other words, why do travel buyers buy?

The short answer is that people buy in order to satisfy their needs. As discussed in Chapter 1, the salesperson has the job of identifying and responding to a buyer's needs. In later chapters we discuss techniques for accomplishing this job; here we provide some background that should make it easier for you to apply those techniques effectively. What needs motivate people in general, and how do they influence buying behavior? And, more specifically, what needs are important to travelers? These are questions we address in this chapter.

Why Do Buyers Buy?

Buyers buy when they expect a purchase to satisfy their needs. Think about the last time you went shopping for a big-ticket item. If you are like most buyers, two types of needs guided you: technical and psychological.

- **Technical needs** are specific features of the product required by the buyer, such as its quantity, date of delivery, and price. If you are buying furniture, you might need four dining room chairs within a week for under $500. If you are buying travel arrangements, you might need lodging for three people next weekend for less than $300.
- **Psychological needs** are the motives that influence the purchase. Are you looking for relaxation or adventure? Do you need to feel important? A particular purchase might help you meet these or other psychological needs.

Which needs have the most influence on a particular buying decision depends on both the person and the situation. Before examining how these decisions occur, let's take a closer look at psychological needs. They are often more difficult to identify than technical ones.

What Are Psychological Needs?

For centuries philosophers and psychologists have been proposing catalogs of human needs. Scholars and scientists still disagree about just what needs are most important and just how they affect people. Abraham Maslow and David McClelland, however, have each offered influential ideas.

Maslow's Hierarchy of Needs. Curiosity and fear. Sex and power. A love of money or a fear of loneliness. All of these might *motivate* a person, moving the individual to act in certain ways. Abraham Maslow proposed a way of thinking about the virtually endless variety of possible needs. According to Maslow, five types of needs motivate people:

- *Physiological needs,* for food, water, sleep, and so on.
- *Safety needs,* such as the need for a secure income.
- *Belongingness needs,* for affection and love.
- *Esteem needs,* including needs for self-respect and for the respect of others.
- *Self-actualization,* or the desire to become all that one is capable of.

These needs, according to Maslow, are not equal. Instead, there is a **hierarchy of needs,** which means that certain needs motivate people only if other, more fundamental needs have been largely satisfied. The most fundamental needs are the physiological ones. If those are for the most part met, a person might be motivated by safety needs. Next come belongingness needs; then esteem needs; and finally self-actualization. In other words, if Maslow is right, people will not be motivated by a desire for social status if they are constantly worried about keeping a roof over their heads.

Is this true? Research suggests that for the most part it is, but not always. Even when more basic needs are not met, people are sometimes moved by Maslow's "higher" needs.

McClelland's Analysis of Needs. Decades of research led David McClelland to suggest another way of analyzing human needs. Consider these comments from three men responding to questions from an interviewer:

Thomas Allison:
Of course, work is important; it's what we're here for—to make things move, to make things happen. I get a big kick out of the things I do; it's fantastic, what you can accomplish.

William Benchley:
I guess I would say what's really important in my work is the ability to work with people and through people; to make plans and then to carry them out. . . . So, what I have to do is get everybody on board and working effectively toward the same goal. . . . I

try very hard to make it clear to other people that I value their opinions, and that they can make a real contribution by working with me. . . .

Arthur Carter:
What I really want to do with my life is be somebody of importance in the community. I'm not overly excited about my particular skill in business, but the money I make allows me to afford the kind of home, car, and recreational activities that influential people have. When you're in a position like that in the community, you really have some control over what goes on around you.*

Work is important to all three of these men, but why? Their comments suggest differing motivations. How would you describe them? Three motives analyzed by McClelland provide one answer:

- **Need for achievement,** which is the need to excel. A person with a strong need for achievement is motivated to master tasks, to set and achieve goals. Allison's emphasis on what he accomplishes at work illustrates this motivation.
- **Need for affiliation,** which is the need for positive relationships with others. If you are motivated by the need for affiliation, people, not tasks, are the focus of your attention, as in Benchley's comments.
- **Need for power,** which is the need to influence and control others. Carter's comments, for example, suggest that he has a strong need for power. Notice that he wants to live as "influential people" do and to have "some control."

Table 2.1 describes some characteristics of people when they are motivated by each of these needs.

Needs in Context. What do these ideas about

*From *Motivational Selling: Exceptional Sales Performance,* © 1986 by The Forum Corporation of North America. Reprinted by permission of The Forum Corporation.

human needs tell you about selling? If you understand a customer's primary motivation, you should be better able to establish rapport with that person. You should also find it easier to focus quickly on those issues which most concern that person. If someone is strongly motivated by the need for affiliation, for example, you might discuss the opportunities for meeting people on a cruise or tour.

Several cautions are important in considering a customer's motives, though. First, be careful not to jump to conclusions. People tend to assume, often wrongly, that other people are just like themselves, with the same needs. And they tend to assume, again often wrongly, that any characteristics they observe are inherent and permanent. In fact, observed characteristics might reflect the effects of an unusual situation. On a bad day, for example, you might become very irritable, and that irri-

**Tips
A Buyer's Decision**

To understand a buyer, you should consider

- *Technical needs.* What specific characteristics of a product are required by the client?
- *Psychological needs.* Do you understand the person's motivation? Has the client shown a strong need for achievement, or affiliation, or power?
- *The situation.* Is there competition for the sale? Is the purchase routine? Is it important to the client? Does the client have time to weigh the buying decision carefully?
- *Your relationship to the client.* What is your history with the client? Does the client have reason to respect your opinion? Does the client know and like you?

Table 2.1

Three Key Needs Motivating Human Behavior

Need	Typical Concerns
Need for achievement: the need to excel in a particular task	Meeting or surpassing a self-imposed standard of excellence
	Striving to make a unique contribution
	Setting long-term goals
	Planning to overcome personal, business, or other obstacles
Need for affiliation: the need to establish, maintain, or restore a positive personal relationship with another person	Being part of a group or team
	Being liked and accepted
	Being involved with people in work situations
	Minimizing conflict
Need for power: the need to influence or control others	Influencing through powerful actions
	Arousing strong positive or negative emotions in others
	Acquiring a reputation or position
	Having control of situations

Sources: Adapted from *Motivational Selling: Exceptional Sales Performance,* © 1986 by The Forum Corporation of North America. Reprinted by permission.

tability may end up looking to others like a need for power. Remember, too, that a customer is likely to be motivated by many needs operating together—including the technical needs we discussed earlier.

How Do Customers Decide?

People rarely do anything for just one reason. Researchers in consumer behavior have tested many ideas about how interacting motives shape buying decisions. No single description explains the process, but we can describe some variations in how people make these decisions.

Variations in Decision Making. In part, how people decide to make a purchase depends on the situation. For example, are there competing sellers? Who is asking the buyer to buy, and

what is that person saying? The decision-making process also depends on characteristics of the buyer and on how the buyer defines the situation. Is the purchase routine to the buyer? Is it important? Does the customer have time to think about it?

Which motives shape a customer's buying behavior depends partly on the state of the competition. If more than one seller can satisfy a buyer's technical needs, psychological needs may determine which seller gets the sale. If a salesperson ends up saying, "I can't believe they didn't buy. Our product would be perfect for them!" chances are the salesperson did not pay enough attention to the buyers' psychological needs.

How the buyer approaches the selling situation is also important. Some decisions are routine. The customer spends little time or energy considering whether to buy or what to buy; habit rules. A traveler who flies from San

Francisco to Los Angeles several times a month every month, for example, may take the same flight every time.

But when habit does not determine a buying decision, what does? Two possibilities are important to salespeople. First, people sometimes buy because they are complying with a request to buy. Second, people may buy because they are persuaded to buy.

Changing Behavior: Compliance. Under certain conditions, people are very likely to do what they are asked to do; they are likely to *comply* with a request, even a request to make a purchase. In recent years hundreds of studies by social psychologists have examined how compliance works. Three conditions that make compliance likely are especially interesting.

First, people are likely to comply if the person making the request has provided something first; people usually feel obliged to *reciprocate*. For example, if an acquaintance gave you a ride last week when you were stranded and this week asked you for a similar favor, what would you say? You would probably feel some obligation to reciprocate and say yes. Stores put this tendency to reciprocate to work when they give customers free samples; salespeople also apply it when they send small gifts to clients.

Second, people are likely to comply with a request if it is *consistent* with a commitment they have previously made. Once a person says yes to a small request, he or she is likely to say yes to a larger one. If John Smith says yes, he agrees with your description of the type of trip he wants, and yes, he thinks that a weekend in Barbados would fit the bill, then he becomes more likely to continue saying yes when you ask him to book the trip.

Finally, as you probably expect, people are likely to comply with a request when the person making the request is someone they view as an authority or someone they know and like. This fact explains why we emphasize two points throughout this book: (1) effective salespeople are professionals, and (2) effective salespeople develop rapport with their clients.

Changing Attitudes: Persuasion. Besides habit and compliance, persuasion may also shape a buyer's decision. In other words, people sometimes buy because an advertisement or some other sales message has created a positive attitude toward the product; the message has given them positive beliefs or feelings about the product.

When and why are people persuaded to make a purchase? Basically, persuasion can occur in either of two ways:

1. People may think carefully about the message and their decision, weighing their choices.
2. People may not take the trouble to think about the decision much but instead look for shortcuts, using cues that seem likely to point to the best choice.

When a purchase is important to people and they have the time and ability to think about their decision, they are likely to take the first route, as Figure 2.1 illustrates. Under these conditions, they are likely to weigh the pros and cons of a purchase, to consider the strengths and weaknesses of one product compared with competing products. With customers in this situation, salespeople who can discuss the details of their product are likely to be effective. For these consumers, if you hope to make the sale on the basis of your winning personality and a colorful, enthusiastic description of a product, you are likely to be disappointed.

In contrast, if a decision is unimportant to consumers, or if they are pressed for time or have a lot of other things on their minds, they often look for shortcuts to making a choice. Instead of thinking critically about a purchase, they might respond to superficial cues. They may be swayed, for example, by how much they like the salesperson or by how colorful a brochure is. A witty video, an endorsement by some trusted figure, or a sales promotion may determine their decision. Under these circumstances, trying to give a detailed analysis of a product may just bore or irritate people. But your friendly smile and vivid, reassuring description may be persuasive.

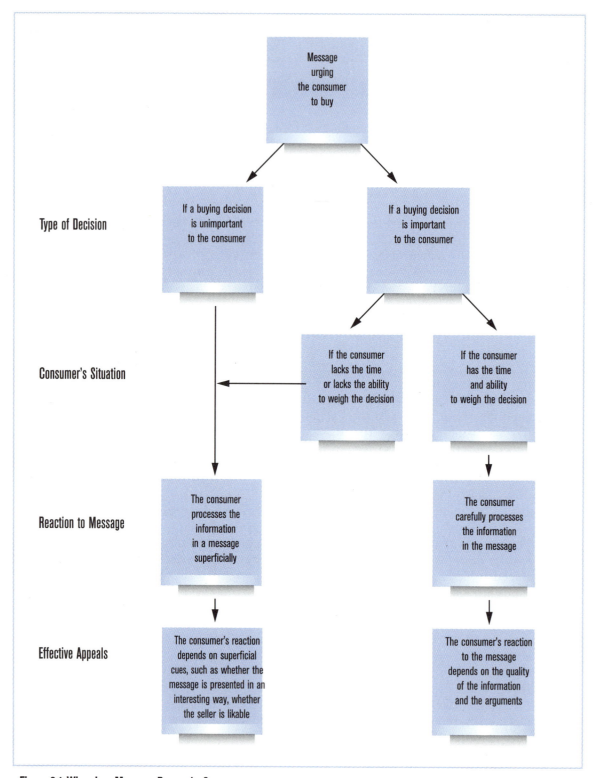

Figure 2.1 When Is a Message Persuasive?
Whether an ad or sales pitch persuades customers to change their attitudes toward a purchase depends greatly on the customer. Suppose the decision is not important to the customer or the customer does not have the time or ability to think carefully about the message. In these cases, the quality of the message does not matter much. When people consider a travel purchase, though, they are likely to have the interest and take the time to weigh the decision carefully.

Time Out

Check your understanding of the discussion so far by filling in the blanks.

1. Decisions to buy depend on two types of needs:

   _____

   _____ .

2. A person with a strong need for

   _____

   might say something like "Our neighbors just came back from a trip to the beach, so we thought we'd take a cruise."

3. A person with a strong need for

   _____

   might say something like "I want to go someplace where my kids and I can get to know each other again."

4. People are especially likely to comply with a request to buy if (1) they have been given something by the person making the request, (2) they previously agreed to a related request, or (3) the person making the request is someone

   _____

   _____ .

5. A person's decision to buy something is most likely to be swayed by trivial features of the product if the decision is unimportant to the person or if

   _____

   _____

   _____ .

Why Do Travel Buyers Buy?

So far, we have introduced some basic ideas about consumer behavior. Our central interest, though, is not consumers in general but travelers in particular. What needs does travel satisfy?

Obviously, there are many answers, depending on which travelers you are interested in. Over the centuries, people have traveled in order to find food and shelter, to trade their crops and crafts, and to satisfy their curiosity about faraway places. They have made pilgrimages to holy places to save their souls and taken tours to fashionable spas to secure their social standing.

Instead of considering the needs of the entire

population of possible travelers, travel sellers first try to organize this huge population into a few major categories. Every profession has a set of categories that helps the practitioners think about the work they do every day—a taxonomy for their work. Lawyers talk about civil versus criminal matters. Accountants talk about accrual versus cash accounting. Travel sellers talk about various *market segments,* which are clusters of individuals with similar characteristics.

Segmenting the Travel Market

To identify market segments and determine their characteristics, many businesses in the travel industry conduct *market research,* which is the collection, analysis, and reporting of data relevant to a specific marketing situation. Market research may involve both primary and secondary data. *Primary data* consist of information collected for the specific purpose at hand. If you send a questionnaire to find out which of your services are most popular, you are collecting primary data. But if you consult a journal to find surveys about the popularity of different services, you are using secondary data. *Secondary data* consist of information that already exists, information that has been collected for some other purpose.

Market research may uncover many ways to segment the population. Here we examine three important approaches.

Demographics and Travel. One way to classify travelers looks at *demographics,* which means the measurable characteristics of a population such as age, income, sex, and so on. For example, in 1995, the average U.S. adult making a trip of more than a hundred miles from home was male, married, older than 35, and had an annual income of more than $40,000. Figure 2.2 gives further information on demographic characteristics of American travelers.

Examining demographic characteristics can give travel sellers many hints about their market and their potential for making sales. They might learn, for example, whether many of their potential customers are likely to travel with children; the answer may suggest whether particular products will attract a lot of customers. For

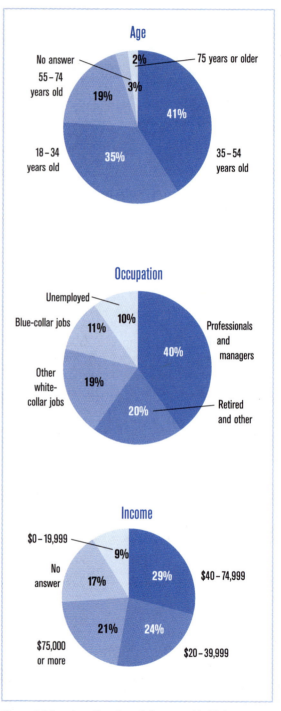

Figure 2.2 American Travelers: A Demographic Picture
Who is traveling, and who makes up your potential market? Demographic data can provide a starting point for understanding a marketplace. Shown here are data on the characteristics of American adults who took trips more than a hundred miles away from home in 1995.
Source: Data from U.S. Travel Data Center, reprinted in *Travel Industry World Yearbook: The Big Picture–1996–97, Volume 40* (New York: Child & Waters, Inc., 1997), p. 33.

American families traveling with children, the most popular types of vacations (according to a 1995 study by the U.S. Travel Data Center) were major theme parks and attractions and family reunions. In contrast, for adults traveling on their own, cruises and overseas trips were the top two choices.

Psychographic Segmentation. Another approach to market segmentation uses **psychographics,** which groups people according to their psychological characteristics such as values, beliefs, and lifestyle. What resources do people have? What is important to them? How do they spend their time and money?

On the basis of questions like these, the VALS 2 Segmentation System was developed by SRI International. It classifies people into categories based on their self-images, their aspirations, their values and beliefs, and the products they use. People in the category called "Achievers," for example, are successful, look for satisfaction to their jobs and families, and favor established products. "Experiencers" value variety and excitement and spend a lot on clothing, fast food, and music.

Stanley Plog has developed one of the best-known systems of psychographic segmentation for the travel industry. According to Plog, travelers can be placed on a spectrum with venturers (once called *allocentrics*) at one end and dependables (once called *psychocentrics*) at the other, as Figure 2.3 illustrates. **Venturers** center their lives on varied interests. They are outgoing, confident, and curious. In contrast, **dependables** focus on everyday problems and value familiarity and comfort. They are inhibited and unadventurous.

Segmentation by Usage. Both demographics and psychographics provide invaluable tools if you are making marketing decisions. They might tell you, for example, that only a handful of families in town could afford a deluxe photographic safari through southern Africa, and that even fewer are likely to be interested in this kind of vacation. Travel counselors, however, might look first to a simpler form of segmentation, by usage.

Segmentation by usage classifies travelers by the purpose of their trips. Looked at this way, the travel market has five major segments:

■ *Business or corporate travel,* which consists of travel services provided to a business.

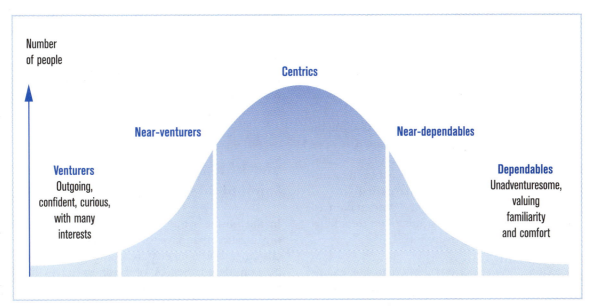

Figure 2.3 American Travelers: A Psychographic Analysis
Are you a venturer? A dependable? Stanley Plog has proposed that these psychological characteristics predict a person's vacation preferences. For an application of this analysis, see Table 2.2, page 38.
Source: Based on Plog Research, Inc.

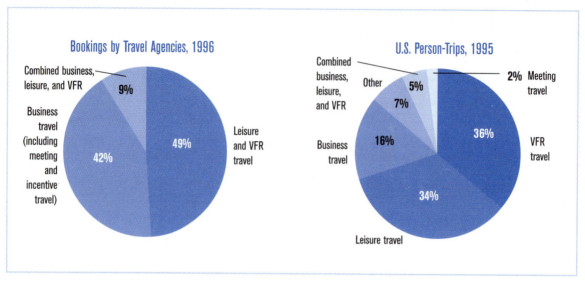

Figure 2.4 Types of Travel: Why Do People Travel?
There are many ways of categorizing the purposes of travel and many ways of collecting data on travel. The first graph here shows an analysis of the purposes of travel booked at travel agencies from December 1995 to February 1996, based on the volume of the bookings. The second graph categorizes the purposes of trips a little differently, and it shows the percentage of U.S. person-trips made for each purpose in 1995.

Source: Data from Louis Harris and Associates and U.S. Travel Data Center as reported in *Travel Industry World Yearbook: The Big Picture—1996–97, Volume 40* (New York: Child & Waters, Inc., 1997), pp. 148, 29.

The travelers are conducting the business of the firm. In 1995, this type of travel accounted for about 42 percent of travel agencies' business (see Figure 2.4).

- **Meeting travel,** which is travel that is undertaken to attend an organized gathering.
- **Incentive travel,** which is travel that is offered by an organization as a reward. Usually, the reward is offered to employees for reaching certain specified goals.
- **Leisure travel,** which is travel bought by individuals or groups for pleasure. The specific aim might range from seeing new and exciting places to sitting on a beach, gambling, golfing, or white-water rafting.
- **VFR travel,** which is travel undertaken to visit friends or relatives. It is often treated as a subcategory of leisure travel.

Often, the uses of travel overlap. For example, a person might extend a business trip to Hawaii in order to visit friends or to spend a few days on the beach. Meeting travel and incentive travel are usually paid for by businesses and amount to a type of business travel.

Despite this overlap among the five types of travel, for each type of travel the needs of the traveler differ. VFR travelers are usually the easiest people to serve. For the most part, they know what they want—to see a friend in California, to visit a grandparent in Arizona, and so forth. VFR travelers may need help in finding the best way to get to their destination, but usually their other requirements are few. Let's take a closer look at the needs of the other types of travelers.

The Needs of Business Travel Buyers

In the business travel market, the company or organization that pays for the travel counts as the customer, but its needs are not the only ones to be considered. Sellers of business travel must meet the needs of (1) the company or organization that pays for the travel, (2) the person who arranges the travel (often a secretary or administrative assistant), and (3) the person actually traveling. Each of these has slightly differing needs.

The Company. The customer for business travel may be a company that has just a handful of travelers who buy a trip now and then, or a large organization that spends hundreds of millions of dollars on travel each year. Companies are most interested in getting the greatest amount of travel possible for the least amount of money, without inconveniencing their travelers. Thus, price greatly affects the travel seller's ability to attract and retain corporate accounts.

Still, a company does have other needs besides a good price. In particular, the company is likely to be concerned with a travel agency's ability to

- Help set up and implement travel policies and procedures. For example, what controls will ensure that an employee cannot charge unauthorized travel to the company?
- Develop a system for handling reservations (by phone, fax, automatically, and so on). For example, the company might want to know how a travel agency will obtain airline tickets in an emergency.
- Use data on travel patterns to identify future cost-saving strategies. Does the agency have a good record for negotiating special rates from frequently used vendors?
- Develop convenient financial arrangements. What are the agency's policies regarding rebating, management fees, and so on?

The Travel Arranger. Travel sellers must also consider the needs of the people within the company who arrange travel. These travel arrangers are interested in making arrangements in the simplest and most efficient manner. They want to speak with people who are experienced and knowledgeable about fares, about travel between airports and city centers, and about other aspects of destination geography. Of course, they are also interested in courtesy and general responsiveness.

The Traveler. Business travelers are not traveling for the fun of it. The 1997 National Business Travel Monitor found that four out of ten business travelers consider business travel to be a hassle; three out of ten experience stress during or after a business trip; and four out of ten don't sleep well on business trips.

Above all, business travelers are likely to be looking for a trip as free of hassles as possible. Their technical needs are likely to include transportation and lodging; convenience and comfort are their key psychological needs. Thus the business traveler is concerned with

- The type of itinerary and travel documentation provided. For example, can the traveler tell at a glance the time allowed for making a connection from one plane to another?
- The accuracy of reservations. Even more than other travelers, business travelers are not likely to have the time or the energy or the patience to deal with the reservation that somehow does not exist.
- Prompt and flexible service. Business travelers may need to change reservations at a moment's notice. They might make a reservation at noon and expect the tickets and boarding pass by 5 P.M.
- Support if problems arise. Is the traveler on his or her own if something goes wrong?
- Services and small conveniences that make it easier to work on the spot. Is the hotel close to the airport or to the site of the traveler's appointments? Does the hotel room have a desk with an office chair? Are local calls from the hotel room free? Is a cellular phone available with the rental car?

Because their trips are working trips, business travelers may also appreciate small, ego-boosting "perks" to counteract the fear of failure and the stress of schedules that often accompany work. Because of the insecurities that come with work, they may be especially eager for hotels with concierge service and exercise facilities, upgrades to first-class service on flights, and other luxuries that make them feel important. Of course, these luxuries can be offered only if doing so is consistent with the policies of the traveler's company.

The Special Needs of Meeting and Incentive Travel

The needs of meeting and incentive travelers are very specialized. Consider this example:

Hale & Co., an executive search firm headquartered in Seattle, has recently seen some troubled times. The chairman of the board left under extreme pressure. Several other key people then quit. Morale is low. The acting chairman wants the company's top managers to spend three nights in a location that will encourage team building and creative problem solving. The chairman is asking for a tranquil setting where the executives can relax, get some exercise, and feel replenished.*

For this meeting, Hale might look to its travel agency for help

■ In finding a site.
■ In selecting activities.
■ In arranging travel to and from and around the site.
■ In registering participants.
■ In coordinating arrangements at the meeting for pricing, food selection, speakers, and so on.

For other meetings, the client's needs might be much simpler, or far more complex, because meetings come in all shapes and sizes. Meetings are held by small civic groups, businesses, and national trade associations. There are meetings (or "workshops") to train employees, meetings (or "expositions") to give information to potential customers, meetings (or "retreats") to boost managers' morale, and so on. One group might need just a motorcoach for transportation to a one-day meeting at a school plus audiovisual services at the meeting. Another might require flights to a distant location; transportation from the airport to the meeting site and back again; lodging; meals; and sightseeing arrangements.

A client who is arranging incentive travel might need help with all of the elements involved in meeting travel, plus some additional concerns. Suppose a clothing company asks for help in designing an incentive travel program to boost the loyalty of its retailers or the sales by its sales representatives. The travel experience that is offered as the reward must be so extraordi-

nary that participants won't think they could duplicate it on their own; otherwise, it would not be worth making the effort that is needed to qualify for the trip. Furthermore, the customer is likely to need help in designing and implementing the incentive plan. In other words, someone must answer a host of questions:

■ Who is eligible for the program?
■ What must they do in order to qualify for the trip?
■ How will the rules be publicized and implemented?
■ How will the winners be announced?

These aren't trivial questions; they may determine whether the program succeeds or not. To be counted as a success, the results of the incentive program must make good business sense for the company or organization sponsoring the trip; the benefits must exceed the costs. Thus, the planner needs

■ To specify goals for the incentive program, such as the extent to which it is likely to boost sales.
■ To determine a planned reward that is large enough to motivate participants to meet those goals.
■ To budget carefully for all of the many costs of the incentive program.

In short, satisfying the needs of those buying meeting or incentive travel is a challenging task. It is also a job with a future, for these types of travel represent a large and growing market.

The Psychological Needs of Leisure Travelers

Like people attending meetings or the winners of incentive travel, leisure travelers may need transportation, lodging, and help with activities. At the least, the successful travel seller must meet these technical needs. Sometimes, that task can get complicated (see the Selling through Service case "Out to Lunch," for example). Usually, though, the technical needs of leisure

---

*Adapted from Institute of Certified Travel Agents, *Sales Skills Development Program,* p. 15.

Selling through Service

Out to Lunch

"Hello, Cranson Travel. Allison Ames speaking. How may I help you?" said the sweet-sounding voice.

"Oh, hi! This is Terry Sandler. I'm going on the Fall Festival tour that you're sponsoring in a few months and I was hoping you could help me with a problem."

Allison suppressed a sigh. It was just about lunch time, and she was eager for a break. But she reminded herself that it was, after all, her job to help.

Mrs. Sandler went on to explain that she had been expecting an elderly friend to join her on the tour, but her friend had recently hurt her hip. "If she's in a wheelchair or if she has to use a cane, will that be a problem? Can she go ahead and book, or is that too risky?"

"Well," said Allison, "That's hard to say. You'd have to be sure that there'd be no trouble with the airline, and the motorcoach companies' policies vary."

"Oh." Mrs. Sandler waited a moment, expecting more information. But Allison's mind was wandering to her lunchtime possibilities.

"Can I do anything else for you?"

"Thank you anyway." And Mrs. Sandler hung up.

If you were Allison Ames' manager and overheard this conversation, what would you say?

■ ■ ■

Allison's conversation amounts to a lesson in how not to sell, how not to give good service, and how not to solve problems! Recall the first three steps in problem solving outlined in Figure 1.5: (1) acknowledge the problem, (2) collect the facts, and (3) take responsibility. Allison did none of these things.

In fact, many U.S. suppliers accommodate the needs of people with a variety of physical limitations. According to federal law, people with disabilities cannot be discriminated against, and they must have access to the same services enjoyed by those without disabilities. Thus, if Allison had followed the seven problem-solving steps, she might have helped both Mrs. Sandler and her friend; she might also have gained Mrs. Sandler's loyalty for her agency as well as an additional member of the tour.

What could Allison have done? She might have begun by saying something like, "Oh, I'm sorry to hear that. We'll need to know more to see what can be done. On this tour, it just might work." She would need to find out more about the mobility of Mrs. Sandler's friend and to check the policies of the particular airline and motorcoach company involved in the tour. In Chapter 3 we discuss some sources of information about such policies. Allison should, at the least, take responsibility for finding the needed information. Mrs. Sandler, after all, is a client, and her friend is a potential customer.

travelers are simpler than those for meeting or incentive travel.

In contrast, the psychological needs of leisure travelers are more complicated than those of any other type of traveler. If you are dealing with business travelers, you basically know at least why they are on the road instead of staying home. But when you are helping non-VFR leisure travelers, two questions are important:

1. Why are they traveling at all?
2. What needs shape their decisions about where and how to travel?

Answers to why leisure travelers are traveling often involve the needs discussed by Maslow and McClelland. Some researchers have tried to develop a more precise picture of the motivation for travel. Motives like curiosity and the need for status, for example, figure in some explanations. But no single analysis is compelling. When Plog Research asked Americans to rate motives for leisure travel, they gave the highest marks to

- Getting rid of stress.
- Enriching their perspective on life.
- Bringing the family closer together.
- Doing what they want, when they want.
- Feeling alive and energetic.

More can be said about why people choose particular destinations. In a 1990 survey sponsored by *Travel Agent* magazine, the three factors most often cited by travelers as the basis for choosing a destination were

- Weather
- Sightseeing
- Beaches

But why do some people look for these things in Miami Beach and others at beaches on the Mediterranean? What needs are they satisfying by their choices? Psychographic analysis can help provide answers.

Applying Psychographics. Earlier, we discussed Plog's analysis of venturers and dependables (look again at Figure 2.3). Venturers, Plog suggests, will be eager to be among the first to discover a new vacation spot; dependables will prefer places that offer reassuring signs of home; and most people will fall somewhere between these extremes. Table 2.2 shows some of the specific destination preferences for people with these differing psychological characteristics.

Plog's analysis also suggests one way in which a person's choice of destination might change over time. A destination "discovered" by a venturer may gradually become popular, losing its appeal to venturers. The spot instead becomes more attractive to near-venturers and to **centrics** (those whose characteristics fall between those of venturers and dependables). When the name of a once-isolated, exotic beach becomes familiar and the area attracts hotels, amusement parks, and fast-food restaurants, it will be a destination for dependables.

What does Plog's analysis mean for the salesperson? Among all the characteristics of your clients that you might consider, you should pay special attention to their desire for adventure and novelty—or, in contrast, their need for familiarity and comfort. When you recommend a destination or activity or lodging to a leisure traveler, try to match its novelty to the adventuresomeness and curiosity of the client.

Special Needs and Special Interests. Demographic characteristics can also help point you to partic-

Table 2.2

Destination Preferences of U.S. Travelers

Venturers	Near-venturers	Centrics	Near-dependables	Dependables
Third World countries	Pacific islands	Sunbelt states	Sunbelt states	Miami
Eastern Europe	Much of Asia	Most of central and	Oahu	Waikiki
Russia	Much of Latin America	southern Europe	Much of the Midwest	Very commercialized
China	Scandinavia	United Kingdom	Las Vegas and other	destinations that can be
Hard-adventure vacations	Alaska and parts of the	All islands of Hawaii	gambling sites	reached by car in the
	western states		Branson, MO	United States
	Soft-adventure vacations			

Sources: Based on Plog Research, Inc., and personal communication.

ular needs of leisure travelers. Depending on their age, for example, leisure travelers may be interested in hotels that offer babysitting services or rooms that are close to elevators and have large-button telephones. They may also be eligible for a variety of discounts.

Clients may also have special interests that influence their travel preferences. Even when salespeople cannot identify clients' underlying psychological motives for travel, their interests may be easy to discover. Among the many possibilities, for example, are

- *Shopping,* which ranks among the top activities of domestic and international travelers. Shopping tours can be organized to almost anywhere.
- *Religion.* Jerusalem, the Vatican, and Mecca, for example, are key destinations for those traveling with religious interests.
- *Entertainment.* The chance to sample the nightlife of a city like Las Vegas or New York or Paris sometimes stands on its own as a reason for traveling.
- *Art.* People will travel halfway around the world to experience great art and architecture firsthand.

- *History and culture.* Many people travel in order to trace their own roots or to learn about the past by visiting museums and historical sites.
- *Food and drink.* The chance to sample different cuisines or take wine-tasting tours attracts many people.
- *Ecotourism.* An increasing number of people are eager for the chance to experience nature's variety and beauty.
- *Active sports.* Skiing, golf, tennis, scuba diving, and windsurfing are among the many sports that people combine with travel.

Increasingly, travel suppliers offer products and services to meet special needs and interests like these. Whether a client is a single person looking to meet other singles, a honeymooner looking for the ultimate in romance, a person with special dietary needs, or a person with a physical disability, there are suppliers geared to meeting that client's needs. The travel counselor, though, must learn to ask about these needs and interests. How to find the right suppliers and how to get information about the client's needs are topics we discuss in the coming chapters.

*C*hapter Wrap-Up

Chapter Highlights

Even experts in consumer behavior cannot say much with certainty about why people buy what they buy, but good salespeople learn to be able to understand their buyers' needs. Later chapters explore the techniques for acquiring this understanding; this chapter has developed a background for it. Here is a review of the objectives with which we began this chapter.

1. **Describe the types of needs that motivate buyers.** Buyers are motivated by both technical needs and psychological needs. The psychological needs can be difficult to identify. Maslow suggests that people are motivated by a hierarchy of needs. Among the psychological needs that should be considered are what McClelland labels the need for achievement, need for affiliation, and need for power. Many needs are likely to work together to motivate a buyer, however, and how they interact depends in part on the situation. Competition for the sale; habit; who asks for the sale and how; the importance of the purchase; whether the buyer is pressed for time—all of these can affect how the buyers' needs interact and what the ultimate buying decision is.

2. **Explain three ways of classifying potential buyers.** Buyers can be classified in terms of demographics, psychographics, or usage; these represent three of the many ways of identifying market segments. The segments are analyzed through market research that may use either primary or secondary data. Demographic segments might include, for example, people of the same sex or people with similar incomes or people of similar ages. Psychographic segments include people with similar values, beliefs, or other psychological characteristics. Usage segmentation might be based on the purposes of travel, such as business or pleasure.

3. **Identify five types of travel buyers.** When travelers are classified in terms of the purpose of travel, the major categories are those engaged in business or corporate travel, meeting travel, incentive travel, leisure travel, and VFR travel. These types overlap. Meeting and incentive travel, for example, are usually also business travel, and VFR travel is often considered a subcategory of leisure travel.

4. **Outline key needs of different types of travel buyers.** Buyers of VFR travel are likely to have few needs beyond transportation. For business travel, the company, the travel arranger, and the traveler all have needs that must be considered. For the company, price is likely to be the main concern; for the travel arranger, efficiency; for the traveler, comfort and convenience. Buyers of meeting and incentive travel are likely to have additional needs, requiring help on such varied issues as site selection, contest design, and on-site arrangements. Leisure travelers present more complicated psychological needs. They may decide to travel in order to satisfy any of a huge array of motives, such as curiosity or the need for status. Plog's research suggests that where they choose to travel depends to a great extent on whether they are venturers, centrics, or dependables.

New Terms. The terms that follow were introduced in this chapter. If you do not recall their definitions, see the Glossary, which begins on page 237.

business or corporate travel
centrics
demographics
dependables
hierarchy of needs
incentive travel
leisure travel
market research
market segments
meeting travel
need for achievement
need for affiliation
need for power
primary data
psychographics
psychological needs
secondary data
technical needs
venturers
VFR travel

Review Exercises

Check-Up

Give yourself a quick test of your memory of a few basic points. Read each of the following statements and indicate whether it is true (T) or false (F). See the answers below the statements.

T   F   1. People who are hungry will never worry about the opinions of others.

T   F   2. Your technical needs determine what you buy.

T   F   3. If you have a strong need for achievement, you are motivated primarily by the desire for social status.

T   F   4. Meeting travel and incentive travel are very specialized.

T   F   5. Salespeople must consider the needs of the company buying business travel as well as the needs of the traveler.

T   F   6. "Dependables" favor destinations that offer novelty.

Answers: 1. F, 2. F, 3. F, 4. T, 5. T, 6. F

Discussion Questions

1. **The Taxonomy of Travel.** How do the needs of VFR travelers differ from the needs of leisure travelers?

2. **Understanding Business Travelers.** You work for an agency with ten employees in a downtown office in a medium-sized city in the Midwest. Early one morning, you answer a phone call for the agency owner. You ask to take a message. The caller represents a local company and tells you that the company is looking for a travel agency to help them in their travel arrangements. There are approximately twenty-five travelers in the company, although five or six people do most of the traveling. What do you think are the key issues that will concern this client in selecting a travel agency?

_____

_____

_____

_____

_____

_____

_____

_____

3. **Understanding Leisure Travelers.** What needs or interests do you think might be met by taking a cruise? Does it matter whether the cruise is a short trip to the Caribbean or a tour of undeveloped Pacific islands?

_____

_____

_____

_____

_____

_____

_____

_____

A Case in Question

Consider again the "Out to Lunch" case discussed on page 37.

1. Did Allison Ames do anything right in her conversation with Terry Sandler?

_____

_____

_____

_____

2. On page 37, we described one way in which Allison might have carried out problem-solving step 1, acknowledging the problem. What would you say to Mrs. Sandler in order to carry out this step?

_____

_____

_____

_____

3. What additional information about the condition of Mrs. Sandler's friend would you want to have in order to advise Mrs. Sandler?

_____

_____

_____

_____

An Exercise in Selling: Tailoring Your Approach

To help you learn to tailor your approach to the needs of clients, here is an exercise in applying the analyses of psychological needs discussed in this chapter. First, break into groups of three or four members each so that you can discuss the exercise easily. Then consider the following statements from four customers:

- *Customer A.* Michael Hadd: "This is the first time we'll be on vacation alone since the kids were born. It seems like everyone we know has shown us pictures of these fantastic hotels and restaurants. Now it's our turn. We want to see how the people who really count do things. Nothing second class."

- *Customer B.* JoLyn Peebles: "I haven't taken a vacation since I completed my thesis five years ago! Well, it's my thirtieth birthday now, and I want to get away from the company for a couple of weeks and forget it all. I'd like to stretch my mind a bit, though, and learn about something completely different. There are so many interests I don't have a chance to follow up on when I'm so busy, I don't want to waste this chance."

- *Customer C.* Warren McCall: "For five years Eleanor was in a nursing home with Alzheimer's. Now she's gone. I'm alone. I have to get away, darn it. I'd really like to go visit the kids, but they're all too busy right now. You know how it is. So I'd just like to get out of here and get around some people."

- *Customer D.* DJ Anderson: "I've been to the usual places with my parents—the Caribbean, Europe, southern California. I really want to go someplace different, off the beaten path. Maybe someplace where I could try climbing or something."

Based on these statements, which, if any, of these customers shows the following characteristics?

1. Venturer _____

2. Need for achievement _____

3. Need for affiliation _____

4. Need for power _____

5. Dependable _____

Now indicate which customer is most likely to find each of the following statements appealing.

1. "This is a little risky, frankly, and the accommodations are on the primitive side, but I think you'll love it." _____

2. "This is one of our most exclusive vacations. This spot is really hot now, and there aren't enough rooms to meet the demand! You're in luck, though, because we have a few set aside." _____

3. "This place is very well run. Everything professionally done. And the location is fantastic. There are more things to choose from to do than I can begin to tell you about." _____

4. "This place is run by the friendliest people you can imagine! And it's contagious. I've had several clients just rave about the friends they made during their stay." _____

Discuss all of your answers with other members of your group. Which characteristic had no match with a customer? It is the topic of Worksheet 2.1, page 45. With other members of your group, complete that worksheet. It asks you to list (1) characteristics of a trip or comments that are likely to appeal to this type of customer; (2) characteristics or comments that should be avoided when dealing with this type of customer.

Worksheet 2.1

Name _____ Date _____

Tailoring Your Approach to the Client

Suppose you are dealing with a client who is a "dependable" in terms of Plog's psychographic spectrum (see Figure 2.3). With other members of your group, list the characteristics of a trip or comments from a travel counselor that are likely to appeal to the client. Then list characteristics or comments to be avoided. Discuss your lists. You may want to duplicate this form before writing on it.

Characteristics and Comments
Appealing to Dependables

Characteristics and Comments
to Avoid When the Client Is a Dependable

_____ _____

_____ _____

_____ _____

_____ _____

_____ _____

_____ _____

_____ _____

_____ _____

_____ _____

_____ _____

_____ _____

_____ _____

_____ _____

_____ _____

_____ _____

_____ _____

C H A P T E R   3

Understanding the Travel Product

Objectives

After reading this chapter, you should be able to

1. Outline a strategy for becoming knowledgeable about travel products.

2. Describe key sources for information on travel.

3. Discuss some key sources for the basic information needed when selling a destination, transportation arrangements, accommodations, a cruise, or a tour.

4. Explain two key principles for evaluating travel products.

Preview

The insights into buyers' needs discussed in Chapter 2 represent one key item in the toolkit for selling. But if salespeople needed only an understanding of these needs, then novelists or psychologists might be the best salespeople. In fact, accomplished travel professionals understand not only their buyers but also their products. They have gained a firm knowledge of the travel industry, world geography, and many facets of travel. This chapter cannot give you that knowledge, but it is a starting point, and it shows how to expand your knowledge over time.

What do you need to know about travel products, and how can you learn it? Those are the key questions addressed by this chapter. We discuss a framework for organizing information about travel, sources for gathering that information, and principles for evaluating travel products.

Getting on Top of the Travel Product

Suppose you decide to buy a car. You go to a dealer and are greeted by a delightful salesperson.

"I'm interested in buying a car," you tell him.

"What sort of car do you want?" asks the salesperson.

"I'm not sure."

"Well, we have all kinds of cars. How about a red one?"

You are a little puzzled by this approach. But wanting to be polite, you ask, "Well, before we talk about color, can we talk about size, and price, and style?"

"We have all those things, too. In fact, we have everything. But to be honest, I haven't driven every type of car, and I don't know too much about all their engines, safety features, and pricing. But I can show you anything we have on the floor and tell you a little bit about them if you just give me more information."

You are beginning to feel a little uncomfortable at this point, but figure you can still make this situation work. So you tell him, "I've been thinking of a Chevrolet convertible, a Cavalier, I think. I really like the way they look and it's in my price range."

Your salesman agrees, "They're really cute. I have a brochure on them I can give you, but I've never driven one. Personally, I drive a Pontiac. It's about the same size and price and you might really like it. Want to try one of them?"

"I'll be back later," you say, running for the door.

This interaction is not as crazy as it might seem at first. It simply involves a salesperson who is trying to sell a product about which he knows little. So instead, he tries to sell the product he knows—the car he drives.

Good sales skills are not a substitute for product knowledge. Instead, they allow you to put that knowledge to work. It is almost impossible to sell a product effectively if you have no knowledge of it.

In travel, there are hundreds of destinations; many types of trips and travel experiences; thou-sands of products, services, and suppliers. No one can travel everywhere or be up to date about every product. You simply cannot know everything. So what do you do?

In truth, no one starting out in any career—not doctor, lawyer, or cook—knows everything about his or her industry. The novice simply needs to know enough. You need to know enough to be helpful, and where to go to get more information if needed. More importantly, you should know what you do not know; you should realize when to seek help. Over time and with study and practice, you will acquire expertise and learn where to find the information you need in order to serve your clients.

Mapping the Questions

How do you get started? You need, in effect, some maps, frameworks for thinking about what you are selling. In the previous chapter, Figure 2.4 provided a first step, a large-scale "map" that divides the travel market into segments based on the purpose of the travel. Using this approach, we identified five segments or travel markets: business or corporate travel, meeting travel, incentive travel, VFR travel, and leisure travel. The needs of the customers, and thus the products bought, differ from market to market.

By thinking through the characteristics of these markets, you can gain a firm grip on what it is you need to know in order to sell to the customers in each. Figure 3.1, for example, shows a checklist of tasks and services that you might be responsible for if you were arranging meeting travel. Most travel markets place fewer demands on salespeople. If you are a travel counselor selling leisure travel, for example, the key products you need to know about can be divided into five categories:

1. Destinations and the activities and attractions they offer
2. Transportation
3. Accommodations
4. Cruises
5. Tours

Gateway Travel
Sue Warn, Meeting Planner

Contact: *Fran Goodrich*
Genetics &
Society Institute

☑ Clarify goals and requirements:

Dates of meeting *Fri. 8/4 - Tues. 8/9*

Preferred location *mountain resort; northeast*

Type of meeting *academic workshops & lectures*

Purposes *1) information 2) recreation 3) establish strong ties among*
group to facilitate future cooperation on research projects

Description of participants *40 postgraduates & professors*

Description of where they will come from *across the U.S.*

Accommodations desired *to be determined*

☑ Select site and facilities

☑ Negotiate with facilities

☑ Budgeting

☑ Handling reservations and housing

☐ Planning the program for the meeting

☐ Planning the guidebook/staging guide/documentation of specifications

☑ Establishing registration procedures

☐ Arranging for and using support services

☐ Coordination with the convention center or hall

☐ Briefing facilities staff

☐ Shipping

☐ Planning setup of function rooms

☐ Managing exhibits

☐ Managing food and beverage service

☐ Determining audiovisual requirements

☐ Selecting speakers

☐ Booking entertainment

☐ Scheduling promotion and publicity

☐ Developing programs for guests and families

☐ Producing and printing meeting materials

☐ Distributing gratuities

☑ Evaluating meeting

Figure 3.1 Learning about Meeting Travel
If you were arranging meetings, you might fill out a checklist like this one in order to keep track of which tasks were your responsibility. Suppose you were responsible for the tasks checked here. What questions would you want to research?
Source: Based on "Managing Meetings," *The Official Business Travel Manager's Reference, A Supplement to Business Travel News*, March 23, 1993, pp. 55–56, and Darryl Jenkins, *Managing Business Travel* (Homewood, IL: Irwin, 1993), pp. 300–301.

Eventually, when you are selling a travel product you will come down to questions about the suppliers of that product. Which tour company or cruise line, which hotel or airline, for example, would best meet the client's needs? The answer will obviously depend on the specific client and the specific trip you are considering. Beyond the particular services offered by a supplier, however, you should be sure you know about two characteristics:

1. *Reputation.* What do you know about the supplier? Do you know whether it is reliable? Does it assure a certain level of quality? In what areas does it have expertise?
2. *Relationship.* What is the relationship between the supplier and you or your company? For example, if you use this supplier, are you assured of preferred availability or support? Whether a travel counselor is trying to learn about travel products or making a recommendation to a client, it makes sense to begin by considering the travel agency's preferred suppliers.

The Selling through Service case on page 51 ("No Room at the Inn") illustrates the importance of these characteristics. Solving the problem described there will be much easier if the travel counselor has an ongoing, positive relationship with the hotel's management.

Suppose client Jerry Ripley is determined to go someplace for a week where he can try white-water rafting and examine unusual architecture. What are the possibilities? Where do you go for the information you need to help him? That is the question we examine next.

Exploring the Answers

If there is one thing the world does not lack today, surely it is information. To find out about travel products, you can draw on basically four types of sources: firsthand knowledge, person-to-person discussions, on-line sources, and printed references.

Personal Experience. Firsthand knowledge is the most appealing source of information, for both you and your clients. Imagine being able to talk to your client about a hotel, cruise ship, or theme park that you have visited yourself. Rather than relying on a brochure to illustrate the features of the product, you can describe a special meal you enjoyed, the comfort of the accommodations, or the newest attraction in the theme park. Your own traveling experiences add a special dimension to your sales encounters.

Luckily, you can gain some of this firsthand experience through ***familiarization trips (fam trips).*** These are trips offered to travel professionals at a reduced rate so that they can inspect hotels and restaurants, sample attractions, and experience the local culture. They may be offered by cruise lines, tour companies, hotels, airlines, or even governments.

A true fam trip is a working trip: you travel with a group, follow a special itinerary, and are expected to participate in scheduled functions and to learn as much as you can. There are also *discounted trips* on which you are expected to do little besides enjoying the trip and sampling services as a typical traveler might. Cruise lines also offer ship inspections, including weekend inspections on which you fly to a port for ship tours, on-board meals, and seminars.

In the rapidly changing world of travel, however, nothing is as constant as change. Properties change hands, cruise lines and airlines consolidate, and restaurants hire new chefs. The value of personal experience is limited by how recently it occurred.

Tips
Sources of Information

To learn about travel products, travel professionals use

1. Firsthand knowledge
2. Personal contacts
3. On-line sources
4. Printed references

Personal Contacts. Like personal experience, person-to-person contact is a very rich yet limited resource. Clients, coworkers, family, and friends—all can add insights. Listen carefully to their assessments to pick up valuable information about everything from the best beaches for snorkeling to the most comfortable meeting facilities.

You might also turn to people in the travel industry outside your office. Representatives of suppliers, tourist boards, and trade associations

---

Selling through Service

No Room at the Inn

Dave Macomber had just settled back at his desk after a hectic day. Starting as a travel agent straight out of school, Dave had been in the business more than ten years. Although he still helped out with reservations occasionally, he was now a representative for large corporate accounts at one of the country's largest travel agencies. His job was to make sure that everything went right for Pemi-United, Inc., no matter what the issue.

The phone rang. "Dave, this is June Miller." June was the travel manager of Pemi-United. Dave has worked diligently to establish a solid professional relationship with her. "Look Dave, I'll be quick. It appears that Joe, our senior vice president, just got walked at the hotel in Chicago. They claim he had no reservation. He was pretty boiled over when he called me. He checked his bags and went out to a meeting. And he told me to get the problem fixed while he was at the meeting. That gives us two hours." What should Dave do?

■ ■ ■

In Chapter 1 we suggested a method for dealing with problems like this. Recall our seven steps in problem solving: (1) acknowledge the problem, (2) collect the facts, (3) take responsibility, (4) select a strategy for solving the problem, (5) test the solution, (6) resolve the problem, (7) follow up. What do you think Dave should do in order to carry out the first few steps?

In step 1, acknowledging the problem, it is important to let the customer know that you understand how he or she feels. In this case, as in many others, it is enough to say something like, "I'm sorry you were inconvenienced."

In step 2, collecting the facts, learning the sequence of events often is not enough. You need to uncover how each person involved perceives the situation. This step can produce a side benefit: letting a disgruntled customer vent a complaint, uninterrupted, may reduce his or her irritation.

In this case, Dave already has quite a few facts. As the Pemi-United account representative, he knows where Joe is staying, when the reservation was made, and when it was confirmed; and he knows that it was not canceled by his office. He knows that walking is the policy of substituting nearby accommodations of equal or better quality if no room is available for a guest with confirmed or guaranteed reservations. And June has told him how Joe feels about the snafu. But Dave still needs to determine how June sees the situation and whether she has any more information. And he needs to find out how the hotel views the problem. Dave also needs to let June know that he is taking responsibility for solving the problem (step 3).

Thus, after checking whether she has anything more to say about the situation, Dave might tell June, "Well, I think I can get back to you within an hour. I've worked a lot with their hotel manager, and the hotel's always been eager to please our clients. It may just be a mixup with a new worker. But I'll straighten it out and call you back." Situations like this one demonstrate the benefits of dealing with suppliers you know and trust and of developing strong relationships with them.

(such as **CLIA,** Cruise Lines International Association; **NTA,** National Tour Association; or **ASTA,** American Society of Travel Agents) are all likely to be experts about some specific travel products.

Keep in mind the strengths and weaknesses of personal discussions. When you are dealing with personal sources, you are likely to be in a good position to judge their reliability and currency. But personal contacts are likely to be limited in what they know and in how up to date they are, and they may not be available when you need them.

On-line Sources. Today, instead of talking with a supplier's representative or someone you know at a trade association, you might contact the organization electronically, via fax machines or computers. *Fax* (or *facsimile*) *machines* electronically transmit documents from one site to another via phone lines. Many trade associations and corporations have a wealth of information that they will fax to you in response to a call. Even more impressive, though, is the information you can easily obtain via computer.

In particular, with a CRS you can retrieve information, make reservations, and obtain tickets via computer. **CRSs,** or **computer reservations systems,** are electronic systems that were set up to handle reservations and link distributors (like travel agencies) and suppliers to a centralized, computerized storehouse of information. A CRS creates and maintains a **database**—an organized collection of data—concerning reservations.

Today's CRSs grew out of efforts in the 1970s to offer travel agencies a single system that could handle reservations for all major airlines. When that effort failed, several airlines began installing their own reservations systems in travel agencies, which leased the equipment from the airlines. Soon, the range of data included on CRSs expanded. Today, the airlines are still the dominant owners of the major CRSs (see Table 3.1), but air travel is only one of the products covered by these CRSs.

In fact, because they are now far more than reservations systems, the major CRSs are often called *global distribution systems,* or *GDSs.* They offer gold mines of information a few keystrokes away. On the major CRSs you can find not only information about the availability of a product

Table 3.1
Major CRSs, 1997

	SABRE	Apollo	Amadeus	WORLDSPAN
Agency locations	32,000+	36,110	41,436	16,350+
Airline partners	None (80% owned by AA parent AMR)	United Airlines, KLM, British Airways, Swissair, US Airways, and smaller carriers	Air France, Continental, Lufthansa, and smaller carriers	Northwest Airlines, Delta Air Lines, TWA
Web site for travel agents	AgentExplorer	Apollo.com	Amadeus.net	Worldspan.com
Total airline participants	424	About 500	Schedules for 739 carriers	About 430
Total hotel participants	224	215	291	197
Total car rental participants	53	44	50	50

Source: Based on *Travel Agent,* December 8, 1997, p. 44.

but also basic descriptions of products and rates for airlines, hotels, rental car companies, Amtrak, Eurail, BritRail, tours, cruises, attractions such as Disney World and Universal Studios, and even events such as the Olympics and Wimbledon.

Even people without access to a CRS can gather much of this information if they can get on the World Wide Web. Travel organizations and companies large and small have sites on the Web. You can use the Web to find out about the best restaurants in New Orleans, an intimate bed-and-breakfast in Colorado Springs, or a little specialty shop selling unique sculptures in Cannes. You can obtain lists of suppliers for luxury travel or a map for a trip from Philadelphia to Pittsburgh.

Using the Web. How do you tap into this wealth of information? You need a computer, a modem, and an account with an Internet access provider (such as AT&T Worldnet or America Online).

Software known as a *browser* (such as Netscape's Navigator) translates information from the Internet into graphic form on your computer screen and allows you to move easily from Web site to Web site.

Once you are connected to the World Wide Web, you can type the address of the Web site you want if you know it (for example, "http://www.icta.com" for **ICTA,** the Institute of Certified Travel Agents). Figure 3.2 shows the home page of the official tourism promotion agency of the state of Florida (http://www. flausa.com). If you do not know the Web site address, you can type the address of a *search engine*—such as Yahoo!, AltaVista, or HotBot— and the search engine will find Web sites for you. You type the topic or company or organization you are interested in, and the search engine lists the related sites.

Suppose, for example, you wanted to find

Figure 3.2 A Home Page on the Web
This is the home page of the official tourism promotion agency of the state of Florida.

out more about the possibilities for leisure travel in Florida. You went to the Web and to the Yahoo! search engine; then you typed "Florida." In 1998, Yahoo! would then tell you that it found 5,487 sites in 70 categories. Table 3.2 gives just a small sampling of the information available.

If you do not find what you are looking for when you use one search engine, try another. One 1998 study found that most search engines index only a third of the hundreds of millions of pages on the Web.

Unfortunately, the quality of information provided by both CRSs and Web sites varies tremendously. Some information is good, and some incomplete, or even wrong. For example, information on a Web site might be months out of date; a CRS might display only one fare for renting a particular type of car when in fact several fares may be available if the renter meets certain conditions. You will need to consult experienced people and learn over time in order to judge how to use the information from particular electronic sources.

Table 3.2
Florida-related Web Sites: A Sampling

Web Site	Information Available
Walt Disney World http://www.disney.com/disneyworld	The official Walt Disney World site that includes vacation planning and ticket information, events and attractions, and maps
St. Petersburg and Tampa http://www.stpete-clearwater.com	Area information including lodging, attractions, and activities for vacationers, meeting planners, and travel professionals
Outdoor Recreation http://www.gorp.com/gorp/location/fl/fl.htm	A guide to Florida's National Parks, forests, and recreational activities
Disney Hotels http://www.tenonline.com/disneyhotels	Web site of the seven official hotels of Walt Disney World
The Florida Keys http://www.fla-keys.com	Comprehensive travel information on Key Largo, Islamorada, Marathon Key, Big Pine Key, and Key West
World Golf Village http://www.wgv.com	Opened in 1998, home to the World Golf Hall of Fame
Florida Camping Guide http://www.floridacamping.com/camping-home.html	A guide to RV parks and campgrounds
Miami International Airport http://www.miami-airport.com	Includes a terminal map, facilities and services, flight schedules, and cargo information
Hotels in Florida http://www.hotelstravel.com/usfl.html	Statewide index to hotels and travel resources, with city and regional breakdowns, major chains' listings, and links to individual hotels
Ticketmaster Florida http://events.ticketmaster.com/cgi/events/state.idc?state=fl	On-line box office with comprehensive events and performance listings

Table 3.3

Popular Periodicals on Travel: A Sampling

Type	Periodical	Address
Trade Periodicals These magazines and newspapers are written for people in the travel industry.	*Travel Weekly*	Reed Travel Group 500 Plaza Drive Secaucus, NJ 07094-3602 (201) 902-1500
	Travel Agent	801 Second Avenue, 12th Floor New York, NY 10017 (212) 370-5050
	Business Travel News and *Leisure Travel News*	600 Community Drive Manhasset, NY 11030-3847 (516) 562-5000
	Travel Counselor	600 Harrison Avenue San Francisco, CA 94107 (415) 905-2200
	TravelAge	500 Plaza Drive Secaucus, NJ 07094 (201) 902-2000
	Travel Trade	15 W. 44th Street New York, NY 10036 (212) 730-6600
	Outbound Traveler	7 Tucker's Wharf Marblehead, MA 01945 (781) 631-1690
Consumer Periodicals These magazines and newspapers are written for the general public. They provide a great deal of information about destinations as well as about trends in travel.	*Condé Nast Traveler*	360 Madison Avenue New York, NY 10017-3136 (212) 880-8800
	Travel and Leisure	1120 Avenue of the Americas New York, NY 10036-6770 (212) 382-5600
	Travel Holiday	28 W. 23rd Street New York, NY 10010-5204 (212) 366-8700
	National Geographic	National Geographic Society 17th and M Streets NW Washington, D.C. 20036 (202) 828-5485

Printed References. Printed material still represents the most comprehensive source of information. Most accessible are advertisements and brochures. You can learn a lot about a supplier by carefully reading its ads and brochures and getting a feel for their approach and quality. Of course, advertisements and brochures are selling tools, not objective information, and must be evaluated with care, as Figure 3.3 illustrates.

For current information on a wide variety of topics, periodicals are an excellent source. Table 3.3 lists some of the most popular ones. For travel professionals, subscriptions to some of these are free for the asking.

For more detailed information and answers to specific questions, you can draw on an amazing number of books and directories. We describe some of the most useful ones in the next section, as we discuss where to look for information on specific types of travel products.

Gathering Data: A Sampling of Sources

Whatever travel market you are interested in, certain topics are likely to crop up again and again. As a salesperson, you are bound to have questions about destinations, about how to get to them, and about the accommodations available there. In this section we offer an introduction to some of the most comprehensive and reliable sources of information on these topics outside of CRSs. (We do not list Web sites because any list would be quickly out of date; each day brings new sites as well as changes to existing ones.) As you gain expertise, you will find your own favorite sources.

The Appendix on page 235 lists the addresses for some of the organizations mentioned in this section. You can locate just about any travel company or travel organization by checking *Fairchild's Travel Industry Personnel Directory* (Philadelphia: Fairchild Books) or *The Travel Agent Official Travel Industry Directory* (New York: Travel Agent). These directories are published yearly.

Destinations

What do you need to know in order to sell a destination to a client? The basic issues concern

- *Accessibility*. How far away is the destination, and how do you get to it?
- *Climate*. You cannot tell a client what the weather will be like, but you can learn about the typical weather prevailing at a destination over a period of time.
- *Culture*. Are the local people known for behaviors or customs that are likely to appeal to travelers or to create problems for them?
- *Costs and standard of living*. How do the costs of lodgings, transportation, food, and everyday expenses at the destination compare with local costs? Can visitors find the services they are accustomed to? Should they expect to encounter deep poverty?
- *Attractions*. What is there to see and do?

For general information about destinations, a world atlas is a most useful tool. For more specific information about particular places, many local and national governments now have Web sites. Local, state, and national tourist offices are a rich resource. National tourist offices offer not only brochures and other travel literature but also seminars, workshops, and well-informed staffs. Profiles of countries and cities around the world are available (in print and on CD-ROMs) from Weissmann Travel Reports in Austin, Texas.

The OAG Travel Planners (Secaucus, N.J.: Reed Travel Group) provide a quick source of information. They are designed to be all-in-one lodging and destination guides particularly suited for business travelers. There are Europe and Asia/Pacific editions as well as the *OAG Business Travel Planner, North American*

New York City

3 Days - Tour NY
2 Meals: 1 Breakfast, 1 Dinner

Collette Advantage
Would you travel to New York City without enjoying breakfast at the famous Tavern on the Green Restaurant?

Are transfers to and from the airport, train station, etc., included?

Day 1: Arrive New York City
You will travel to America's largest and most exciting metropolis, NEW YORK CITY. Upon arrival, you will have time for shopping before you check into your hotel. This evening, you will enjoy a pre-theater dinner before attending a BROADWAY SHOW. Meals included: Dinner.

Day 2: New York
This morning a local tour guide will take you, via motorcoach, on an interesting sightseeing tour of Manhattan. You will pass through such areas as GREENWICH VILLAGE, THE WALL STREET DISTRICT, LITTLE ITALY, and CHINATOWN. You will also view the UNITED NATIONS, THE WORLD TRADE CENTER, THE EMPIRE STATE BUILDING, and THE CHRYSLER BUILDING, as well as countless other famous New York landmarks. Following your tour, you will visit the METROPOLITAN MUSEUM OF ART before traveling to 5TH AVENUE, where you will be at leisure to explore the many famous shops.

Will your clients be satisfied with a tour that does not allow them to get out and visit these sites?

Will your clients be comfortable being on their own?

Day 3: Sightseeing - Depart for Home
You begin the day with an outstanding breakfast at TAVERN ON THE GREEN RESTAURANT. This is sure to be a highlight of your tour. Next, you will visit the STATUE OF LIBERTY and ELLIS ISLAND. This afternoon, you depart for home with many pleasant memories of the "Big Apple." Meals included: Breakfast.

Is the menu limited to specific items? Can the restaurant meet special dietary needs?

Your Hotel
Day 1, 2 Southgate Towers, New York City, NY

On some dates an alternate hotel may be used.

Where is this hotel and what class of accommodation does it provide? What types of rooms are available?

Land Rates Per Person*

	Twin	Single	Triple	Child
March 1–Nov 12	$499	$759	$489	$299
Nov 13–Dec 3	$549	$809	$539	$349
Dec 4 & 11	$569	$829	$559	$369
Dec 5–10 & 12-28	$549	$809	$539	$349

What is included in the tour price?

*Please note: When Radio City Music Hall is open, it will be included in your tour at an additional cost of $60 per person. On certain dates, the Radio City Music Hall performance will be scheduled for the afternoon when there is no evening performance.
*Due to the room configuration in New York City, some rooms may have a pull-out couch which will be used as a second bed.

Departs Fridays, March–December

Figure 3.3 Using Ads and Brochures
Ads and brochures can be useful selling tools if you remember that you are not the only one using them that way: the advertiser, after all, is using them to make a sale. Read them carefully. Watch for language that dresses up limitations to seem like strengths, and look for ambiguities.
Source: Reprinted by permission of Collette Tours.

Edition, which includes maps, ratings for hotels, information on ground and air transportation, and general facts about cities such as local attractions and climate.

For travel abroad, the federal government is often the most convenient source of specialized information. If you want to know about the documents required when traveling overseas, or regulations about what can be brought back into the United States, or the customs of a particular country, or whether the country is safe for traveling, government offices and publications can help. Table 3.4 lists some specific sources.

Guidebooks are another important resource. *The Lonely Planet, Let's Go,* and *Berkeley* series,

---

Table 3.4

U.S. Government Help for Travel Abroad

Topic	Sources of Information
Regulations on going into and out of the country	The government pamphlet *Your Trip Abroad* includes advice on obtaining a passport and preparing for a trip.
	For other information on passports, contact U.S. Customs (P.O. Box 7407, Washington, D.C. 20044), a local Customs office, or the National Passport Information Center (900-255-5674).
Regulations on bringing goods into or out of the country	For information on regulations about what can be brought across U.S. borders and the charges (*duty*) for bringing articles across borders, see the government pamphlets *Know Before You Go* and *GSP and the Traveler.* For additional questions, contact U.S. Customs (P.O. Box 7407, Washington, D.C. 20044) or a local customs office.
	For information on restrictions on bringing fruit, vegetables, livestock, or poultry across the borders, contact the U.S. Department of Agriculture.
Conditions for travelers in other countries	For advice about how to minimize the chance of becoming a victim of terrorism or crime, the government offers the pamphlet *A Safe Trip Abroad.*
	For information about travel to specific areas and countries, the government offers the *Tips for Travelers* series of pamphlets.
	Information regarding which countries are dangerous to visit is provided in U.S. Department of State travel warnings. Information about these warnings as well as emergency services is also available from Overseas Citizens Services at 202-647-5225.
	Information about every country in the world—including health conditions, political disturbances, crime, areas of instability—is provided in the U.S. Department of State's consular information sheets.
	For information on health issues, contact the Centers for Disease Control and CDC's International Travelers' Hotline (404-332-4559) or U.S. Public Health Service (301-443-2403).

Note: Most government pamphlets can be requested from Superintendent of Documents, U.S. Government Printing Office, Washington D.C. 20402.

for example, offer guides that emphasize budget travel. Guidebooks in the *Insight* series provide superb photographs along with essays that give excellent overviews of a country or area. But some of the best-known, comprehensive series of guidebooks include

- The *Baedeker* guides, which emphasize how to get to a destination and what to see when you get there. This series covers countries of Europe, the Caribbean, Asia, and Africa.
- The *Fodor* series, which includes guides to most destinations in the world. Its three-in-one travel kits contain guidebooks, language cassettes, and phrasebook dictionaries. Fodor's coverage of most destinations includes hotel and restaurant reviews as well as comments on nightlife, shopping, and attractions.
- The *Michelin* guides, which come in two main types. Michelin's *Red Guides* provide listings of hotels and restaurants; the *Green Guides* give historical and sightseeing information. There are Michelin guidebooks for specific countries as well as regions. Western Europe is covered best by the series.
- The *Birnbaum* guides, which emphasize tourist services, sources of information, and brief descriptions of important sights. Their "Diversions and Directions" sections include some comments on special-interest travel.
- The *Frommer* "Dollar-a-Day" and city guides emphasize accommodations, restaurants, and sightseeing tips. The Frommer series also offers country and regional guides that include the authors' insights, recommendations, and advice, along with walking maps and pricing and sightseeing information.

If your starting point is not a particular location but special interests or special needs, you might find out about appropriate destinations by checking the Web or *Specialty Travel Index* (San Anselmo, Calif.: Alpine Hansen)—a directory of special-interest travel published twice a year. For information related to travel arrangements for people with disabilities, you might contact SATH (Society for the Advancement of Travel for the Handicapped) or see the *International Directory of Access Guides* (New York: Rehabilitation International USA).

Transportation

Besides information about destinations, travel sellers also need facts about various types of transportation; we focus here on airlines and railroads. What do you need to know about them? As a travel seller, you are likely to face questions about their itineraries, schedules, and prices. The answers can often be found in electronic sources.

Some Web sites claim to be able to find the lowest fares for flights; but at least as of 1998, people (aided by machines) still beat machines at this task. *Travel Counselor* magazine set up a challenge: travel counselor versus the Web. It dialed three self-booking sites on the Web and asked for their best fares for three trips. It also asked three travel counselors to do the same—without telling them that it was a test. The results, the magazine reported, were clear: "In each case, the agents found the best fares, the most creatively, in the least amount of time" (*Travel Counselor*, June 1997, p. 12). If the best you can do for your client is to hand the problem off to a computer, you have not mastered the travel product.

Among printed sources of information on air travel, basic references are

- The *Industry Agents' Handbook* (Arlington, Va.: ARC), which describes the procedures and regulations related to the sale of airline tickets.
- The *OAG Desktop Flight Guide: North American Edition* (Secaucus, N.J.: Reed Travel Group), which gives schedules for more than 250,000 flights in North America, as well as information on minimum connecting times, meals, seating charts, and fares. It is published twice a month.
- The *OAG Desktop Flight Guide: Worldwide Edition* (Secaucus, N.J.: Reed Travel Group), which gives not only schedules for more than 750,000 flights worldwide but also information on credit card acceptance, baggage allowances, international time zones, airport duty-free shops, and exchange rates.

The U.S. government also offers helpful advice about air travel. In particular,

- For statistics on the performance of airlines,

see *Air Travel Consumer Report* from the Office of Aviation Enforcement and Proceedings at the U.S. Department of Transportation. The FAA also provides aviation news, including extensive safety data, posted on its Web site.

■ *Fly-Rights: A Consumer Guide to Air Travel* is a small booklet provided by the Office of Consumer Affairs at the U.S. Department of Transportation. It summarizes information and advice about passengers' rights, overbooking, lost luggage, and other issues most likely to concern passengers.

Information on rail travel is also easily available through both printed and computerized sources. Amtrak's Arrow reservations system, for example, is linked to majors CRSs. Printed sources of information include the following:

■ The *Official Railway Guide* gives detailed information about timetables, fares, services, and rules for Amtrak and VIA Rail Canada. It also includes schedules for the National Railways of Mexico and selected international routes. It is published eight times a year by Amtrak.

■ The *Thomas Cook European Timetable* (available in the United States from the Forsyth Travel Library) includes schedules for trains in Britain and Europe, along with maps and ferry schedules. It is published in Britain each month.

■ The *Thomas Cook Overseas Timetable* (also available from the Forsyth Travel Library) gives schedules for rail routes in more than 150 countries outside Europe as well as schedules for bus, shipping, and ferry services in places not served by rail. Also included are maps and information on issues such as entry requirements, climate, and currency. It is published in Britain six times per year.

Accommodations

Is there a good hotel close to the Evanston airport? Would one of the lodgings inside Shenandoah National Park offer a suitable room for a client, or should you stick with hotels outside the park? Travel sellers frequently face

questions like these. Once you start looking for facts about accommodations, you are likely to find a mountain of information.

The accommodations industry these days offers rooms for every taste and budget. Besides hotels, motels, bed-and-breakfasts, and inns, there are resorts and spas. And even spas come in many types—from U.S. spas, which usually emphasize beauty and fitness, to European spas, which tend to have a medical focus; from destination spas, where the spa itself is the main attraction, to resort spas, where the spa is just one of many amenities.

What do you need to know in order to sell accommodations? As a start, become familiar with the major hotel chains. Many chains operate hotels geared to different price ranges under different names. For example, the Marriott chain includes Fairfield Inns for economy-minded travelers and Marriott Hotels, Resorts, and Suites for those looking for first-class lodging. Choice Hotels International offers EconoLodges for the low-priced end of the market as well as mid-priced Quality Inns.

To evaluate a particular hotel, you should learn about

■ The type of accommodations offered.
■ The location.
■ Food service.
■ Amenities.
■ Price.
■ Special advantages.

You can find information about many hotels and resorts from CRSs and other electronic sources, as well as from many of the reference books mentioned in previous sections. The sales representatives for hotels are also good resources. Three hotel references guides, however, are especially useful:

■ The *Hotel and Travel Index* (Secaucus, N.J.: Reed Travel Group) gives the basic facts about 45,000 hotels, resorts, and inns along with hundreds of maps and thousands of ads, many of which include photographs. It is published quarterly.

■ The *Official Hotel Guide (OHG)* (Secaucus, N.J.: Reed Travel Group) gives detailed profiles of 30,000 hotels and resorts, which it classifies

● Marriott's Camelback Inn   427 R   Ⓔ SWB/DWB $89-345   (MAR)(UI) ....Wynn Tyner, Gen Mgr
5402 E Lincoln Dr, 85253, 15 min from airport, Tel: 602-948-1700, Fax: 602-950-1198 AE MC VS

• **Marriott's Camelback Inn Resort,**
Golf Club & Spa   **453 Rooms   Map D, Dot 93**

5402 E Lincoln Dr   POST CODE: 85253   PHONE: (602)948-1700   FAX: (602)951-8469
Moderate Deluxe Secluded Desert Resort & Golf Club (1936) set on 120 private acres, between
Mummy & Camelback Mountains - 3 miles from downtown Scottsdale & 15 from Sky Harbor Int'l Airport -
Individual casitas with air conditioning, phone, radio, remote-control color cable TV (movies), safe,
kitchenette & patio or balcony - Units for nonsmokers - Wheelchair access - 5 Restaurants - Lounge -
Meetings to 2200 - Business Center - 36 holes of Championship Golf - 6 Tennis Courts - 3 Outdoor Pools -
European Health Spa - Playground - Concierge - Supervised Children's Program - Shops - Laundry - Free
Parking - $35 million renovations in 1997
RATES: EP S/D/TWB $109-280/324-380 Ste 200-1025/500-1700 - Max rates Jan 1-Jun 8 - Tax
10.25%   **COMM:** R-10   **CREDIT CARDS:** AE CB DC DIS ENR JCB MC VISA
RESERVATIONS: REPS: UI MAR   **Toll-Free:** (800)24-CAMEL   **CRS:** Apollo, Sabre,
SystemOne, Worldspan

MARRIOTT'S CAMELBACK INN, 5402 E. Lincoln Dr., PARADISE
VALLEY, near *Marriott's Mountain Shadows,* four miles W of downtown Scottsdale and 10 miles NE of Sky Harbor Airport, is one of the
Southwest's oldest, most traditional convention resorts, with a service-
oriented staff that genuinely cares about the welfare of its guests.
Mountain views enhance this cluster of desert sandstone casitas. The
large Western lobby with its polished flagstone floor was under rehabilitation at inspection to make it more accessible to those in wheelchairs.
The nonworking tower clock gives visual counterpart to the hotel's
motto: "Where Time Stands Still." The lobby features a beehive fire-
place, paintings hung on adobe brick walls, and stenciled beams overhead. Yet more mountain vistas accompany Continental specialties in
the highly regarded *Chaparral* restaurant, where jackets are requested
in season. The less formal room next to it serves all meals in a
Southwestern setting, and a health-food outlet at the spa, a fancy cof-
feeshop-bakery, and daily al fresco buffets provide plenty of variety.
One lounge beams big-screen events for sports fans, and the restaurant
lounge resounds with piano tunes several nights a week. Drinks are
served poolside and at the 19th hole. Of the three plunges, the newest is
the most spectacular, ringed with multilevel sundecks and two
whirlpools. The elaborate spa offers a spectrum of treatments and services in addition to its own whirlpools and cold plunges, saunas, exercise classes, and fitness equipment. Six lighted tennis courts, a nine-
hole pitch-and-putt course, bicycles, lawn games, a playground, a game
room, and shops enhance leisure time, and two 18-hole golf courses are
just five minutes away by car. Groups of up to 1500 can gather in the
meeting area adjoining one pool. Golf carts link lowrise accommodations wings scattered about on different levels. All units are equipped
with TVs, dual-line phones, safes, ironing boards, refrigerators,
microwave ovens, and one king or two double beds. The spacious combination baths feature glass block accents. Privately owned, the pueblo-
style units are primarily in large flat-roofed casitas of one or two stories.
Octagonal rooms with Native American flair have cathedral ceilings
and solid Western furniture. Rooms with sundecks on the second story
fetch about 20 percent more than others. Many have come through
thorough beauty treatments and have new Southwestern and wrought-
iron furnishings in place — these are the ones to request. The best rates
are bundled into the many breakfast, golf, and spa packages. This hotel
has more regional charm than any other large resort in the area, leaving
little to be desired overall. 423 units. $119-$355 single or double. Wynn
Tyner, mgr. (C-10) Marriott, Utell. Phone (800) 242-2635, (602) 948-
1700. Fax (602) 951-8469. ★★★★★

Figure 3.4 Guides to Hotels

The *Hotel and Travel Index* (top), *Official Hotel Guide* (middle), and *Star Service* (bottom) take different approaches to the task of describing hotels. Each has advantages, as you can see in these three descriptions of one hotel, the Marriott's Camelback Inn.

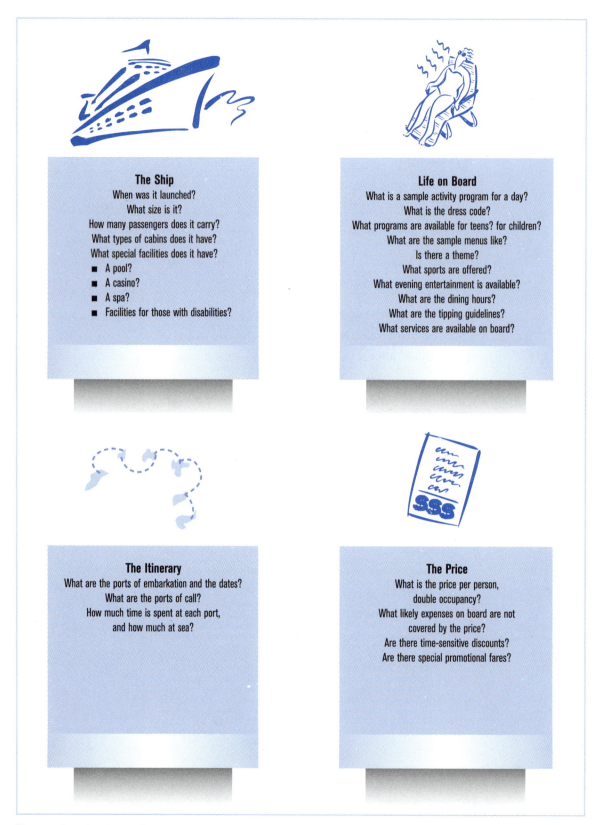

The Ship
When was it launched?
What size is it?
How many passengers does it carry?
What types of cabins does it have?
What special facilities does it have?
- A pool?
- A casino?
- A spa?
- Facilities for those with disabilities?

Life on Board
What is a sample activity program for a day?
What is the dress code?
What programs are available for teens? for children?
What are the sample menus like?
Is there a theme?
What sports are offered?
What evening entertainment is available?
What are the dining hours?
What are the tipping guidelines?
What services are available on board?

The Itinerary
What are the ports of embarkation and the dates?
What are the ports of call?
How much time is spent at each port,
and how much at sea?

The Price
What is the price per person,
double occupancy?
What likely expenses on board are not
covered by the price?
Are there time-sensitive discounts?
Are there special promotional fares?

Figure 3.5 Learning about a Cruise
A cruise has many components. These are some of the questions you would want to answer before selling a cruise.

into ten categories, from moderate tourist class to superior deluxe. It also includes hundreds of maps and a section on specialty travel. It is published once a year in three volumes.

- The *Star Service* offers subjective reviews by travel writers and correspondents, with ratings, of about 10,000 hotels (and more than a hundred cruise ships). As Figure 3.4 shows, it provides a more detailed and more subjective view of hotels than *OHG* or the *Hotel and Travel Index*.

Cruises

Figure 3.5 outlines key questions about a cruise. The numbers of cruise ships and shipping lines change constantly, along with their names, itineraries, sizes, schedules, and services. To keep up to date with current cruise products, you should

- Visit ships and go on cruises. Take advantage of ship inspections and seminars at sea.
- Study videos as well as brochures offered by cruise lines.
- Talk to cruise line representatives. Often they will offer seminars when a new cruise comes on-line.
- Examine the special supplements on cruises published each year by major newspapers such as *The New York Times* and by trade periodicals.
- Check with CLIA (Cruise Lines International Association), a major source of information.
- Refer to cruise directories. *Star Service* also includes helpful information on cruises.

The major directories of cruise lines are

- *CLIA Cruise Manual,* which is updated annually by CLIA. A reference guide to CLIA's member cruise lines, the manual gives information on cruise ships and their companies, including deck plans, menus, and policies regarding discounts and credit cards.
- The *Official Cruise Guide* (Secaucus, N.J.: Reed Travel Group), which is also published annually. It offers profiles of hundreds of cruise ships, with color-coded deck plans as well as maps of ports of call. Also included is information on sailing schedules, rates,

reservations policies, booking information, and more.

You can also turn to the Web for information. Major cruise lines have their own Web sites. Most of these sites offer all the basic information about a cruise that would be found in a brochure, but it is more specific and more up to date.

Tours

Any travel arrangement that packages several features together as a unit—such as transportation and lodging—may be called a *tour*. There are custom-designed tours and prepackaged, mass-marketed tours. There are guided tours and independent tours, tours that package together only an air flight and rental car with a choice of hotels and tours that include flights, motorcoaches, sightseeing, meals, lodging, and more. Thus, to sell a tour you might be interested in some or all of the questions in Figure 3.6.

You can find information about the thousands of tour operators and tours from on-line as well as printed sources. In particular,

- The *Official Tour Directory* (New York: Thomas Publishing), which is published twice a year, describes tour operators and tours and includes some tour brochures bound into it.
- The *USTOA World Tour Desk Reference* is an annual listing of members' programs, services, and destinations published by **USTOA,** the United States Tour Operators Association.
- The *WATA Master-Key* (Geneva, Switzerland) is published annually by the World Association of Travel Agencies.

You might also contact the NTA (National Tour Association), whose members are mostly operators of motorcoach tours. Also, tours are listed in many of the reference books discussed earlier.

For information on specific tours, brochures are indispensable. *Worldwide Brochures: The Official Travel Brochure Directory* (Detroit Lakes, Minn.: Worldwide Brochures) can help you find whatever brochure you might need. Of course, you can also request brochures from tour operators. Many of them are now on the Web.

The Transportation
What is the type and class of air travel, if any?
What are the departure and arrival points?
Are transfers included?
What is the type and class of ground transportation?
What is the luggage allowance?
Is luggage handling provided throughout?

The Price
What is the price per person?
Is there a supplement charged
for those traveling alone?
Are tips included or optional?
What service charges and taxes, if any,
are not included in the price?
What meals and sightseeing options
are included in the price?

The Itinerary
What are the departure and return dates?
What special events and side trips are included?
Is the traveler on his or her own, or does a group travel
together?
If it's a group tour,
- is there an escort, host, or guide?
- What locations are visited?
- How much time is spent at each stop,
and how much time is there between stops?
- What leisure time is allowed?

The Accommodations
What class of accommodations is provided?
Where are the hotels located?
What choice of room types is offered?
What is the location of the rooms offered?
Do the hotels offer any special amenities?
Is there a choice of meal plans?
How many meals are included?
Are the meals offered at the hotels or at restaurants?

Figure 3.6 Learning about a Tour
What do you need to learn about a specific tour before selling it? Here are some of the questions you should be able to answer.

Time Out

Check your understanding of the discussion so far by filling in the blanks.

1. In selecting suppliers, a salesperson should consider both

   _____

   _____.

2. Four key types of sources of information on travel are

   _____

   _____

   _____

   _____

   _____.

3. A travel counselor selling leisure travel should know how to find information about (1) destinations, (2) transportation,

   (3) _____.

   (4) _____.

   (5) _____.

4. Your client wants to travel to an island that underwent a violent coup last year. How do you find out the risks of traveling there?

   _____

   _____

   _____

   _____.

*E*valuating Travel Products

So far, we have discussed what you need to know as a salesperson and where to find the "facts." The point, though, is not to become a walking encyclopedia but to sell, which means helping your client. To do that, you must analyze and interpret facts until you find benefits and determine value.

Finding Benefits

A CRS or a directory will list the ***features*** of a product, which are its objective, inherent characteristics. A salesperson is interested in its ***benefits,*** which are the consequences of characteristics that are positively evaluated by the client.

If you are spending a weekend at a hotel at the beach, is the fact that the hotel provides fax machines, irons, and clothes steamers a benefit? Is the fact that it is close to a national wildlife sanctuary a benefit? These are all features, but whether they are benefits depends on the traveler's perception. Whatever a travel supplier may intend, a feature is not a benefit until the client says it is.

As you explore the characteristics of any travel product, think about its features in terms of its possible benefits for clients. Ultimately, you will want to be able to describe these benefits when you sell the product, as we describe in Chapter 5. And thinking about the product's benefits has another advantage: if you interpret information in terms of benefits as you gather it, you are more likely to be able to recall the information when you need it. Research on memory shows that the more you think about and organize information, the better your ability to retrieve it.

Determining Value

At the end of the day, clients are interested, not in benefits alone, but in value. **Value** reflects the difference between the benefits and the perceived costs. A client may consider the chance to go scuba diving to be an intriguing benefit but a poor value if it requires staying at a hotel that costs an extra $50 a night. To other clients, a fourteen-day tour of Australia for $2,400 may represent a better value than a seven-day tour for $1,000 because the shorter trip would force them to miss some desired activities. Thus, like benefits, value is subjective.

The Role of the Salesperson. Although value lies in the eye of your client, successful salespeople help their clients determine value. Suppose, for example, you are a travel counselor meeting with Richard and Irene Donahue, a couple in their sixties who are looking for a week in the sun, hoping to swim a little and relax a lot. They are traveling alone from Philadelphia and would like to spend no more than $1,800. You have just suggested a visit to Florida, when suddenly Richard exclaims that he knows "just the thing."

"Our neighbors went a couple of years ago. I'd forgotten all about it. They took the Big Blue trip. Remember, Irene? They loved it. It sounded like the trip of a lifetime. That's what we want, isn't it, Irene?"

"Yes, let's do that."

"Can you book us?"

This certainly sounds like an easy sale! But suppose that this hypothetical Big Blue package costs $945 each and offers a four-night cruise from the Florida coast to the Bahamas as well as three nights at Walt Disney World Resort. The brochures emphasize "romantic dancing," "nonstop entertainment," "the best kids' program afloat," as well as unlimited admission to all Disney theme parks. In short, suppose this is a trip made to order for a young couple with children.

Is it a good value for the Donahues? A significant part of the cost goes for features that are not likely to bring them any benefits, such as babysitting services and special entertainment for children on board. The "romantic dancing" and entertainment come at the cost of staying in a modest room. And most of the passengers on the cruise are usually considerably younger than the Donahues. Are they likely to find the company congenial or the entertainment to their taste?

Suppose you doubt that the Donahues will end up seeing many of this cruise's features as benefits. You doubt that the product the Donahues are ready to buy will end up being a good value to them. Should you care?

One key to successful selling is helping your clients find a product that meets their needs at a price they can afford. If you can help clients do that, you have a good chance of having satisfied clients. And satisfied clients are repeat clients. If you book the Donahues on a vacation that will fall short of their expectations, you win short-term gains at the price of a long-term loss. You might earn a commission from this one booking at the cost of losing the potential for repeat business with the Donahues. And you will not be serving their best interests.

What could you say to the Donahues in this situation? You might say something like the following:

Travel counselor: Of course, I'd be happy to make a reservation for you. I've sent a lot of

young families on that trip. It's a great value for parents who want a real family vacation with nonstop fun for the kids. But you know, there's another possibility that I think you might enjoy more. You're looking for a week of warm weather, with opportunities to swim if you want or just relax and enjoy the sun. Right?
Mr. Donahue: That's the ticket.

And then you could proceed with your recommendation. It should be based both on what you have learned about the features offered by suppliers and their costs and on what you have learned about the Donahues. Successful salespeople, in short, help clients assess benefits, costs, and ultimately value.

Detecting Costs. Is a nine-day tour of national parks that includes hotels, ground transportation, and meals for $1,200 a good value? Finding the answer takes some time and expertise. Keep in mind that when you find a benefit, you will almost certainly find a cost as well (see Figure 3.7). For example,

■ The benefit of a cheap airfare is likely to bring the cost of restrictions on when your customer can fly.
■ The benefit of an oceanfront view may bring the cost of a higher price.

■ The benefit of camaraderie on a group tour may bring the cost of restrictions on freedom.
■ The benefit of the adventure in visiting an exotic, isolated beach may bring the costs of inconvenience in getting there and in finding good food.

Many costs are not obvious, especially to nonprofessionals. A client may not realize, for example,

■ That the price quoted in the brochure for a cruise might not include the cost of port taxes, tips, and shore excursions.
■ That a change in exchange rates (for example, the value of the Japanese yen or British pound in American dollars) may raise the actual cost of travel abroad.
■ That even an "all-inclusive" resort may charge fees or "membership dues" for certain activities, and it may not include the cost of all meals, taxes, and tips in its quoted price.
■ That the price quoted in a tour brochure may not include the cost of all transfers.
■ That there may be a cancellation penalty if a client cancels participation in a tour before departure.

Spotting hidden costs is a sure way to win friends and influence people.

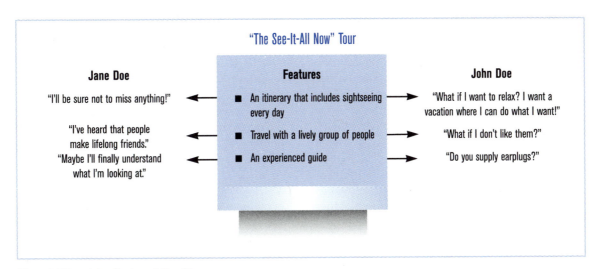

Figure 3.7 Perceiving Costs and Benefits
Any feature is likely to have both costs and benefits. What matters is how the client sees it.

Chapter Wrap-Up

Chapter Highlights

Success as a salesperson depends in part on having a good understanding of the product. But it is simply not possible to know all the travel products available because the "product line" includes the whole world, a world that is constantly changing. Good salespeople learn enough to be helpful and develop a strategy for learning more. Helping you do the same is the goal of this chapter. Here is a review of the objectives with which we began.

1. **Outline a strategy for becoming knowledgeable about travel products.** A first step is to think about each of the main travel markets—business, meeting, incentive, VFR, and leisure. In each market, customers need somewhat different products and services, so the knowledge required of the salesperson also differs. If you understand the needs of each market, you can develop a systematic way of thinking about it in order to organize your search for information. Above all, be ready to realize when you don't know enough and to seek help. Over time—with study, practice, and experience—you will gain the necessary expertise.

2. **Describe key sources for information on travel.** Firsthand experience is an important source. Familiarization (or fam) trips are one way of acquiring this experience. Discussions with other people—including sales representatives for suppliers and contacts at trade associations as well as family, friends, clients, and colleagues—represent a second source of information. On-line sources, including the Web and CRSs, and an immense variety of printed sources—from ads and brochures to periodicals and directories—represent other key places to search for travel information.

3. **Discuss some key sources for the basic information needed when selling a destination, transportation arrangements,** accommodations, a cruise, or a tour. For all of these travel products, CRSs and Web sites offer an increasing amount of information. For destination information, sources include a world atlas, national tourist offices, *OAG Travel Planners and* guidebooks. Printed sources for transportation arrangements include the *OAG Desktop Flight Guides, Official Railway Guide,* and the *Thomas Cook* timetables. When selling accommodations, the *Official Hotel Guide, Hotel and Travel Index,* and *Star Service* are among the most useful sources. For cruises and tours, all of the questions important in selling destinations, transportation, and accommodations are likely to be relevant. Crucial information can be found in such well-established directories as *CLIA Cruise Manual, Official Cruise Guide,* and *Official Tour Directory.* In addition, trade associations (such as CLIA, USTOA, WATA, and NTA) and brochures are key sources of information on cruises and tours.

4. **Explain two key principles for evaluating travel products.** The evaluation of a travel product should take into account not simply its features but its value, which depends on the benefits and perceived costs of the product. However, benefits, and thus value, are not inherent characteristics of the product. Instead, they depend on the customer's perception of the product and vary from person to person.

New Terms. The terms that follow were introduced in this chapter. If you do not recall their definitions, see the Glossary, which begins on page 237.

ASTA	features
benefits	ICTA
CLIA	NTA
CRSs (computer reservations systems)	USTOA
database	value
familiarization (fam) trip	

Review Exercises

Check-Up

Give yourself a quick test of your memory of a few basic points. Read each of the following statements and indicate whether it is true (T) or false (F). See the answers below the statements.

T   F   1. To sell travel products effectively, you do not need to be an expert in geography.

T   F   2. The opinions of friends and colleagues are too subjective to be a useful source of information about travel.

T   F   3. CRSs are useful only if you want to obtain airline tickets.

T   F   4. The Web is the most reliable source of information on travel.

T   F   5. Brochures are a very helpful but biased source of information.

T   F   6. Ultimately, the salesperson must be interested in benefits, not features.

Answers: 1. T, 2. F, 3. F, 4. F, 5. T, 6. T

Discussion Questions

1. **Mapping the Issues: Meeting and Incentive Travel.** The local Mary Kay Cosmetics representative, who is a friend of yours, has decided to set up a sales contest for her fifty part-time sales representatives. She wants to use travel as an incentive to increase sales. What issues would you need to know about in order to help her?

2. **Gathering Information: Leisure Travel.** An accountant for whom you have been handling a small amount of business travel calls to discuss his upcoming spring vacation. He and his family have heard a lot about Jamaica from their friends and are thinking of either going there or traveling to Bermuda.

     a. What would you need to know about travel products to help them plan this trip?

     _____

     _____

     _____

     _____

     b. Where would you look for information?

     _____

     _____

     _____

     _____

3. **Finding Answers: Hotels.** *The Hotel and Travel Index, OHG,* and *Star Service* are all very popular and useful guides to accommodations. Each has its own strengths.

     a. If you needed to find the phone or fax number for a hotel you had already selected, which of these guides would you look at first?

     _____

     _____

     _____

     _____

     b. If you were planning a long, expensive vacation for a client, which guide would you prefer as a source, and why?

     _____

     _____

     _____

     _____

A Case in Question

1. In the "No Room at the Inn" case described on page 51, suppose the hotel finds a room for Dave's client. What else should Dave do?

_____

_____

_____

_____

2. Look again at the "Out to Lunch" case in Chapter 2 (page 37). Suppose you were arranging a tour for Mrs. Sandler's friend, who recently hurt her hip and cannot walk unaided. Where would you look for information?

_____

_____

_____

_____

Exercises in Selling

1. **Evaluating Tours.** In order to practice evaluating travel products, gather tour brochures from a local travel agency or a tour operator. Choose two similar tours of similar length from different tour operators and compare them by filling out Worksheet 3.1, "Tour Evaluation," on page 73. Then answer the following questions:

   a. Is there a significant difference in the price or other costs of the two tours?

_____

_____

   b. What is the most significant difference in the features of the two tours?

_____

_____

_____

_____

c. What benefits might be associated with this difference?

_____

_____

_____

_____

d. How would you describe a client who is likely to perceive these as benefits?

_____

_____

_____

_____

2. **Evaluating Cruises.** As further practice in evaluating travel products, gather information about two Caribbean cruises of similar length. You might obtain brochures or videos or visit Web sites. Compare the two cruises by filling out Worksheet 3.2, "Cruise Evaluation."

Worksheet 3.1

Name _____ Date _____

Tour Evaluation

Fill out this form as part of the exercise described on page 71. You might want to duplicate this form before writing on it.

	Tour 1	Tour 2
1. Tour operator	_____	_____
	_____	_____
2. Destinations visited	_____	_____
	_____	_____
	_____	_____
3. Number of meals included	_____	_____
4. Leisure time available	_____	_____
	_____	_____
5. Types of hotels included	_____	_____
	_____	_____
6. Deposit and payment schedule	_____	_____
	_____	_____
	_____	_____
7. Special features	_____	_____
	_____	_____
	_____	_____
	_____	_____
	_____	_____

Worksheet 3.2

Name _____ Date _____

Cruise Evaluation

Fill out this form as part of the exercise described on page 72. You might want to duplicate this form before writing on it.

	Cruise 1	**Cruise 2**
1. *Dates*	_____	_____
2. *The ship*	_____	_____
Age of ship	_____	_____
Size of ship	_____	_____
Special facilities	_____	_____
	_____	_____
3. *Life on board*		
Style, atmosphere	_____	_____
Dining	_____	_____
	_____	_____
Sports	_____	_____
	_____	_____
Entertainment	_____	_____
	_____	_____
Attractions for special groups	_____	_____
	_____	_____
Special services or amenities	_____	_____
	_____	_____

	Cruise 1	Cruise 2

4. *Itinerary*

Consecutive days at sea _____ _____

Ports of call and time at each _____ _____

_____ _____

_____ _____

_____ _____

_____ _____

_____ _____

5. *Rates*

Per person double occupancy _____ _____

Tipping guidelines _____ _____

Other costs _____ _____

_____ _____

Possible discounts _____ _____

_____ _____

PART 2

The Selling Process

The Sales Cycle: Getting Information

Objectives

After reading this chapter, you should be able to

1. Discuss the goals and difficulties of the first four steps of the sales cycle.

2. Identify the five basic *W*s and other key questions to ask in order to determine a client's needs.

3. Explain four guidelines for effective listening.

4. Interpret several common forms of body language.

5. Identify six principles for getting the information you need from an interview.

6. Apply techniques for effective listening and questioning to the sales cycle.

Preview

Selling is a skill that can be taught and learned, much like riding a bicycle or playing a musical instrument. The previous chapters described what you need to know in order to sell travel; now we turn to selling itself, explaining what you do when you sell and how you can learn to do it well.

Recall that in Chapter 1 we described eight steps in the selling process; here we examine the first four steps in detail. They require two key skills: listening and questioning. In this chapter we explain techniques for improving your ability to do both. Then we describe how to apply these skills to the sales cycle.

The Sales Cycle: An Overview

Laurie was enthusiastic as she talked to Arlene Inman, a middle-aged woman who was interested in taking a trip to Scandinavia.* A week earlier, Arlene had picked up brochures about Scandinavia at Laurie's travel agency and taken them home to show to her husband. Now Arlene was describing to Laurie the "little trip" that she and her husband wanted to take to northern Europe "during the last two weeks of summer."

"Is there anything you definitely want to see when you're there?" Laurie asked.

"Well, my husband would like to see Sweden and Norway, and I would like to see the Tivoli Gardens."

"Great. Is there anything else that you want to do?"

"Well, yes." Arlene went on to say they would like to visit a historic ship, country gardens, and country inns.

"Scandinavia is breathtaking," exclaimed Laurie. "Is it just going to be the two of you traveling?"

"Just the two."

"Do you have a particular budget in mind?"

"Well, not really, but something within reason."

"Mn-hmm. Have you traveled very much in Europe?"

Arlene mentioned several trips they had taken, independently and with a group.

"Do you have particular types of hotels in mind—five-star or perhaps something more economical?"

"We always stay in luxury hotels. That's half the fun of the trip, isn't it?"

"Yes, it is. Well, you know, I think there are two ways you can do this trip." Then Laurie described the choice between traveling independently or with a group.

"Is there a difference in price?" asked Arlene. Laurie noted that traveling with a group costs a little less and is "a different kind of travel experience."

"I think that's worth looking into."

"Was there anything in the brochure that was particularly attractive to you?"

Arlene mentioned one of the tours but added, "It didn't have everything we wanted, though."

"Well, let's see. That's four cities in ten days. The price is $3,200 per person. Is that in your budget?"

"Well, it's in the ballpark."

Another tour in the brochure, Laurie suggested, "has it all. It's a 21-day all-inclusive tour with motor coach of Scandinavia. Look." Laurie went through the itinerary described in the brochure. "How's that?" she concluded.

"Sounds great!"

After summarizing the benefits of the tour, Laurie concluded, "It's $5,000 per person. September is close. Would you like me to call the tour operator and book you?"

"Well, I don't know how my husband will feel about traveling in a group." Arlene decided that she had to discuss the trip with her husband.

The next day, Arlene called.

"I thought I'd give you a call. We loved everything about the trip, but we have two problems. First of all, Harry has to be back for medical meetings, so we have only two weeks. And secondly, we really liked that $3,200 price rather than the $5,000."

Laurie suggested traveling sooner, when the price would be cheaper, but Arlene explained that they couldn't get away then. So Laurie suggested that they "take the 14-day trip that we talked about that you liked. The price is right, and the time is perfect. It gives you almost everything. You'll miss the Tivoli Gardens, but you'll get everything else."

But Arlene objected. "Isn't there any way to get us to Tivoli Gardens?"

"You could take a different route home, seeing the Tivoli Gardens on your own, but that would cost extra." The total package, Laurie estimated, would come to about $4,000 each.

"I don't know. It sounds awfully expensive. I just don't know." Arlene paused. "Laurie, maybe we should go to just one country—say, Sweden."

Laurie kept her patience. "Well, a trip to one country would give you a closer look. But you wouldn't get to see all the other places in the

---

*Adapted from *Selling Tours and Vacation Packages,* prepared for the United States Tour Operators Association by The Institute of Certified Travel Agents, © 1994, Institute of Certified Travel Agents. Videocassette.

area. But if you do want to go to one country in Scandinavia, Sweden is a good choice."

"Oh, I'm so confused. Maybe I just better think about it."

What we have here is a failure to *communicate*—to share information—and to sell. Making a sale requires the ability to obtain information from the customer, interpret that information to understand the customer's needs, and give back to the customer information that meets those needs. In short, selling is a particular type of communication.

What went wrong in the communication between Laurie and Arlene? Although Laurie was pleasant and polite, she still has not made the sale and has not helped Arlene obtain the trip she wants. Despite all of the time they have spent talking about the trip, neither is closer to meeting her goals. Why? As the discussions in this chapter will illustrate, Laurie might have

fared better if she had paid closer attention to the eight steps of the sales cycle.

Figure 4.1 illustrates these steps, which we introduced in Chapter 1. In effect, the sales cycle shows how selling proceeds when the communication is effective. Reality, of course, is more complicated than our diagram of this cycle. Sometimes, for example, steps must be repeated. And the steps overlap, flowing into each other. For example, as you identify customers (step 1), you should also begin establishing rapport (step 2).

Still, the cycle provides a useful framework for understanding selling situations. Each step in the cycle does depend on the step before it, so later steps in a sale can be complicated if you skip earlier ones. For example, you must determine the client's needs (step 3) before you can find a product to meet those needs and make a good recommendation (steps 4 and 5). If you understand where you are in the sales

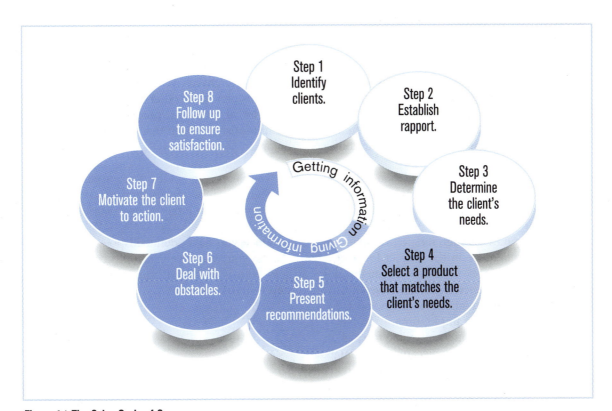

Figure 4.1 The Sales Cycle of Success
The eight steps shown here provide a framework for understanding your role in selling situations. Each step depends on the step that preceded it, but the steps are neither isolated nor absolute. In other words, the steps overlap, and in some situations certain steps should be skipped or repeated. Exactly how you move through the cycle depends on the client's response.

cycle, you can identify the skills you should exercise at that time.

Notice in Figure 4.1 that the sales cycle can be summarized in terms of two activities: getting information and giving information. In steps 1–4, the basic task is gathering information so that you can build a relationship with the client and serve the client's needs. In the rest of this chapter we examine these first four steps and the skills they require.

*B*uilding the Relationship: Steps 1–4 _____

Without a customer, there is no sales cycle, and the customer can "leave" the cycle at any point. It is up to the salesperson to be sure the customer stays. The first four steps of the sales cycle go a long way toward meeting that goal. In these first steps, your key task is to learn enough about the customer to establish a successful sales relationship.

Step 1: Identifying Customers

As we discussed in Chapter 1, the first step of the sales cycle has two parts: finding new potential customers and determining whether they are "buyers," not "shoppers." The first part, finding new customers, is called *prospecting*. Often, it is considered not part of the sales cycle, but a preliminary stage.

As a travel counselor, for example, you might prospect for new customers by taking some of the following steps:

- Review your customer files or database to see who might be in the market for a new travel experience. Clients who might not have been interested in certain types of trips a short time ago might be good prospects for them today. For example, until a few years ago few people thought of going to spas; in the 1990s, though, spas became increasingly popular. And many people could imagine themselves enjoying a cruise only after the movie *Titanic* became a smash hit in 1998.
- Review your customer files or database to find people who might be able to refer new business to you.

- Look beyond your current clients to identify people or groups who have travel needs that you can meet. What local organizations might be interested in offering their members a chance to travel as a group? What companies need a professional to coordinate their travel arrangements? Are there any specific market segments (for example, seniors, adventure travelers) that you could reach with an idea for a trip?

The second part of this first step—determining whether the customer is ready and able to make a purchase—is often called *qualifying* your customers. In other words, before spending a lot of time with potential customers, you should satisfy yourself that they meet three conditions:

1. They have a need for your product.
2. They have the means to purchase it.
3. They can make the buying decision.

Once you have identified potential qualified clients, you want to persuade them to do business with you, which brings us to the second step in the sales cycle.

Step 2: Establishing Rapport

When they can, people do business with people they like, so the ability to establish rapport with customers is essential to successful selling. *Establishing rapport* means finding a link with the customer and making it strong. If you have created rapport, the customer is comfortable with you, trusts you, and believes what you say.

You cannot do this all at once; establishing rapport is a goal that continues throughout the sales cycle. For example, in step 3, when you ask questions to determine the client's needs, the answers should help you learn how to strengthen a link with that person. When you present your recommendations, when you deal with objections—indeed, at every point in the sales cycle—you should be strengthening your rapport with the client.

Still, we isolate establishing rapport as the second step in the sales cycle because, at this point, it is the most important task. Why? If you have not begun developing rapport, the next steps may be difficult. For example, a client is more likely to respond to your suggestions with an open mind and a candid answer if you have developed a strong link with that client. And first impressions are often the strongest. They can shape the entire relationship and thus can, ultimately, make or break a sale. If you do not begin establishing rapport at the beginning of your sales relationship, first impressions may create barriers to your later efforts.

Creating a Link. How do you establish rapport? First, acknowledge the client. If you are dealing with the client in person, make eye contact. Start with a warm and friendly greeting, giving your name. Then discover your client's name. To do so, you might use the "fill in the blank format"; for example,

> *Travel counselor:* Hi, my name is Stacy, and you are _____?

People respond with their name, and there you have it. Use the name during the conversation to maintain a personal link.

A busy office can frustrate attempts to follow these guidelines. The moment that a client walks into the office or the instant that the telephone is answered, the customer is forming impressions. If you ignore the customer when he or she enters or if you answer the phone abruptly, establishing rapport will be an uphill battle. Think of the times when you have been ignored as a customer and how you felt.

When a busy office makes it impossible to greet the customer and start the sales conversa-tion immediately, what do you do? Even if everyone in the office is occupied, make sure to establish eye contact with the client. Let the client know that someone will be with him or her as soon as possible. (The office should have a comfortable waiting area, with interesting brochures and magazines or perhaps a video playing destination tapes.) If there will be a lengthy delay, let the client know that. Finally, when you are free to work with the client, thank the person for waiting and proceed with your greeting.

What if your "customer" is actually a group, such as a local club? In that case, try to be sure that the key decision maker acts as your contact with the group. Then focus on establishing rapport with this person.

Developing the Link. Once you know the client's name, show concern for his or her needs by asking how you can help. When the client responds, try to reinforce whatever is said. For example,

> *Travel counselor:* What can I do for you, Mr. Evans?
> *Client:* I'm hoping to find a trip I can afford for sometime next month. Mostly to relax. I was thinking maybe of Mexico and just going to a beach for a week.
> *Travel counselor:* Oh, there are a lot of gorgeous beaches in Mexico.

The salesperson is getting in step with the customer by showing empathy and enthusiasm. Remember that in order to build a relationship, you need to be sincere and to respond in a way that comes naturally to you. Thus, to reinforce what the customer says, pick out the part of it that you can identify with.

Some small talk may be appropriate. Your goal is to make the customer feel comfortable with you.

After the first stages of the interaction, you should continue to build rapport. Following four simple guidelines should help:

- Begin and end each conversation with a smile. Emotions are often contagious.
- Use the client's name frequently.
- Do not waste the client's time. Be prepared,

Tips
Developing Rapport

Think of developing rapport as a three-step process:

1. Acknowledge the client in a warm, friendly way, and learn the customer's name.
2. Show enthusiasm and empathy.
3. Continue to strengthen your link with the client by listening carefully and responding to your client's concerns.

and be ready to find someone who can help if you do not know an answer.

■ Express empathy and respond to the client's concerns.

Carrying out this last guideline requires that you listen very carefully to the client, an activity that we consider in detail later in this chapter.

Step 3: Determining Needs

After identifying potential qualified clients and beginning to develop rapport with them, your next step is to identify their needs. Like Sherlock Holmes, you will use your powers of deduction aided by thorough questioning.

The Five Basic *W*s. For the travel industry, the essential bits of information about your clients' needs are called the *five basic Ws:* Who? When? Where? Why? and What? In other words, you need to know the following:

■ *Who* is traveling? How many people are traveling? Are they adults or children? What are the travelers' names?
■ *When* are the dates of travel? What are the departure and return dates? Is everyone traveling together? How quickly must you act?

Are they going immediately or at a peak time?
■ *Where* is the destination?
■ *Why* is the client traveling? For example, business travelers may be taking the trip in order to attend a meeting, to make a sale or presentation, or to attend a seminar. Vacation travelers may be looking for romance, an educational experience, an adventure, or just a chance to "get away from it all."
■ *What* type of accommodations and services does the client need? The answers may indicate the client's budget and expectations.

Clients volunteer some information. You must seek out other facts. In any case, you should make sure you get answers to the five basic *W*s before proceeding.

Points for Probing. Once you have the basic questions out of the way, pin down the specific needs of the client. Start asking more probing, open-ended questions. ***Open-ended questions*** are those that cannot be answered by a simple yes or no or with simple facts. For example, if you are a travel counselor dealing with a customer for leisure travel, you might ask,

■ What was your best vacation? Why?
■ What do you like to do on vacation?
■ What are you looking for from this vacation?

This type of questioning encourages your clients to talk about themselves and their experiences, to "open up." From their answers to open-ended questions, you can add depth and detail to your image of them and their needs. You may get a sense, for example, that they are motivated by a need for affiliation, as discussed in Chapter 2, or that they are "venturers" rather than "dependables."

The sheer variety of needs and the number of elements that can go into a travel experience can make the "determining needs" stage difficult. The customer in the dialogue at the opening of this chapter, for example, wanted luxury, but she also had a budget and restrictions on her time.

Exactly what you need to ask obviously depends on the client and the travel products. If your client needs only a room at a hotel, for example, determining the client's needs is fairly simple. But even when selling just a hotel room, you should go beyond the five *W*s and ask also about the following:

- The budget or price range.
- Any particular requirements (such as smoking or nonsmoking rooms).
- Any specific preferences (such as a type of bed).
- Any special requests (such as interest in the availability of a whirlpool or tennis courts or the ability to bring a pet along).

What if you are arranging a tour for a client, as Laurie was trying to do for Arlene in the dialogue at the opening of this chapter? For a tour, the possible questions multiply, as Figure 4.2 illustrates.

Special Needs. As you probe, be on the lookout for special needs. For example,

- Does the business traveler need particular communications technology or laundry services?
- If the clients have children, will they require babysitting services or special amusements?
- If the clients are religiously observant, do they need a special diet or a place of worship nearby?
- Is their mobility impaired in any way?

For leisure travelers in particular, probe for special interests. During the last decade, the travel and tourism industry has developed attractions and activities to suit every taste, especially expensive ones. If you ask the right questions, you might find that you can suggest travel products even better suited than your client expected. A client who likes both wine-tasting and river-cruising, for example, might be surprised that you can recommend a floating wine-tasting seminar along the Rhine and Moselle Rivers from Düsseldorf, Germany, to Basel, Switzerland.

If your customer is actually a group, you should determine the needs of the *average* member. First you will need to develop a profile of the average member in terms of age, interests, economic status, and so on. This picture of your customer should guide your efforts through the rest of the sales cycle.

The Question of Budget. Some travel professionals like to add a sixth question to the five basic *W*s, one about the budget.* Early in the sales interaction, they ask a question such as "How much do you want to spend?" or "Do you have a total budget in mind for this trip?" If the question is answered, the salesperson reaps two benefits. First, he or she can focus quickly on the appropriate type of arrangements or destinations. And second, the salesperson can avoid embarrassing or alienating the customer by suggesting a trip that costs too much.

Still, avoiding or postponing an explicit question about the budget is sometimes a wise approach. Some clients wildly overestimate how much travel costs. Some understate what they are willing to pay in order to get the best deal. Some do not have a good idea of what they want to do or what they want to spend. And for many clients, what they are willing to spend depends on what they are offered for the money. In short, a client's initial response to a question about the budget may be very misleading.

When, then, is the best time to deal with the budget? It depends. When you ask about the fifth *W*—the type of accommodations and services—you should get strong clues about the client's budget. In fact, throughout the conversation, you should look for signals about the budget. If necessary, once you have established strong rapport with the client, you might be comfortable making your questions about the budget more explicit. In any event, if you carry out the next step (step 4) effectively, you'll be certain that you understand the client's budget.

Step 4: Matching a Product to the Client

Now that you have obtained information about the client, you should be ready for step 4, deciding what to recommend to the client to meet his or her needs. (This is sometimes called "estab-

*This section is adapted from Patricia J. Gagnon and Bruno Ociepka, *Travel Career Development,* 6th ed. (Wellesley, MA: Institute of Certified Travel Agents, 1998), p. 206.

Gateway Travel

Tour Group	Customer Profile
Traveler(s)	*Heléne and Jack Hodgson*
Dates of travel	*one week including Nov. 19—their anniversary*
Price/Budget	*$2500*
Destination goals	*Caribbean*
Travel experience	*Moderate. Traveled together in France and Switzerland*
Logistics	*7 days. Husb. & wife only. Prefer to leave a few days before Nov. 19th—their anniversary*
Ambiance	*Moderate degree of luxury. Romance a must.*
Group vs independent	*Will consider group tour if they don't feel like they're on a group tour*
Special needs	*None*
Special interests	*Want to do what they did when "first in love"— "leisurely" days on the beach—long and elegant dinners. Bike riding. "Skinny dipping at night."*

Figure 4.2 The Needs of Travelers on Tour: A Checklist

If you are selling a tour, you want to learn at least enough about your client's needs to complete a profile like this.

Source: Adapted from *Selling Tours and Vacation Packages: Participant Guide,* prepared for the United States Tour Operators Association by the Institute of Certified Travel Agents, © 1994 by the Institute of Certified Travel Agents, pp. 2.3, 3.11.

lishing product fit.") You put together what you know about the travel product with what you have learned about the client in order to decide what to recommend to the client. For example, Figure 4.3 shows the scheme that we have found helpful for planning leisure travel. You begin at the outer circle, identifying what the client wants to do on the vacation, working toward the inner circle, until you end up at the center of the target, selecting the appropriate suppliers.

Before making a recommendation, though, you need to be sure that you have correctly

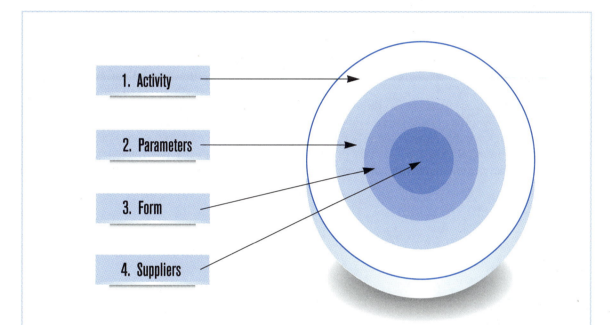

1. **Activity: What does the traveler want to do on vacation?**
   Most clients have ideas of their own about what they want to do. There are three possibilities:
   - To sun
   - To see
   - To do
   By identifying their desired activities, you can narrow down the possible destinations.

2. **Parameters: What are the time, distance, company, budget, and ambiance desired for the vacation?**
   If your clients have a four-day holiday and live in Seattle, a trip to the Bahamas is almost impossible because it would take too long to get there. If a family is on a tight budget, they will probably not go to an island such as St. Bart's, which is on the expensive end of the market. Thus, these questions help you narrow the possible destinations even further and point you toward the possible accommodations to consider.

3. **Form: Will a packaged trip suit the customer, or should it be custom-designed?**
   If a packaged trip will meet the client's needs, it is likely to offer two advantages over a custom-designed trip: a packaged trip allows "one-stop shopping," and it's probably less expensive.

4. **Suppliers: Which suppliers would best meet the client's needs?**
   Besides determining whether a supplier offers what the client needs, remember to consider the supplier's (1) relationship to you or your company and (2) reputation for reliability and quality.

Figure 4.3 Finding the Trip for Leisure Travelers
Determining what to recommend to leisure travelers means considering many needs and many possible products. One way to simplify the task is to follow the sequence shown here.

identified the customer's needs and that the client will respond favorably to your ideas. To do so, you restate the client's needs, using some of the client's own words, and elicit feedback. For example,

> *Travel counselor:* Mr. Evans, you said you were looking for a relaxing week at the beach for yourself, and you'd like to see a little of Mexico. But you don't want to do a lot of sightseeing or travel, so you'd like to find a place with good food and a few things to do at night close by. Is that right?

Notice that the salesperson is doing two things: paraphrasing what has been said and eliciting feedback to this interpretation of the information gathered so far. Thus, at this point in the sales cycle, getting and giving information

merge. You can use this step to probe further, to create a fuller picture of the customer's needs and how to meet them.

If you carry out this step effectively, you are also strengthening your relationship with the client. By restating the client's needs and asking for confirmation, you show (1) that you were listening attentively and (2) that you have understood what the client said. By sending these messages, you continue to build rapport with the client.

At this point, clients can have one of two reactions, as Figure 4.4 illustrates. They may confirm that you understand their needs, or they may tell you that you don't. If they confirm, you can move on to step 5, making your recommendation (which is discussed in the next chapter). If they do not confirm your statement of their needs, return to the previous step, determining needs, because something was missed along the

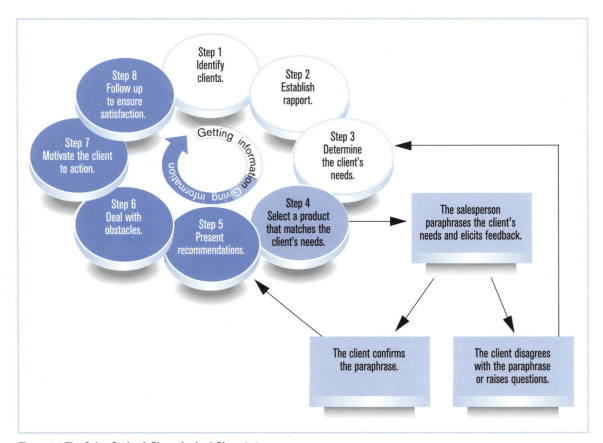

Figure 4.4 The Sales Cycle: A Closer Look at Steps 3–4
By step 4 of the sales cycle, you should have an idea of the travel products that would suit your client's needs. But before presenting that idea, you should offer the client your understanding of what he or she has said, your picture of what the client needs and what kind of trip he or she is looking for. The client's reaction determines whether you return to step 3 or go on to step 5.

way. Continue questioning until you have a better picture of your client's needs; then restate those needs and ask for confirmation again.

Eventually, you will "get it." When the customer seems positive and excited about your description of what they are looking for, then you can move on to the next steps: making your recommendation, dealing with obstacles, motivating the client to action, and following up to ensure satisfaction.

Time Out

Check your understanding of the discussion so far by answering the following questions.

1. What are the first four steps of the sales cycle?

   _____

   _____

   _____

   _____

   _____

2. Look again at the scenario at the beginning of this chapter. Did Laurie ask questions about each of the five *W*s?

   _____

   _____

3. Which step of the sales cycle did Laurie skip?

   _____

   _____

*L*earning to Listen

Communication is a two-way street. No matter how well you talk, your communication will fail unless you also know how to listen. Consider this conversation between a travel counselor and a client:

"As you can see in the brochure, the hotel has a modern gameroom with just about everything you could imagine."

"My kids will love that gameroom!"

"Of course some people are more interested in the golf course and lighted tennis courts."

"The gameroom's enough for us."

"And there's a fantastic view from the oceanfront room."

What has happened? The salesperson is so preoccupied with explaining the product that the client's possible willingness to commit to the sale has been overlooked. At the least, a salesperson must learn how to "hear" signals that the customer is ready to buy.

In fact, perhaps the greatest skill a good salesperson can have is the ability to listen and to listen well. Listening requires that you use not only your ears and brain to hear but also your mind and eyes and feelings in order to understand.

Steps for Effective Listening

So how do you become an effective listener? According to an old saying: "There's a reason we have two ears and one mouth: it's to listen more and talk less." But talking less is only one part of effective listening. Think of someone you consider a good listener. Chances are, that person pays attention, really hears what you are saying, and makes you feel that he or she cares.

To develop these characteristics of good listeners, follow four basic guidelines: (1) concentrate, (2) avoid assumptions, (3) read between the lines, and (4) elicit feedback and respond. You can remember these guidelines by the sentence "Use CARE when you listen." Let's look at each.

- *C = Concentrate.* Focus all of your attention on the speaker. Try to avoid distractions like ringing telephones, other conversations, or a cluttered desk. Use techniques that help you pay attention to the speaker, such as maintaining good eye contact and nodding your head intermittently. You might even take notes. Most importantly, avoid the temptation to interrupt the speaker.
- *A = Avoid assumptions.* When you jump to conclusions or make judgments or assumptions, you are no longer listening. Keep personal judgments and assumptions under control. Do not let them cloud what you hear. Know the warning signs your body sends you when you become emotional, such as rapid breathing or a clenched jaw.

- *R = Read between the lines.* In face-to-face communication, studies show that only 7 percent of the message comes from words. What else is there? Most of a message comes "between the lines," through body language such as gestures and through how the words are said (inflection, emphasis, speed, and so on). Take the sentence, "I said Sally could read that." Repeat the sentence, placing the emphasis on a different word each time. The meaning changes. In order to listen well, you must pay attention to such messages beyond the words.
- *E = Elicit feedback and respond.* Finally, to make sure you have understood what the speaker has said, put what you have heard into your own words and ask for the speaker's response. The speaker will either agree with your assessment or correct it.

If you follow these guidelines, you should end up with an accurate idea of what the speaker is trying to communicate.

Reading Body Language

For the most part, all you need in order to master the steps for effective listening is the desire to practice them. Reading between the lines, though, may require some trial and error. In particular, many people know little about reading **body language,** which is nonverbal communication consisting of eye contact, facial expressions, posture, gestures, and *personal space* (the distance that you typically maintain between yourself and others).

The elements of body language do not have absolute interpretations. Their meaning can vary with the culture, the context, and the individual. (Table 4.1 gives some examples of cultural differences in the interpretation of body language.) Despite these variations, nurturing the ability to "read" body language can help salespeople greatly. Let's examine some of its key elements.

Eye Contact. Most people believe that if someone does not look them in the eye while they are speaking, then that person is not paying attention or is not in step with them. Downward or

Table 4.1

Body Language around the World: A Sampling

Country	An Element of Body Language
Great Britain	Maintaining eye contact throughout a conversation is considered both polite and a sign of attention.
Finland	Folding your arms across your chest is a sign of arrogance.
Germany	Keeping your hands in your pockets when speaking is a sign of disrespect.
Greece	It is an insult to wave with an open palm and extended fingers (American-style). Use the index finger with palm closed.
Poland	When a man flicks a finger against his neck, it means you're invited to join him for a drink.
Russia	The thumb placed between the index finger and the middle finger is an obscene gesture.
Turkey	To say no, Turks raise their chins, close their eyes, and tilt their heads back.
Indonesia	Speaking with your hands on your hips is considered a contemptuous posture indicating anger and aggressiveness.
Thailand	It is considered rude to pat someone on the head, which is considered the most sacred part of the body.
Vietnam	It is considered rude to point, especially with one's feet.

Source: Based on Nancy L. Bragani and Elizabeth Devine, *European Custom and Manners* (Deephaven, Minn.: Meadowbrook Press, 1992) and *Pacific Rim,* © 1994 ICTA.

shifty looks may indicate distrust or a lack of self-confidence.

This does not mean that you and the person you are talking with should stare at one another continually. But you should spend a comfortable amount of time looking directly at each other's eyes and face. For good communication, experts suggest that speaker and listener should maintain positive eye contact about 70 percent of the time.

Facial Expressions. Often, facial expressions tell a lot about what a person is thinking. They can run the gamut from a friendly smile to a fiendish frown.

Smiles come in three basic types: simple, upper, and broad. The *simple smile* shows no teeth and generally says that you are smiling to yourself. The *upper smile* shows only the upper teeth and is the smile most often used in greeting. The *broad smile* shows both upper and lower teeth and indicates amusement and acceptance. Watch your customer's smiles and read into them how well the customer is accepting what you say.

Other important facial expressions include the following:

- When a person *frowns,* the eyebrows are drawn together and the lips are compressed. Frowns generally indicate disagreement, although they can also indicate thought.
- *Raised eyebrows* often signal surprise. They usually say that the person hadn't thought about what was said. Thus, raised eyebrows may indicate that this is a good time to clarify or otherwise expand on your comments.

- A *poker face* expresses no emotion. If a client offers you a poker face, you should look for other clues to the message "between the lines."

Posture. How a person stands, walks, and sits can tell you many things, even before any words are spoken. An erect stance and a brisk walk often indicate a confident and secure person. Someone who is feeling low will often shuffle along, looking down.

Watch, too, how a customer sits; that can tell you how well the sale is progressing. Leaning back, with arms crossed in front of the body, usually indicates a negative response. Add to that a frown, clenched hands, and minimal eye contact and you have a customer who is not going to buy. In contrast, when a customer leans toward you, shows a relaxed arm and an open hand, and is making good eye contact, that customer is responding positively to what you are saying.

Sometimes a change in posture rather than the posture itself conveys a message. If customers lean toward you when they had been leaning back, or lean back and relax when that had been leaning toward you, that is a sign of interest.

Gestures. The meaning of some gestures seems obvious. If a client takes out a credit card or checkbook, that person is ready to buy. How a customer handles brochures may indicate his or her interest level. Is the customer folding back pages, making notes, or underlining the brochure (high interest)? Or is the customer idly flipping through the pages (low interest)?

Other gestures are not so easy to read. Here, though, are some guidelines that will usually stand you in good stead:

- Thoughtfulness, an attempt to reach a decision or to evaluate what is being said, may be indicated by tapping the cheek, stroking the chin, pinching the bridge of the nose, or other hand-to-face gestures. Continue to probe or present recommendations to judge whether the customer will respond in a positive manner.
- Frustration or aggressiveness may be sig-

naled when a customer clasps a fist, holds the wrist of a fisted hand, or puts a fist to his or her chin.
- Defensiveness is often the correct interpretation when you see arms crossed in front of the chest or tightly crossed legs or when customers move papers or a handbag between them and you.

Mirroring. In essence, **mirroring** is body language between individuals in which they assume each other's position. Suppose you are having a conversation with a friend seated face to face. After a while, you may find that your body positions are identical, though reversed, as if you were looking in a mirror. Often, when one person changes position, the other person soon assumes the same position.

The more precise and identical the mirroring, the greater the degree of empathy and agreement. Subtle mirroring can help a salesperson develop rapport with the customer.

Encouraging the Speaker

Being a good listener means more than grasping what the speaker is saying. Good listeners make the other person feel comfortable talking. That is why people like good listeners, and it goes a long way toward turning good listeners into good salespeople. Here are two ways to encourage the speaker.

First, remember that communication goes two ways. Just as you get messages from the speaker's body language, your body language is sending messages to the speaker. Lean toward your client to indicate your interest, and make eye contact periodically. Know what your own body language is saying. In particular, your facial expressions will tell the speaker a lot, just as the expressions on the speaker's face give you much information.

Second, let the speaker know you are listening by giving acknowledgments such as "I see," "Uh-huh," or "Okay." If you are communicating by telephone, such verbal acknowledgments become even more important. Chapter 6 discusses the special challenges of selling by telephone.

Time Out

Check your understanding of the discussion so far by filling in the blanks.

1. To listen well, the salesperson should concentrate, avoid making assumptions or jumping to conclusions,

    _____

    _____

    _____

    _____ ,

    and elicit feedback and respond.

2. "Reading between the lines" means paying attention to how something is said and to

    _____

    _____ .

3. Body language includes posture, gestures, eye contact, as well as

    _____

    _____ .

How to Ask Questions

Unless you are extraordinarily lucky, even the most sensitive listening will not tell you all you need to know about a customer. Skillful questioning is also required in order to gather enough information to meet a client's travel needs. (The Selling through Service case on page 94 illustrates some of the problems that can arise when people don't know how to ask the right questions.) Let's look first at how questions should be phrased.

Phrasing Your Questions

What's wrong with this dialogue?

"And when will you be holding this meeting?"
"Well, we have it tentatively penciled in for May 15-19. But we have some flexibility still, if it makes a difference to where we could go or what we could do. We're open to ideas."
"How many people will be coming?"
"It's really hard to say right now. You see, we're still trying to . . . well, fifty would be my best guess right now."
"Do you want to have swimming and golf available?"
"That would be good."
"Do you need any other sports?"
"I guess not."
"Do you want all meals for everyone on the site?"
"Yes."

At least so far, the salesperson has asked only closed-ended questions.

Closed-ended questions can usually be answered with a yes or no or with simple facts. In contrast, *open-ended questions,* as we discussed earlier, are questions that get someone to "open up" with more specific information. Open-ended questions generally begin with *how, what, tell me,* or *why*. Like reading only the headlines in a newspaper, asking only closed-ended questions leaves you ignorant of details and context and can be misleading.

To get the best picture of the customer, you should use a combination of types of questions. Figure 4.5 shows how closed-ended questions can be converted into open-ended questions. You should also use ***feedback questions,*** which seek the confirmation of details that have come up in the conversation. For example,

> *Salesperson:* So you want a very sociable tour so you can meet people, is that right?

The client can answer yes, offer minor corrections, or object.

Remember to phrase feedback questions so that clients are likely to give you a positive answer. By getting clients to say yes to your

Selling through Service (continues on next page)

The Fish that Got Away

It was not a good day. Timothy Cunningham had been hoping to leave early for the weekend. Instead, he was answering a reporter's questions. "I can't exactly explain what happened," he said. As director of sales for the River Scenes Boat Company, Timothy knew he would soon have to find out.

Meanwhile, the local paper thought it had a good story. One of Timothy's agents had sold a trip to the Shuntee Elementary School for more than a hundred children, plus teachers and chaperons. The trip included a boat ride in the capital city's harbor, a trip to the Museum of Science, and, last but certainly not least, a visit to the aquarium, where a sea lion show promised to be a special treat.

Everything had gone fine until the students reached the aquarium. Then Muriel Gaines, the teacher in charge of the trip, had gone to the ticket collector in the lobby, explaining that they had reserved tickets for the students. The ticket collector, Sue Holmes, checked her list of special guests for the day, and found nothing about the school.

"We have no record of that," she said. "The tickets are $3 each for the children, $7 for each adult, and you'll have to wait with everyone else. We're full now, but in about half an hour, we'll begin letting more people in. You probably won't get anyone in until the next group, though. There's quite a crowd."

Muriel objected, explaining again that they had reserved tickets. Again, Sue said that they weren't on the list. Muriel protested, "But we should be! I have more than a hundred students waiting outside in that blasted heat!" She argued that they had paid and expected to be admitted. Sue decided that a slight retreat was the best strategy.

"I'm sure we can straighten this out. Why don't you wait over by the water fountain? Let me contact our tour liaison."

Half an hour later, the aquarium's director of tour sales, Duncan Davies, appeared.

"What's the problem?" he began, reasonably enough. Muriel and Sue started their competing explanations.

"When did you make these reservations?" asked Duncan.

"Two months ago!"

"Did you confirm by mail or phone?"

"By mail."

paraphrases, you move them closer to saying yes to the sale itself.

Also, in phrasing your questions you should adapt your style to fit the customer. Use words the customer used. If your client talks about wanting to "examine recent archaeological excavations in Mesoamerica," there's no reason for you to talk about "looking at old stones and bones." Try to use the **communications style** preferred by the client—the type of words, eye movements, and other body language typically used by that person when communicating.

Recognizing a person's communications style is another way of "reading between the lines." One way to look at communications styles classifies them into three types: visual, which is the most common style; auditory; and kinesthetic/feelings.

- *Visual communicators* tend to use words such as *look, see,* or *imagine* when speaking. They tend to look up as they speak or think.
- *Auditory communicators* select words that refer to sounds, such as *hear, listen,* or *tune out.* They tend to look side to side (as if trying to see the ears).
- *Kinesthetic/feelings communicators* choose

Selling through Service (continued)

"Oh, well! . . . I just don't know. I'd like to let the kids in and straighten this all out later, but we have a full crowd waiting ahead of you."

"But River Scenes told us it was all set!"

"Who?"

"River Scenes."

Duncan looked again at the day's reservation list. It included the name of the agency, not the school. Still, there were problems. "But you were supposed to be here two hours ago," said Duncan.

"No, we told the agency we would be here at 3."

"But you were supposed to talk to us!"

The argument went on. The children milled around in the heat, making fans out of fliers. But Muriel and Duncan still had not decided just who had said what to whom.

"It doesn't matter now, anyway," sighed Sue. "It's too late for them to go in. It's fifteen minutes before closing."

So the children got back on their buses for the two-hour ride home. And Timothy Cunningham was trying to figure out what to do. The call from the reporter was the first he had heard of the fiasco.

"River Scenes will be sending an apology to the school and the children," he told the reporter, "and we'll arrange with the aquarium to send them free tickets to come again."

■ ■ ■

Could you have done a better job handling this situation? Recall the steps for problem solving that we discussed in earlier chapters: (1) acknowledge the problem; (2) collect the facts; (3) accept responsibility; (4) select a strategy; (5) test the proposed solution; (6) resolve the problem; (7) follow up. The second step seems to have eluded both Sue and Duncan. Much of the confusion and wasted time could have been avoided, for example, if Sue had asked Muriel who had made the reservation. Unearthing the facts requires skills in listening and questioning much like those needed to determine a client's needs. In this case, better questioning might have clarified the situation sooner.

At least Timothy, the River Scenes director, has done something right: he is accepting responsibility for the problem, and he is planning to follow up with the client. But how would you evaluate the problem-solving skills of Duncan, the aquarium's director of tour sales? What problem-solving steps did he take? If you were Muriel, the teacher in charge of the trip, what impression would you have of the aquarium and its staff?

Replace the closed phrase with an open phrase.	
Closed Questions	**Open Questions**
Have you been to Cancun?	**Why have you** chosen Cancun?
Do you need a car?	**How do you** plan to get around the city?
Is there anything else I can do for you?	**What is there** that would make this trip memorable?

Figure 4.5 Converting Closed to Open Questions
To turn a closed question into an open one, restate the question by beginning with *why, how,* or *what.*

words such as *feel, understand,* or *handle* to convey the message. They look down and most often to the right.

In short, when you are interviewing clients, remember to follow these guidelines for phrasing questions effectively:

1. Use a combination of open-ended, closed-ended, and feedback questions.
2. Phrase your feedback questions so that it is likely the client will answer yes.
3. Adapt your style to fit the client.

Carrying Out an Interview

How you ask your questions can be almost as important as the questions themselves. Look again at the sample dialogue in the opening of the previous section. Unlike that salesperson, you should gather information in a conversational yet direct way. You do not want to sound as if you are taking an order at a fast-food drive-in. By weaving the basic questions into your conversation, you maintain rapport while gathering the information you need.

You should also try to retain control of the conversation. How? Consider this dialogue between a client and a travel counselor as they plan a meeting:

> *Client:* Do you know some good resorts that are not more than a few hours away?
> *Travel counselor:* Oh, of course, there's a huge selection within that distance.
> *Client:* But do you know some that are a little off the beaten track, someplace sort of serene?
> *Travel counselor:* Yes, that's no problem. But it might be good if we back up a bit here. Can you give me an idea of the purpose of the meeting? What are you trying to accomplish?

To retain control, never answer more than two questions without asking one yourself. But remember to limit your own talking.

You should also remember to listen with CARE as you interview. If the answers are vague, be sure to ask follow-up questions. Sometimes, customers cannot or do not express their needs clearly. Look again at how Arlene answered the first few questions at the beginning of this chapter. Did you expect that a $4,000-per-person trip would fall beyond her budget? At other times, clients do not have answers to your questions, as in the following example:

"When are you planning to take your vacation?"

"Well, I usually take the first two weeks of July. But, Martha, my sister, can't go then. Jimmy, her youngest, is taking swimming lessons and she needs to be around to shuttle him back and forth to the pool. Let's see . . . August is too hot . . . and September is too busy, what with school starting and all. I just love autumn around here, don't you? So October's out. Gee, then we're into the holidays. I don't know."

In cases like these, the salesperson needs to help clients pinpoint and articulate their own needs. That requires both listening and questioning carefully. When clients do not have an answer to your questions or cannot answer clearly, you need to continue to probe. In the case that opened this chapter, for example, Laurie might have had more success if she had probed further when

Tips
Interviews
That Work

To gather information, follow these guidelines as you ask questions.

■ Combine open-ended, closed-ended, and feedback questions.

■ Phrase your questions so that the client is likely to say yes.

■ Adapt your style of questioning to your client.

■ Weave your questions into the conversation.

■ Retain control of the conversation.

■ Listen with care.

■ Follow up vague answers with further questions or suggestions.

Arlene did not give specific answers. The conversation might have gone something like this:

Laurie: The price is $3,200 per person. Is that in your budget?
Arlene: Well, it's in the ballpark.
Laurie: Arlene, when you say it's in the ballpark, is that higher or lower than you expected?
Arlene: Well, it's OK, but it's just about at the maximum we'd want to spend.
Laurie: Good; then we know just what to look at.

Now Laurie would know that the $5,000-per-person trip would not be a good match, so she might make a better recommendation.

As another example, let's go back to the case of Hale & Co. that we mentioned in Chapter 2.

Hale & Co., an executive search firm in Seattle, is in trouble. The chairman of the board left under pressure; several other executives soon quit; morale is low. The acting chairman has asked Alex Hernandez, Hale's manager of corporate travel, to arrange for the company's managers to spend three nights out of town. He hopes to rebuild team spirit, encourage some problem solving, and give everyone a chance to replenish themselves. When the travel agent asked who was attending this retreat, Alex estimated that there would be "fifty people." (Adapted from ICTA, *Sales Skills Development Program*, p. 15.)

Is that answer adequate? No. Arranging a trip for fifty managers, for example, would be very different from arranging one for thirty managers plus spouses and children or friends.

When answers are vague, be ready with follow-up questions that require more specific information from the client. The goal is to get enough information to help clients make their travel plans. Sometimes recapping the travel needs they have expressed so far or asking for additional detail will be enough to accomplish that goal. Table 4.2 gives some other suggestions for what to do when clients are uncertain about their own needs.

Table 4.2

When the Client Cannot Answer

If the Client Does Not Know	The Salesperson Might
Where	Review needs with the client. Provide more information. Make suggestions. Make an appointment for the future.
When	Make transportation reservations on the most likely dates, provided there is no cancellation policy.
How long	Make definite reservations for outbound transportation and either reserve the most likely return date or leave the return temporarily open.
Who, how many	Make reservations for the greatest number likely to travel. It is always easier to cancel one person from a party than to obtain a duplicate booking for another traveler later.
What kind, what class	Ask more questions. Provide more information.

Source: Based on Patricia J. Gagnon, CTC, and Karen Silva, *Travel Career Development,* 5th ed., a publication of the Institute of Certified Travel Agents (Boston: Irwin/Mirror Press, 1992), p. 193.

Applications to the Sales Cycle

So far, we have discussed some techniques for listening and questioning that will help you gather information and build a relationship with clients. Now let's see how these techniques can be applied to steps 2-4 of the sales cycle.

Suppose that travel counselor Brad and customer Don Brown are having their first meeting. As Mr. Brown enters, Brad makes eye contact, stands up, extends his hand, and offers a warm and sincere welcome.

> *Brad:* Thanks for stopping by. I'm Brad, and you are _____?
> *Brown:* Don Brown.
> *Brad:* Have a seat, Mr. Brown. What can I do to help you?
> *Brown:* My wife and I are planning our summer vacation. I'd like to get some information about taking a cruise.
> *Brad:* Cruises are very popular among our

clients, and I'm sure we can help you find the one that's right for you and your wife.

Notice that Brad has put the client at ease and encouraged him by reinforcing what the client said. Later, Brad might recommend something other than a cruise in order to meet the Browns' needs, but at this point he is most concerned with developing rapport with Mr. Brown. Like all steps in the sales cycle, however, establishing rapport does not stand alone. While Brad is creating a link with his client, he is also beginning step 3, determining needs. After only one question, Brad knows that Mr. and Mrs. Brown will be traveling together during the summer.

Of course, Brad needs to know more about Mr. Brown's psychological and technical needs. Let's follow how Brad goes about determining them.

> *Brad:* You mentioned that you and your

wife will be traveling, Mr. Brown. Will there be anyone else traveling with you?

Brown: Why don't you call me Don? No, it will just be the two of us.

Brad: Fine, Don. And what's your wife's name?

Brown: Helen.

Brad: And your address and phone number?

Brown: 1234 Oak Street. And the phone is 555-9901.

Brad: Great, Don. Now when during the summer are you looking to take your vacation? Do you know how long you'll have?

Brown: The week of July 15th, and we'll have about ten days total.

Brad: July is a very popular month for cruises. If we find the right vacation for you today, would you be ready to make a decision, or would you need to discuss it with your wife?

Brown: We've discussed this already. If you can put this all together, and I like what I hear, I can make the decision.

Brad now knows exactly who is traveling, when, and for how long. He also has the client's address and phone number, which he can add to the agency's database, and he knows that Mr. Brown can make the decision on his own. But he does not yet have answers to all of the five basic *W*s (who, when, where, why, and what). While Brad gathers that information, he will also begin thinking about what product would meet Mr. Brown's needs and continue to develop his link with him. Let's continue with the conversation.

Brad: Great, Don. Let me ask—how did you and your wife decide on a cruise for your vacation? There are lots of cruises, so I'd like to get an idea of what you and your wife like to do on vacation.

Brown: Well, we work hard all year so we really like to relax on vacation. Good friends of ours just came back from their first cruise and couldn't stop raving about it. It sounded perfect for us too. My wife loves to shop, and I go along with her, of course, and we both like to have some nightlife—you know, some dancing and maybe a show or two. Our friends also talked about the food and the service.

Brad: So that sounds like the kind of vaca-tion you would like too, is that right?

Brown: Yes. We hear cruises are a good value, too.

Brad: That's true, Don. May I ask where you and your wife have traveled on past vacations?

Notice that Brad is

- Using (but not overusing) the client's name as he continues to build rapport.
- Attempting to weave his questions into a conversation.
- Using open-ended, closed-ended, and feedback questions.
- Reflecting the client's communications style in his own questions.

Tips
Questions for Leisure Travelers

To determine the needs of a leisure traveler, consider asking these questions.

- Who will be traveling?
- When will you be traveling, and for how long?
- Where will you be going?
- Why are you traveling?
- What travel arrangements will you need (transportation, accommodations, other services)?
- Where have you traveled before?
- What type of hotel do you usually stay in?
- What activities are you looking for?
- Tell me about your best vacation and why you liked it.
- Describe your ideal vacation.
- What did you especially like about your last trip?
- What are you looking for from this trip?

Brad is also listening carefully. He limits his own talking and encourages the speaker.

Brad still needs to question Mr. Brown further in order to determine other needs. He will probe to find out what the Browns liked or did not like about past experiences and what they are looking for from this vacation. He will ask where they stayed in the past to help determine the type of accommodations to suggest, and he might ask Mr. Brown if he has a total budget.

As he gathers this information, Brad develops an idea of what he should recommend to Mr. Brown. In other words, he cycles into step 4, finding a product to match the client's needs. Before presenting a recommendation, he offers a picture of the Browns' needs and elicits feedback to that picture, as follows:

Brad: Don, let's take a look at what we've got here. You said you and your wife like the idea of a cruise vacation. You're looking for something relaxing, yet you want a choice of activities for both of you, including shopping and nightlife. Is that right?
Brown: Yes, that's it.

Brad: And you told me you've already been to Nassau, St. Thomas, and Puerto Rico, so you want to try someplace new, right?
Brown: Yes, somewhere tropical where we haven't been before.
Brad: You always stay in first-class beachfront resorts with oceanview rooms, and you both enjoy exploring places with lots of local crafts. Yes?
Brown: Yes.
Brad: Well, Don, I've got just the cruise for you!

Notice that Brad phrased his feedback questions so that Mr Brown would say yes in response.

Brad will go on to describe the ideal cruise he has in mind for the Browns, using some of Mr. Brown's own words and phrases, without mentioning a specific cruise line or ship. From this point on in the sale, giving information is the key task. These later steps in the sales cycle and techniques for presenting information are the subjects of the next chapter.

Chapter Wrap-Up

Chapter Highlights

Like any skill, selling requires that you know the steps involved in the skill, learn some basic techniques, and then practice. The first four steps in selling and techniques for carrying them out were the subjects of this chapter. Here is a review of the objectives with which we began.

1. **Discuss the goals and difficulties of the first four steps of the sales cycle.** In the first four steps of the cycle, the underlying goal is to build a relationship with the client as you gather information. The first step, identifying customers, includes prospecting and qualifying possible clients in order to identify people who have the interest and

ability to buy. In step 2, establishing rapport, you aim to form a link with the client so that the client sees that you are friendly, concerned, and trustworthy. A busy office is a common problem that can create a roadblock to building rapport. In step 3, your goal is to obtain information about the client's psychological and technical needs. The multitude of factors that influence travel requirements and the almost endless variety of motivations can make this step difficult. Furthermore, clients may not know what they want, or they may be unable to articulate their needs. In step 4, you and the client confirm that you have understood the client's needs and the type of travel product to be recommended. The information gathered in these first steps provides the basis for the remaining steps of the sales cycle.

2. **Identify the five basic *W*s and other key questions to ask in order to determine a client's needs.** The five basic *W*s of travel are who is traveling, when, where, why, and what type of accommodations and services they will require. (Some salespeople consider "What is your budget?" to be a sixth basic question; but often it is wise to avoid or postpone asking explicitly for a budget.) You should also ask about the client's previous travel experiences and ideal trip. For example, you can probe the client's needs more fully by asking questions such as, Where have you traveled before? What type of hotel do you usually stay in? What activities are you looking for? Can you describe your ideal vacation? What did you especially like about your last trip?

3. **Explain four guidelines for effective listening.** First, concentrate on the speaker, remembering to talk less yourself. Second, avoid making assumptions or jumping to conclusions. Third, "read between the lines" by paying attention not only to what is said, but also to how it is said and to the speaker's body language. Finally, elicit feedback and respond. The salesperson who is a good listener will always be more successful than one who is not.

4. **Interpret several common forms of body language.** Eye contact, facial expressions, posture, gestures, and personal space are all part of body language. A broad smile, good eye contact, and relaxed posture usually indicate agreement; a frown, avoidance of eye contact, clenched hands, and arms crossed in front of the body are all likely to indicate a negative response. The more empathy there is between two people, the more precisely they tend to mirror each other's body positions.

5. **Identify six principles for getting the information you need from an interview.** First, to question effectively, combine closed-ended, open-ended, and feedback questions. Second, phrase the questions in the style used by the customer. Third, weave the questions into a conversation. Retaining control of the conversation is a fourth principle. Also, be sure to listen with care. Finally, follow up vague questions.

6. **Apply techniques for effective listening and questioning to the sales cycle.** The ability to listen and to question effectively is key to carrying out the first steps of the sales cycle. In particular, being a good listener is essential in order to develop rapport and determine needs (step 2). Determining needs also requires that you ask lots of probing questions. At the least, you must get answers to the five basic *W*s, but the good salesperson also aims to discover the customer's underlying wants and needs.

New terms. The terms that follow were introduced in this chapter. If you do not recall their definitions, see the Glossary, which begins on page 237.

five basic *W*s
prospecting
qualifying
body language
closed-ended
   questions
communication
   style
mirroring
open-ended
   questions
feedback questions

Review Exercises

Check-Up

Give yourself a quick test of your memory of a few basic points. Read each of the following statements and indicate whether it is true (T) or false (F). See the answers below the statements.

T   F   1. Each step in the sales cycle must be completed in sequence, one at a time, one after the other.

T   F   2. You begin to develop rapport when you understand a client's needs.

T   F   3. To become an effective listener, you should be careful not to talk too much.

T   F   4. All over the world, the interpretation of postures, gestures, and facial expressions is the same.

T   F   5. To conduct an effective interview, use only open-ended questions.

Answers: 1. F, 2. F, 3. T, 4. F, 5. F

Discussion Questions

1. **Analyzing the Sales Cycle: A Group Exercise.** Break into groups of three or four members each. Using Worksheet 4.1 on page 109, identify actions to take and actions to avoid when moving through each of the first four steps of the sales cycle of success. Compare your answers with those given by other groups. Discuss why you listed each action.

2. **Analyzing the Sales Cycle: A Case in Point.** Reread the scenario that opened this chapter and then answer the following questions:

   a. Look over your completed Worksheet 4.1. Did Laurie omit any of the "Actions to Take" on your list?

   _____

   _____

   _____

   b. Did Laurie take any of the "Actions to Avoid" that you listed?

   _____

   _____

   _____

c. How would you describe Arlene's needs?

_____

_____

_____

_____

d. Are there additional questions that you would have asked Arlene before recommending a group tour? If so, what are they?

_____

_____

_____

_____

3. **Reading Body Language.** Imagine that you are about to greet a new customer.

a. What should your body language be like? (Be specific. Describe your use of eyes, facial expressions, body position, and gestures to convey a message.)

_____

_____

_____

_____

b. What body language would indicate that your customer is interested and feels positive about the encounter so far? (Again, be specific. Include descriptions of eyes, facial expressions, body position, and gestures.)

_____

_____

_____

_____

_____

4. **Asking Questions.** Reread the description of Hale & Company's situation on page 97. What questions would you ask in order to determine enough about the company's needs to make a recommendation?

_____

_____

_____

_____

5. **Carrying Out an Interview.** Try rephrasing the dialogue at the beginning of "Phrasing Your Questions," page 93, into one that is more conversational.

_____

_____

_____

_____

6. **Finding a Match: Cruises.** If you completed Worksheet 3.2 in Chapter 3 (page 75), pick one of the Caribbean cruises that you analyzed. Now consider whether it would meet Brad's needs.

Brad's needs	Features that meet those needs
_____	_____
_____	_____
_____	_____
_____	_____
_____	_____
_____	_____
_____	_____
_____	_____

7. **Finding a Match: Destinations.*** Suppose Fran is a 29-year-old woman from Michigan who wants to take a flight to a two-week vacation spot in February by herself. She is planning to spend $2,000. Her favorite vacation was a wildlife photo trip in Africa. Her most disappointing vacation was a family reunion at a lake resort in the upper Midwest. She travels as often as she can and last took a trip to Honolulu. She has also visited Disney World and Club Med in Cancun and went camping in Yellowstone. Fran wants her travel counselor, John Wakely, to recommend a destination for this year's vacation.

John has just been planning trips for other clients to Costa Rica and to the area from San Francisco to Los Angeles in California, so he thinks of these destinations first. Costa Rica offers places of ecological interest, volcanoes, a different culture, beaches, the opportunity for great photographs, and warm weather in February. California also offers warm weather, beaches, and some fabulous scenery—as well as theme parks, shopping, and nightlife.

a. How would you place Fran in terms of Plog's psychographic chart on page 33?

_____

_____

_____

_____

b. Does a San Francisco–Los Angeles vacation seem a good match for Fran? Why or why not?

_____

_____

_____

_____

c. Would you recommend Costa Rica as a destination for Fran? Why or why not?

_____

_____

_____

_____

_____

*This exercise is adapted from *Understanding Client Needs: Travel Industry Core Course* (Wellesley, MA: Institute of Certified Travel Agents, 1998), pp. 28, 49-52.

A Case in Question

Consider again the case on page 94, "The Fish that Got Away."

1. If you were Duncan, the aquarium's director of tour sales, what would you have said in order to acknowledge the problem?

    _____

    _____

    _____

    _____

    _____

    _____

2. If you were Duncan, how could you have taken responsibility for the problem?

    _____

    _____

    _____

    _____

    _____

    _____

3. The problem in this case seems to have begun with the communications—or miscommunications—between the travel counselor for River Scenes and the school and between the staffs at River Scenes and the aquarium. What were the miscommunications, and what questions might have avoided them?

    _____

    _____

    _____

    _____

    _____

Exercises in Selling

1. **First Steps.** Break into teams of two for practice in prospecting for clients and developing rapport with them. Assume that you have joined a new travel agency and want to identify groups that are potential clients for group excursions abroad.

a. Where would you look for leads? List four sources:

_____

_____

_____

_____

b. Assume that one of these sources has generated a lead. Together with your partner, act out the initial encounter between the travel counselor and the new potential customer. One of you will take the role of the travel counselor; the other, the potential customer. The travel counselor should qualify the potential client and begin developing rapport.

2. **Determining Customer Needs.** Break into groups of three and try your hand at gathering information from four types of clients by role-playing encounters. For each encounter, one member of the group will act as the travel counselor, one as the client, and one as the observer. Rotate the roles so that each member of the group has an opportunity to be the counselor, the client, and the observer. Before you begin, decide who will take each role for each of the four encounters.

When you take the role of the travel counselor, do *not* read the profile of your client. Remember to act as naturally as possible.

When you play the client, read the profile carefully and jot down notes. Be ready to respond to the travel counselor's questions and comments, and offer additional information if asked. Feel free to personalize the character if you like.

Observers should use Worksheet 4.2 (page 111) to evaluate the performance of the person playing the travel counselor.

After each encounter, discuss the observer's evaluation. If the observer gave you a total score above 28, you gather information well. Consider practicing techniques for which you earned only a fair or poor mark from the observer.

Here are descriptions of the four clients.

■ *Client profile A.* You and your spouse, both public school teachers, are thinking about taking a cruise during the February school vacation. This will be your first cruise. Now that your two children are out of college, you'd like to be a little extravagant. You have nine days and want to spend them relaxing as much as possible. You and your spouse both enjoy snorkeling, love to dance whenever you get the chance, and like the idea of sampling a variety of new places in a short time.

■ *Client profile B.* You are an executive of a Fortune 500 company and have just come back from its semiannual Board of Trustees meeting. The stress of preparing for the meeting has put you on edge. You need a change of scenery, if only for a long weekend. Money is not a real concern. You just want to get away for a few days, work out some tension, and have fun.

■ *Client profile C.* Your sister has been clamoring for you to visit her ever since her twins were born. You have postponed visiting her because you are not fond of the heat in Florida. But you have been hearing about Disney World, Epcot, and Universal Studios for so long that you are ready to see them for yourself. You need help figuring out an inexpensive way to combine a visit to your sister in Tampa with some fun.

■ *Client profile D.* You are a single, middle-aged woman who works for an international health organization. As part of your job, you have visited every continent, advising local health organizations. But your business travels have never left much time for traditional sightseeing, for savoring a country's culture, or for exploring the hinterland. Now you have a month off, a large travel budget, and a desire both to relax and to explore someplace in a little depth.

Worksheet 4.1

Name _____ Date _____

Analyzing the Sales Cycle

Complete this worksheet in order to answer the first Discussion Question on page 102. You may want to duplicate this page before writing on it.

	Actions to Take	**Actions to Avoid**
1. Identifying Customers	1. _____	1. _____
	2. _____	2. _____
	3. _____	3. _____
2. Establishing Rapport	1. _____	1. _____
	2. _____	2. _____
	3. _____	3. _____
3. Determining Needs	1. _____	1. _____
	2. _____	2. _____
	3. _____	3. _____
4. Matching Product and Client	1. _____	1. _____
	2. _____	2. _____
	3. _____	3. _____

Worksheet 4.2

Name _____ Date _____

Determining Clients' Needs

As the observer for the exercise described on page 107, your job is to evaluate the ability of the "travel counselor" to gather information in order to meet the customer's needs. Circle the response that best describes the counselor's performance. You may want to duplicate this page before writing on it so that you can evaluate several performances.

	Good	Fair	Poor
Develop rapport	3	2	1
Ask the right questions to determine needs	3	2	1
Concentrate on the customer	3	2	1
Avoid assumptions	3	2	1
Use appropriate body language:			
Facial expression	3	2	1
Eye contact	3	2	1
Posture	3	2	1
Gestures	3	2	1
Elicit feedback	3	2	1
Encourage the speaker	3	2	1
Use appropriate style of communication	3	2	1
Combine types of questions	3	2	1
Weave the questions into a conversation	3	2	1
Follow up and clarify answers	3	2	1

Total points: _____

Comments:

_____

_____

_____

_____

The Sales Cycle: Giving Information

Objectives

After reading this chapter, you should be able to

1. Discuss the goals and difficulties of steps 5–8 of the sales cycle.

2. Describe several strategies for asking a client for a commitment to buy the travel product.

3. Identify six guidelines for presenting ideas persuasively.

4. Outline steps for answering objections to your ideas.

5. Apply the techniques discussed to the sales cycle.

Preview

After you have created a relationship with your client and gathered information, how do you make the sale? That is the subject of this chapter. In Chapter 4 we described how you build rapport and gather and analyze information during steps 1–4 of the selling process. In the next steps of the cycle, your focus shifts to giving information. In particular, you need to present a recommendation and answer the customer's questions and objections.

How best can you give this information? We will describe several guidelines and techniques for presenting ideas and handling objections persuasively. First, though, let's take a closer look at the last four steps necessary to make a sale.

*M*aking the Sale: Steps 5–8

"I've got just the cruise for you!" That was the last statement we heard of the conversation between travel counselor Brad and his client at the end of Chapter 4. We saw how Brad had progressed through the first four steps of the sales cycle. He had established a relationship with the client, Don Brown, gathered information about his needs, paraphrased those needs, and received confirmation of that paraphrase. Now we turn to the remaining steps of the sales cycle. In these steps your underlying task is to give information back to the client so that the client will buy the travel product and will be happy with the purchase.

Step 5: Presenting Recommendations

Recall that in step 4 the salesperson confirms an idea of what to recommend to the client by paraphrasing what the client has said and asking for confirmation. If you have correctly identified the needs of your client, he or she should be agreeing with everything you say. If your customer says, "No, that's not right," then you go back to determining needs through more questioning. By watching body language and listening carefully to the customer's responses, you should have a good sense of how the customer will react to your actual recommendation.

Your goal in step 5 is to make the recommendation and to do it in a way that is persuasive. Because of the intangibility of the travel product, this task is likely to be more difficult than if you were selling a car or some other tangible product. When you go to buy a car, you can see it, touch it, and even take it for a test drive before you commit your hard-earned dollars. But in the travel industry, customers commit their money before they have any tangible contact with the product.

Effective salespeople find ways to make the intangible travel product seem tangible. For one thing, they describe very specific ways in which the recommended products will meet the clients' needs. They try to help clients imagine what they will do or see or feel if they buy the products. As an example, consider how travel counselor Brad offers his recommendation to Don Brown:

Brad: Well, Don, I've got just the cruise for you! I've selected a ship that cruises the western Caribbean, with stops at Cozumel, Grand Cayman, and Jamaica. They're all places you haven't visited before, with plenty of local crafts shops and areas to explore once you're there. The ship itself offers a wide variety of activities for you and your wife to choose from. You can be as busy as you want, or you can just relax. I suggest we make a reservation for an outside stateroom so you can watch the ocean while you're in the cabin. How does all this sound?

Brown: Sounds great. I'm ready to go home and pack, Brad!

Brad has not even mentioned which cruise line he is thinking of, yet Mr. Brown is ready to start packing for a vacation that is months away.

Of course, you cannot count on your recommendation being accepted this readily. As you present recommendations, watch your clients closely, and ask for feedback. Generally, they will do one of two things, as Figure 5.1 illustrates: they will send a buying signal, or they will offer obstacles to your recommendation.

A ***buying signal*** is a sign that your customer is ready to make a commitment to buy the product. Buying signals can be both verbal and nonverbal. *Verbal signals* consist of statements such as "That sounds good to me," "Can I bring my own golf clubs?" or "What restaurants can you recommend for dinner?" *Nonverbal buying signals* include head nods, eye contact, leaning toward your desk, and touching a brochure.

Table 5.1 describes some of the most common buying signals. These signals tell you when it is time to stop selling. Do not become so preoccupied with presenting the recommendation

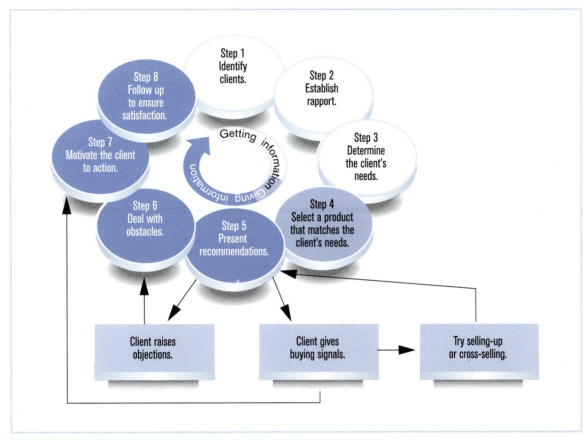

Figure 5.1 Another View of the Sales Cycle: Steps 5-7
The client shapes the course of the sales cycle. You should be ready to skip or to repeat steps in light of the client's responses.

that you miss the opportunity to make the sale.

If your client gives buying signals, you can move to step 7, motivating to action (see Figure 5.1). First, though, if your client is happy with your recommendation, consider whether the client might be interested in other travel products. In other words, you should consider two possibilities:

- **Selling-up,** which means upgrading, suggesting a more expensive or inclusive version of a product. For example, you might suggest a more luxurious hotel or hotel room, a larger rental car, or a cabin on a higher deck on a cruise ship.
- **Cross-selling,** which means offering additional products. Your clients might not be aware, for example, that they can go ahead and ask you to arrange their theater tickets, travel insurance, city tour, or transfer service from the airport.

Brad, for example, might have said the following after Don Brown reacted enthusiastically to Brad's recommendation:

Brad: You know, Don, you mentioned that you have ten days for this vacation. This ship leaves from Fort Lauderdale. Here's an idea. Why don't you spend a few days either before or after your cruise in Fort Lauderdale? One of our agents just came back from there and said there's a lot to see and do. We can make arrangements for you at a great hotel, get you tickets for the IMAX Theatre, and even arrange a rental car. How does that sound?

If, instead of giving buying signals, the client offers an obstacle to your recommendation, you must deal with it, which is step 6.

Table 5.1
Reading Buying Signals

Form	Buying Signals	Nonbuying Signals
Gestures	Touching a brochure Marking a brochure Nodding Taking out a check or credit card	Refusing to touch a brochure or to look at it Flipping idly through a brochure Reading a brochure very closely, indicating a need for more information
Facial expressions	Smiling	Frowning Minimal eye contact
Body position	Leaning in with relaxed arm and open hand Leaning back and relaxing	Leaning back with arms crossed in front Fidgeting
Verbal expressions	Statements of approval such as "That sounds good to me"; "I'm ready to start packing." Questions indicating serious interest such as "Can we get theater tickets for two nights?" or "How much luggage can we bring?"	Objections

Step 6: Dealing with Obstacles

Don Brown was an ideal client. He knew what he was looking for when he entered the travel agency and therefore made Brad's job simple. Not every client is that easy. If you follow the steps of the sales cycle, however, you increase the chances that you can avoid obstacles to the sale. But you should be prepared to deal with obstacles nonetheless.

Some Typical Obstacles. Obstacles can take several forms. Indifference is one. If the client lacks interest in what you are saying, you might not have uncovered his or her true needs yet. Step back and ask more questions to reconfirm your understanding of the client.

Skepticism is another obstacle. If the client doubts the validity of something you have said, back it up by referring to a source of your information. To confirm your statement, for example, you might turn to a brochure, magazine article, photograph, or contract.

Obstacles can also take the form of specific objections to your recommendation. If the client does raise objections, do not be discouraged. Instead, remember that an objection is not a rejection; try to think of it as an opportunity. It provides a chance to clarify information and indicates that the client is still interested. The objection may become a step toward completing the sale.

Also, eliminate the instinct to reject the client's concern outright. If the customer states, "I don't think I'd like a resort that far away from the city," you may feel like responding, "Don't worry, there are shuttle buses to take you downtown whenever you want." You shouldn't. The customer has a legitimate concern—whatever will she do so far from the city?—and you should address that concern, not dismiss it out of hand.

Some Common Objections. One very frequent objection is that the client wants to check with someone else. Often you can avoid this obstacle by doing what travel counselor Brad did: as described in Chapter 4 (page 99), early in the sales conversation Brad asked whether Mr. Brown was prepared to make a decision himself. If Mr. Brown had indicated that his wife had to be consulted, Brad would have stopped and made an appointment to get together with both Browns.

Price is another very common objection, and it too may be avoided by thoroughly determining the customer's needs before recommending a product. If you present a recommendation and the customer's response is "Wow, that's a lot more than we wanted to spend," chances are you did not find out the client's real price range during step 3. If you think you did get that information, did you reconfirm it in step 4? In other words, did you feed back a price range or category and get a positive response from your client?

Even if you did all of this, however, the client may still raise objections. Often, objections come from misinformation and misconceptions. *Misconceptions* are preconceived ideas such as "cruises are too expensive." *Misinformation* can stem from either a client's misinterpretation of correct information or a salesperson's presentation of false information. Objections can also arise when salespeople gather the right information but still make poor recommendations. Sometimes, though, clients simply want to procrastinate, or they might feel guilty about

indulging in the trip, or have second thoughts about their budget.

Suppose, for example, that despite his enthusiasm, Don Brown suddenly had doubts about the price of the cruise that Brad had recommended. The conversation might then go something like this:

> *Brown:* You know, that's a lot of money.
> *Brad:* Yes, I agree, the cost for the package may seem a little high when you first look at it. But remember everything that is included.

Brad would once again stress the benefits of those features that give Don a reason to buy the cruise. Remember that customers are more concerned with what they are getting for their money (value) than with the actual amount, as long as it is within their budget.

Handling objections is one of the trickiest tasks a salesperson faces. But if you learn how to recognize objections and to deal with them, they are never as tough as they seem initially. Later in this chapter we look at specific techniques for responding to objections effectively.

Eventually you will reach a point where all of your client's concerns have been addressed and you receive buying signals. Now (as Figure 5.1 shows) you can move on to the next step in the sales cycle.

Tips
Preparing for Obstacles

You are more likely to make a sale if you are prepared to spot and deal with the following common obstacles:

- Indifference.
- Skepticism.
- Specific objections, which often stem from (a) price, (b) misconceptions, (c) misinformation, (d) poor recommendations, (e) the client's tendency to delay or avoid decisions or feel guilty.

Step 7: Motivating to Action

Throughout the sales cycle you have been moving toward the point at which money "changes hands"; it is to this action that you wish to motivate your customer. Your efforts to develop rapport, your questioning to determine needs, and the way you have presented your recommendations and dealt with obstacles have led you and your customer to the point where the next logical step is the reservation and payment. That is the time to ask for the client's commitment to buy the product.

Often, this "motivating to action" step is called the **close** or **closing the sale.** Note, though, that these terms have a misleading finality. If you "close" the sale, does that mean you have finished with the customer? Absolutely not! You have worked too long and hard. You want a long relationship with the client.

Even before step 7, you indirectly ask for the commitment to buy the product through your feedback questions. Every time you ask, "How does that sound?" and the customer responds positively, he or she is implying a willingness to buy. This technique of asking questions throughout the sales process in order to gain the client's agreement and move the client closer to the purchase is called a *trial close.* The more times you get your customer to say yes, the closer you are to obtaining a commitment.

How do you know when a customer is ready to commit to the sale? Is there a "magic moment" when it all comes together, when bells and whistles and fireworks go off? Not exactly. But buying signals like those summarized on page 116 will tell you when to go ahead and ask for the purchase. Travel counselor Brad, for example, closed the sale with Don Brown by saying:

> *Brad:* You sure sound excited, Don. Let me call Getaway Cruises and see what cabins are available for the week of July 15th.

Generally, if you have read your customer well, there should be no resistance, and the sale will be made.

Still, asking for the commitment to buy can be difficult. Among the possible strategies for closing the sale are the direct close and the assumptive close.

- In a *direct close,* you ask the client for the sale directly.

> *Travel counselor:* Shall we go ahead and make these reservations?

- In the *assumptive close,* you assume the sale has been made. This close can take several forms. For example, the *choice close* is a form of the assumptive close in which you offer the client a choice based on the assumption that the sale is made.

> *Travel counselor:* Will you be paying by credit card or check?

Similarly, in the *complimentary close,* you compliment the client in a way that assumes that the client has decided to make the purchase.

> *Travel counselor:* I think you've made a great decision in picking this cruise of the Caribbean.

If the client has not "made the decision," he or she will let you know.

When clients resist making a commitment to buy, some salespeople turn to tougher closing strategies. For example, they might warn clients that if they do not make a decision now, the price might rise or their preferred flight or cabin or hotel might be sold out. The nationally known speaker and consultant Marc Mancini (*TravelAge West,* June 24, 1996, p. 18) suggests some gentler approaches such as

- The "You deserve it" close. Clients may have worked hard all year to take a trip like the one you've described; remind them of this. Or say something like, "Your family deserves this kind of trip."
- The "I'll throw it in" close. If the travel package is large enough, you can afford to give something free in order to avoid losing the client's business. You might offer free travel insurance, for example, or a $50 credit to spend on board a cruise.

Which closing strategy is best? That depends on the situation and the salesperson. No one strategy fits every situation or every salesperson. Each salesperson develops his or her own selling style, and successful salespeople adapt their style to the situation.

Step 8: Follow Up to Ensure Satisfaction

At last—the sale has been made! Still, the sales cycle is not complete, as the Selling through Service case on page 119 illustrates. Travel professionals aim to establish long-term relationships with clients. Keeping existing clients is far less expensive than finding new ones,

Selling through Service

Calling Collect . . .

It was a collect call from Hawaii. Susan had no idea what the caller could want. In fact, for a moment, she had no idea who was calling. But Norton is not a very common name, and she quickly remembered a Norton family for whom she had arranged a trip to Hawaii a few weeks ago. That was the first time she had worked with them.

"I'll accept the charges," she said with some hesitation, wondering why they were calling.

"Well, Susan," Mrs. Norton began in a voice that was anything but pleasant. "The hotel is perfectly fine, but we are unhappy with the view from our room. We specifically asked for a waterview room. And we cannot see the water from our room unless we almost break our necks. We want you to fix the problem."

Susan quickly scrambled for her file on the Nortons. She had booked the trip through a well-known tour operator. Then the conversation came back to her. Susan remembered that she had offered the Nortons the choice between waterfront and waterview. They had selected the less expensive alternative, "waterview," without asking any questions or making any comments about the choice.

Susan was frustrated. If she had only asked more questions, she might have learned that having a good view was important to the Nortons. And if she had paraphrased the terms when discussing her recommendations, perhaps they would have objected to getting only a "waterview" room.

Then, in a flash, Susan was irritated, not with herself, but with the Nortons. If the view mattered so much, why hadn't they said so? If they didn't understand the choice, why hadn't they asked? Now what should she do? Should she tell the Nortons to call the tour operator? Should she call the operator or the hotel? If you were Susan, what would you do?

∎ ∎ ∎

For one thing, Susan should put aside her irritation with the Nortons. Recall the problem-solving steps that we outlined in Chapter 1. The first three are to acknowledge the problem, collect the facts, and accept responsibility. After carrying out these steps, Susan needs to select a strategy for solving the problem.

We've examined the first three steps in earlier cases, so let's consider step 4, selecting a strategy to solve the problem. Recall that in Chapter 1 we described three basic strategies: doing what the client wants; finding an alternative way to reach the client's goal; or redefining the client's goal and finding a way to reach that goal. Thus, in this case, Susan's possible strategies are

- To obtain a waterfront room for the Nortons at no extra cost to them (the Nortons' request). She might contact the tour operator's on-site representative and explore the possibility of getting them an upgrade at the tour operator's expense.
- To obtain a waterfront room for the Nortons at the Nortons' expense (an alternative way of reaching the Nortons' goal of getting a waterfront room). Susan might call the hotel directly to find out if a waterfront room is available and move the Nortons to it at the Nortons' expense.
- Explain the difference in price between a waterfront and waterview room and point out how much the Nortons are saving by staying in the waterview room (a redefinition of the Nortons' goal).

In order to select a strategy intelligently, Susan should consider the benefits and drawbacks of each possible solution. Is the solution feasible? Is the customer likely to agree to it? In this case, what are the gains and losses of each possible solution for each of the parties involved?

but keeping clients requires following through on a sale.

In fact, when the client says yes, much of your work still remains. If you are a travel counselor, there are reservations to make, documents to complete, tickets to generate, credit cards to process. You must do everything in your power to see that the trip your customer booked will be a success.

Your goal at this stage of the sales cycle is to ensure that the client will be satisfied and return to do business with you again and again. We call this *following up* or *managing after-sale satisfaction*. Remember, satisfied customers are repeat customers, and repeat customers mean more business for you. Satisfied customers may also provide word-of-mouth referrals, generating more business.

Some basic techniques for following up with the client include

- Checking that the sale is processed accurately. Are all documents accurate and complete? Are you certain that clients understand any actions they must still take—such as being sure that a deposit is made by a certain date or renewing a passport?
- Keeping in touch with the customer after the sale to answer questions or solve problems.
- Providing additional information after the sale but before the trip, such as new magazine articles about a destination.
- Delivering documents in a timely way.
- Seeking feedback from customers after a trip. You might call them to find out how the trip went or ask them to complete a formal evaluation.
- Letting clients know if new travel opportunities come up that match their interests.
- Congratulating the client on special occasions such as birthdays or anniversaries. These simple gestures go a long way toward building rapport and securing loyalty.

The follow-up on a sale is an important linkage between sales and customer service. In fact, it is often hard to differentiate sales from customer service. You could say that good selling is good service.

Time Out

Check your understanding of the discussion so far by filling in the blanks.

1. Steps 5–8 of the sales cycle are

    _____

    _____

    _____

    _____

2. Common buying signals include

    _____

    _____

3. If the client agrees with your recommendation, you

    _____

    _____

4. Obstacles to a sale include

    _____ ,

    _____ ,

    and specific objections.

5. Some common sources of objections to recommendations are

    _____ .

Presenting Ideas

There you are. New on the job, you are faced with a tall, elegant, gray-haired man, a twenty-year veteran of the travel industry. He is now the travel manager for a large corporation. You want to persuade him that you should make the arrangements for an upcoming corporate meeting. You have discussed his needs and are ready to offer your paraphrase of those needs and your ideas for meeting them. What do you say? More generally, what is the best way to give information so that the customer will say yes to your ideas and, ultimately, to the sale? This section offers some guidelines.

Persuasive Presentations

First of all, try to use language that your clients can identify with. In particular,

- Adopt the words and communications style used by your client. If your client talks about finding a place where he can "get people together to relax and talk things over," there is no need for you to talk about "facilitating interdepartmental communication and synergy."
- Eliminate travel industry jargon. Instead of talking about a "round-trip transfer," mention that the traveler would be taken from the airport to the hotel and then back to the airport at the end of the trip. Instead of recommending "an outside cabin," suggest a "room with an ocean view."

Second, throughout the conversation, elicit feedback and be alert for signs that your customer is surprised or perplexed by what you are saying. In order to be persuasive, you need to understand how your client is reacting to your comments. Remember to listen and to watch the customer's body language.

Third, phrase your questions so that your customer is most likely to say yes. For example, instead of asking, "Does that sound too elaborate for you?" you might ask, "Does that sound good so far?"

Fourth, be prepared with two ideas—but present only one at a time. Begin with the idea that you believe the customer will react to most favorably. Your second idea should also meet the customer's needs, but offer it only if the first recommendation is rejected.

Fifth, resist the temptation to oversell. Your job is to present information not only persuasively but also credibly. You want not only to make this sale but also to serve this client and keep him or her as a future client. Table 5.2 describes some dangerous statements.

Finally, in discussing your ideas, do everything you can to make the intangible seem tangible. You cannot offer your customers a "test ride," but you can try to make them see themselves experiencing what you are describing. The successful salesperson

- Uses words to create mental pictures. For example,

  Travel counselor: This hotel is right on the beach and every room has an ocean view. You and your wife can enjoy those sunsets you've been dreaming about right from your own private deck! Or bring your coffee and newspaper out there in the morning while your wife gets dressed. Sounds peaceful, doesn't it?

Figure 5.2 describes some specific techniques for creating mental pictures.

- Emphasize benefits.
- Use visual aids such as brochures and videos.

These last two techniques for making the intangible tangible deserve a closer look.

Features and Benefits

One of the best ways to make the travel product tangible is to identify the benefits of a product's features. As we discussed in Chapter 3, a *feature* is part of the design of the product; a *benefit* is what the feature does for the customer. For

Table 5.2
Some Statements to Avoid

Form of Overselling	Examples	Comment
Exaggerations, overgeneralizations, lies	"It's the greatest value in New Orleans." "It's always lovely at this time of year." "You don't have to worry about malaria; you'll never catch it in a week."	Watch out for a common error of inexperienced salespeople: making generalizations about things they know nothing about.
Guarantees of enjoyment by referring to another client's experience	"I know you'll enjoy this trip because Mr. and Mrs. Smith did."	Mr. and Mrs. Smith may have enjoyed the trip for reasons that have nothing in common with this client's needs or expectations.
Guarantees of anything beyond your control, such as the weather, the service, or the client's reaction	"It's always beautiful there in May." "You'll love it!"	"You'll love it" is a dangerous expression. Don't promise something unless you can deliver it.
Criticism of the competition	"The trouble you mentioned having with that last travel agency is typical, I'm afraid!"	If a client criticizes the competition, do not answer the comment directly. Instead, return to a discussion of the client's needs.

Source: Adapted from Patricia J. Gagnon, CTC, and Bruno Ociepka, CTC, *Travel Career Development*, 6th ed. (Wellesley, MA: ICTA, 1998), p. 210.

example, a feature of a cruise might be that the ship calls at three ports. A benefit of this feature is that the client can visit three different islands without packing and unpacking more than once.

Turning Features into Benefits. Customers buy because of what the product does for them—the benefit of the product, not the features. As an example, let's look at some features of a conference center proposed for a meeting. Suppose that you want to recommend a conference center that (1) is small and independent, (2) is at a remote location, (3) includes all meals in the price, and (4) offers day- and nighttime activities.

If you simply list these features, your customer might think, "So what?" You want your customer to get excited about the recommended purchase. To achieve that goal, you need to emphasize the benefits of these features. What are they?

Features	Possible Benefits
Small and independent	Personalized service; unique design and furnishings; intimate atmosphere
Remote location	Decreases possible distractions; encourages camaraderie; offers refreshing tranquility
All meals included	No need to search for restaurants for dining; no need to monitor budget for meals
Day- and nighttime activities	Wide variety of things to do both day and night; activities can be as active or lazy as you like

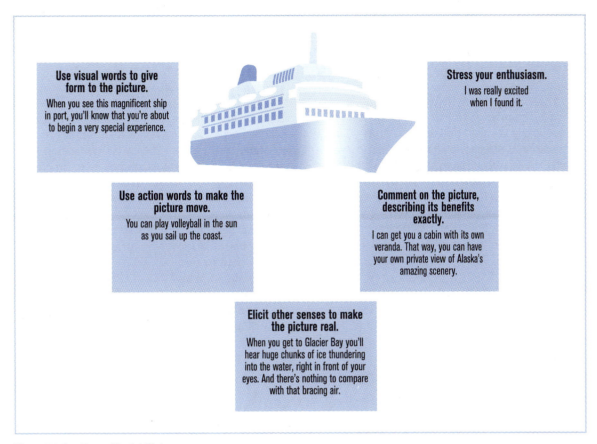

Figure 5.2 Creating a Mental Picture
"If your client imagines himself on a trip," writes Marc Mancini, "he's more likely to actually take that trip. Your job as a salesperson, then, is to help a client paint an imaginary picture of a voyage, with himself right at the center." Here are his tips for how to create that picture.
Source: Adapted with permission from Marc Mancini, "Sales Clinic: Putting in the Picture," *TravelAge West,* April 1, 1996, p. 57.

Thus, you might recommend this conference center to a client by saying something like the following:

> *Travel counselor:* This conference center certainly looks as if it will fit all the needs for your meeting. Because it's small, you'll really be able to receive personalized service, and people won't feel lost in the crowd. With this remote location there's less of a chance for distractions. And you'll come in under budget because all your meals are included in the price. There's also a wide variety of day- and nighttime activities, so everyone can relax at their own pace during their free time.

You describe the features of the travel products, emphasizing the benefits those features will provide.

Adjusting to the Client. Our hypothetical conference center might appeal both to corporate managers and to a square-dancing club. The same cruise might be attractive to honeymooners and to a family—if you emphasize different benefits. Make sure the benefits you describe meet the customer's needs and motivations.

Often, the benefits of a feature can be expressed in different ways in order to appeal to different needs. What is the benefit of having all meals included in the price? For the client who is worried about not knowing where to go in a strange place, the benefit is that the client will know where to go for dinner every night. But for the client concerned with budget, this feature gives the benefit of guaranteeing that the last meal will be as complete and satisfying as the first. For the first client, you might say something like the following:

Travel counselor: One of the great things about this vacation package is that all your meals are included in the price. You know, you mentioned that searching out new places to eat every night doesn't appeal to you. Having all your meals at your hotel would certainly solve that problem, don't you agree?

But for the budget-conscious customer, you might describe this same feature as follows:

Travel counselor: The great thing about having all your meals included in the price is that you won't have to worry about budgeting your money over the course of your vacation. You can be sure that every meal will be as complete and satisfying as the first. That's important to you, right?

Remember to point out benefits that meet a customer's special needs. In your conversation with your client, you might have picked up signals that the client has a strong need for achievement or for affiliation. You might have learned that the client has a bad hip that limits the time he or she can spend walking or that the client is trying to lose weight. Perhaps the client has a special interest in antiques or in skydiving. This information has shaped your recommendation, but now is the time to apply your understanding of the client again. Use it to make your presentation persuasive.

Differences in cultural background, in values and lifestyle, can complicate your presentation. Be careful to avoid stereotyping your clients or assuming that they share your values or expectations. You might consider the opportunity to have free time away from children to be a great benefit; your customers might be insulted at the idea. You might be enthusiastic about the all-night bar in a city; your customers might be more interested in finding religious services to celebrate the Sabbath on a Friday or Saturday.

In short, good salespeople always keep the customer in mind. They analyze features and emphasize those benefits that meet the needs of a particular client.

Using Brochures and Videos

Here is an all-too-common scene. A customer enters a travel agency and asks about a vacation to some sunny spot. The travel counselor, ever agreeable, hands the customer five brochures and says, "Look these over. When you find something you like, call me and I'll make the reservations."

What's wrong with this picture? This agent is acting like a doctor who gives you a medical text to read to find out what's wrong with you. Who is the expert?

Brochures are a widely used tool for making the travel product tangible, but they are valuable only if they are used correctly. Unfortunately, many novice salespeople use travel brochures as

Tips
**Presenting
Ideas Persuasively**

Whenever you have a message to present, your chances of being persuasive are increased by following these guidelines:

- Avoid jargon and adopt the communications style used by the other person.
- Pay attention to the other person's reactions and elicit feedback.
- Phrase feedback questions so that the other person is likely to say yes.
- Be prepared with two ideas.
- Present only one idea at a time, saving the second in case the first is rejected.
- Make the intangible seem tangible by creating mental pictures, describing the benefits of features, and using visual aids.

a crutch. They either hand them to customers or just read along with the customers.

How do you use brochures as an effective sales tool? Here are some guidelines.

- Study the brochures of those travel products sold most frequently.
- Annotate the brochures. Good salespeople will have their own copies of brochures, which have been marked up, clipped, and otherwise personalized with information.
- Wait to present the brochure until you know the product will suit the customer. In other words, after you have matched a product to the client (step 4) and begun to make your recommendation (step 5), if you sense a positive reaction from the client, take out the appropriate brochure.
- As you discuss the brochure, remember to emphasize benefits.
- Watch the customer's reactions.

Travel videos provide another powerful aid for selling. Like brochures, they should be used only after you know what to recommend to the client and only as tools, not as replacements for your own selling efforts. To use them effectively,

- Preview all videos before showing them to be sure that they are interesting, accurate, and relevant to the client.
- Show the video to reinforce certain sales points, to illustrate benefits that you have already discussed, or to enhance the client's enthusiasm.
- Discuss the video with the client, emphasizing the benefits illustrated.

Travel videos have a special appeal to travel agencies. Besides using them to advance the sale, some travel agencies sell them or rent them. And some agencies give videos as gifts to clients as part of their efforts to follow up on the sale.

Selling to Groups

Presenting an idea to a group of people rather than an individual offers some special challenges. Perhaps you are proposing an incentive trip to a committee of managers or suggesting an idea for a tour to a local club. How do you "adjust to the client" when you are talking to a variety of people? Should you aim for a group discussion to develop a consensus? How do you hold your audience's attention? Here are a few pieces of advice.

- Aim your presentation at the average member of the group.
- Come prepared with one specific package to recommend.
- Before your presentation, be sure you can deliver what you are recommending. If you are selling a trip, check out the specific destination, dates, and price so that you can guarantee that transportation and accommodations are available. Bookings for a group involve special procedures, penalties, pricing, and due dates for reservations and payments, as well as possibilities for discounts and extra amenities.
- Use visual aids. Posters, slides, films, or videos will help keep your audience's attention and make the travel product seem tangible.

Time Out

To check your understanding of the discussion so far, reread the description of the conversation between Arlene and Laurie at the beginning of Chapter 4, page 80. What are three weaknesses in Laurie's presentation of her ideas?

_____

_____

_____

_____

Responding to Objections

No matter how smoothly you think a sale is progressing, many client will throw some obstacles in your path. Perhaps they object to your paraphrase of their needs (step 4), or maybe they see drawbacks to your recommendation (step 5). How do you deal with objections? Even before you say anything, you should take several steps, which Figure 5.3 summarizes.

First, anticipate objections and prepare helpful responses in advance. Table 5.3, for example, shows some objections that anyone selling cruises should be ready to handle.

Second, take a positive attitude. Do not look at the objection as a dead end to the sale. Do not take resistance personally and become defensive. Instead, think of the objection as an opportunity to clear up any misconceptions and to present the client once again with reasons to buy.

Third, listen to the objection completely without interrupting.

Fourth, "get in step" with the client by restating the concern and empathizing. Show that you are listening to the concern.

Fifth, evaluate the objection. Make sure you understand it and the extent of the customer's concerns. How important is it to the customer? Is the objection really just an obstacle, or is it a condition? ***Conditions*** are obstacles that cannot be overcome. If it takes two weeks to sail between two points and your client has only one week, you will not sell that trip to the client. Physical barriers and insufficient money or time are common conditions. Be sure you devote your time to handling obstacles rather than wrestling with conditions.

After you have taken these five steps, you are ready to respond to the objection.

Forming Responses

Let's examine some specific methods for responding to an objection. One of the most successful is known as the ***"yes, but" method.*** It has two main components. First you agree that the objection is worthy of concern; then you show how it can be handled.

Suppose you have established that a cruise would fit a couple's needs, but then they respond,

> *Client:* Maybe not. We've heard that lots of people get seasick on a cruise.

What do you do? You might get in step with them by saying,

> *Travel counselor:* You know, Mr. and Mrs.

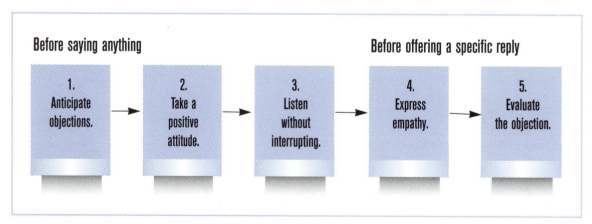

Before saying anything   **Before offering a specific reply**

| 1. Anticipate objections. | 2. Take a positive attitude. | 3. Listen without interrupting. | 4. Express empathy. | 5. Evaluate the objection. |

Figure 5.3 Handling Objections: Getting Ready to Respond
Whatever the client's objection, a sale is not a battle of wills. The salesperson's job is not to overcome the concern and win a debate but to work with the client to come up with a solution. These are the steps that will prepare you to find that solution.

Smith, a lot of first-time cruisers have that same concern, and I can understand why you might be hesitant. Getting seasick could spoil your vacation.

Then you go on to the "but" stage. You might mention modern technology and medicines that permit a comfortable and ultimately enjoyable cruise. For example,

> *Travel counselor:* But today's cruise ships are so large and they have equipment that will stabilize the ride, so you'll hardly notice you're at sea at all. If you're still leery, we can provide special wrist bands that alleviate motion discomfort.

Stacy in our office uses them all the time. You could also speak with your doctor about prescribing a special patch for you to wear. What do you think?

Another technique is to *ask questions*. When the customer raises an objection, simply ask, "Why?" The customer must then think about the objection and provide further information. For example,

> *Client:* I think the quality of the accommodations on this cruise are not quite up to my taste.
> *Travel counselor:* Why don't you think they're for you?

Table 5.3
Frequent Objections to Cruises

Objections	Possible Replies
"Cruises are too expensive."	Explain how much is included in the price of a cruise and the value it represents. Cite some budget cruise lines or special promotions. Break down the cost of a land-based vacation and compare it with the cruise's price.
"Cruises are boring."	Cite everything that goes on during a cruise. Show the client a "daily activities" sheet from a cruise that you've taken. Recommend a cruise line that features few full days at sea and many activities that would appeal to your client.
"Cruises aren't for _____" (young people, or singles, or children).	Recommend a cruise line that gives special attention to the profile and needs of your client.
"I don't like water."	Is this a fear of sinking? If so, emphasize the safety features on modern cruise ships. Is this a fear of being seasick? If so, explain that modern medications are very effective at countering motion discomfort. Describe Sea Bands. Suggest a short "try-out" cruise or one with minimal motion, such as a river cruise or a cruise along inlets.
"I hate all of that forced socializing."	If it's within the client's budget, recommend an upscale cruise line with open seating. Explain that on most cruises you must socialize with people you don't know only at dinner.
"Cruises are too formal and stuffy."	Explain that formal dress is required for only one or two evenings on a cruise. Suggest a cruise line that takes a very relaxed approach to attire.

Source: Adapted with permission from Marc Mancini, "The Sales Process: Overcoming Objections," *Educational Sales Manual: How To Sell to First-Time Cruise Clients,* a special supplement to *Travel Counselor,* July 1997, p. 43.

When the customer responds, you can then ask more probing questions. This method works best to distinguish excuses from real objections.

Compensation is another approach to objections. Agree with the client, but then show a benefit that balances the objection.

> *Client:* I think the quality of the accommodations on this cruise are not quite up to my taste.
> *Travel counselor:* I agree that these cabins may not be what you're used to. But, you know, this ship was specifically designed for the low-cost weekend cruise you're looking for. So with the smaller cabin you'll save money.

Be careful, though, that you show empathy with a client's concern and do not brush it off abruptly.

If a client interrupts your presentation with an objection, *postponement* is sometimes the best strategy. For example,

> *Travel counselor:* That's an interesting point. Before we discuss that further, I'd like to talk about just two things that will help you understand these accommodations from a different viewpoint. Okay?

Finally, when a client is clearly wrong, *direct denial* may be the best approach.

> *Travel counselor:* I'm not sure where you got that information. Several cruise magazines rated the quality of the accommodations on this ship very highly.

This type of response, though, should be used cautiously and sparingly. No one likes to be told they're wrong.

Overcoming Hidden Objections

Some clients may find it difficult to criticize or disagree openly with what a salesperson says. And often clients are reluctant to make a commitment, whatever they say at first. In both cases, there are hidden obstacles to a sale. How can you uncover them so that they do not prevent a sale? It helps to recognize two techniques often used to hide objections.

First, clients often disguise their doubts or obstacles by asking questions. For example, a client who asks, "Will there be time for shopping?" may have several motivations for asking that question. Answering a question by asking one may uncover an objection lurking behind the client's question. In this case, instead of answering yes or no, the salesperson may ask, "How important is time for shopping to you on this trip?" This creates another opportunity to probe and then to move the sale along.

Second, clients frequently disguise objections by saying that they need time to think things over. What do you do? You might say something like the following:

> *Travel counselor:* I understand that you don't want to rush into anything. But could you explain exactly what you need to think over?

If the customer responds by offering another objection, you have successfully identified a hidden obstacle and can proceed. If the customer is vague or reluctant, then go over various possibilities. For example,

> *Travel counselor:* Ms. Barnett, is it the dates that you are not sure of?

or

> *Travel counselor:* Bob, are you not comfortable with the hotel we've selected?

Probe until the customer says, "Yes, that's it." Congratulations! You have uncovered a hidden objection, which you can now address.

How do you know when an objection has been handled to the client's satisfaction? The customer will usually say something like, "Oh, okay" or "I see." Watch body language to see if your customer is nodding. Sometimes the customer remains silent. Ask if he or she has any other concerns or hesitations. This is an opportunity to get everything out in the open rather than playing a cat-and-mouse game, with client and salesperson chasing each other all around the sale.

Time Out

Check your understanding of the discussion so far by filling in the blanks.

1. Before you reply to an objection, you should be sure to

   _____

   and listen to the objection without inter-rupting.

2. The "yes, but" method of replying to objections consists of first agreeing that the objection is worth considering and then

   _____ .

3. Other techniques for replying to objections include asking questions, and

   _____ ,

   _____ ,

   and

   _____

   _____ .

Applications to the Sales Cycle

Let's see how the techniques we have discussed for presenting ideas and handling objections can be applied to steps 5–7 of the sales cycle, which we described at the beginning of this chapter. We'll look one more time at Brad and his client, Don Brown. Recall Brad's recommendation (step 5):

Brad: Well, Don, I've got just the cruise for you! I've selected a ship that cruises the western Caribbean, with stops at Cozumel, Grand Cayman, and Jamaica. They're all places you haven't visited before, with plenty of local crafts shops and areas to explore once you're there. The ship itself offers a wide variety of activities for you and your wife to choose

from. You can be as busy as you want, or you can just relax. I suggest we make a reservation for an oceanview stateroom, so you can watch the ocean while you're in the cabin. How does all this sound?

Notice that Brad used several of the techniques we discussed for presenting ideas effectively. He avoided jargon and tried to make the intangible seem tangible by emphasizing how the features of the trip will create benefits for Mr. Brown. And he elicited feedback.

Now let's suppose that the rest of the sales conversation between Brad and Don Brown took a direction a bit different from our description earlier in the chapter. After hearing Brad's recommendation, Don Brown responds,

Brown: That sounds pretty good.

Because Don has responded favorably to his recommendation, Brad decides to try selling-up, as follows:

Brad: Maybe we should reserve a stateroom with a balcony. What do you think?

This time, though, Don Brown begins to raise objections.

Brown: Well, I've got a few questions. I don't know about that balcony room. It sounds kind of expensive.

Perhaps Brad should have described the benefits of taking a balcony room. In any event, Brad now finds himself at step 6 of the sales cycle, handling objections. How does he do it?

Brad: You're right, Don. It sounds expensive, but think about what's included in the price of the cruise. You're probably spending less than you would with an oceanfront room at a resort hotel in the Caribbean, as you've done in the past. Remember, all your meals and entertainment are included, so most of the cost of your vacation is paid up front. Does that help?
Brown: Yes, I understand that, but won't a balcony be too much extra? I mean, I like the idea, but, you know?
Brad: I understand. It does seem like it would be a lot more money. But it's really only a difference of about $180 per person for the balcony. That's only $25 a day. And to be able to sit on your own private space, soaking in the sun and the ocean breezes—well, don't you think you and your wife would really enjoy that, since that's the type of room you usually stay in?

To handle Don's objection, Brad used the "yes, but" method. He agreed that Don had a legitimate concern about the cost of the trip, but then attempted to show why the price should not deter Mr. Brown. But Brown's response indicated that Brad had not addressed Brown's real concern: the extra cost of the balcony. Brad applied the "yes, but" method again to deal with

this objection. Notice that he used concrete language, emphasized benefits, and again asked for feedback. Let's return to Don Brown's response.

Brown: Putting it that way, Brad, I can see your point. I didn't realize the price difference was so little. But I have another question. Some friends took a cruise that went to Grand Cayman, and they said it was kind of boring. Is there anyplace else we could go?
Brad: Of course, there are other options. But let me ask you, Don, do you know why they thought it was boring?
Brown: Well, they said all there was to do was snorkel or dive and they really weren't into that. And neither are we.
Brad: I understand your concern. The Cayman Islands are noted as a great place for diving, but there are a lot of other opportunities there. Here, this brochure on the islands shows some of the other things to do. You mentioned shopping and beaches as being important to you. Well, there's good shopping right as you step off at the pier. And Grand Cayman is famous for its Seven Mile Beach, where you and your wife can relax. What do you think—does it sounds like something you'd like?
Brown: It sounds like a lot of fun.
Brad: Do you have other concerns, or does that answer all your questions?
Brown: Oh yes, I think you've covered everything.

If Brad had been less confident about his recommendation, he might have retreated to a different suggestion once his client asked for another option. Instead, though, Brad handled the new objection by asking a question. He learned more about his client's concern, and he was able to address it by drawing on what he had discovered earlier in the sale about Brown's needs and wants. Then he checked to be sure there were no hidden objections.

What happens next? Brown's responses amount to a strong buying signal; so Brad moves to his closing.

Brad: Good, then let's check with the cruise line to make sure we can get you that balcony stateroom for July 15th.

Brown: Sounds great!

Of course, Brad's work is far from finished. He must process the sale and follow up to ensure that the Browns are satisfied (step 8). But Brad can feel pleased that so far he has succeeded in meeting his client's needs and that the client has made the purchase.

*C*hapter Wrap-Up

Chapter Highlights

Although each step in the sales cycle is linked to the other steps, giving information becomes a primary task in the second half of the sales cycle. In these steps the salesperson must present ideas and answer objections. This chapter focused on techniques for giving this information in a way that moves the client to make the purchase. Here is a review of the objectives with which we began the chapter.

1. **Discuss the goals and difficulties of steps 5–8 of the sales cycle.** In steps 5 and 6, you communicate your recommendation to the client, seek to learn any obstacles to it, and communicate your response to those obstacles. The fact that travel is an intangible product complicates the task of presenting a compelling recommendation. And clients may raise objections to a recommendation because of misconceptions, misinformation, or poor recommendations. You need to be ready to go back through the cycle, to keep building rapport and clarifying needs as the situation requires. Use obstacles as an opportunity to clarify information and move the sale along. If the customer seems satisfied with your recommendation, consider selling-up or cross-selling. When you receive buying signals, you are ready for step 7, the closing, when you obtain the commitment to the sale. Every step in the sales cycle has been leading to this step, but many salespeople have trouble bringing themselves to ask for a commitment to buy. Once you have that commitment, it is tempting to think that your work is done. But a final step remains: following up to ensure customer satisfaction.

2. **Describe several strategies for asking a client for a commitment to buy the travel product.** In the direct close the salesperson asks for the sale directly; in contrast, in the assumptive close the salesperson asks a question or makes a statement that assumes that the sale has been made. Among the forms that the assumptive close can take are the choice close (in which that salesperson offers a choice that assumes the sale has been made) and the complimentary close (in which a compliment assumes that the sales has been made).

3. **Identify six guidelines for presenting ideas persuasively.** First, use language that the client can identify with. In particular, adjust your communications style to suit the client and avoid jargon. Second, as you offer ideas, listen to the client, watching body language, and elicit feedback. Third, phrase feedback questions in a way that encourages the customer to answer yes. Fourth, although you should always have two ideas to recommend, present only one at a time. Fifth, avoid overselling, such as exaggerating or making guarantees about aspects of a trip that are beyond your control. And finally, make the travel product as tangible as possible by creating mental pictures with your description, emphasizing benefits, and using aids such as brochures.

4. **Outline steps for answering objections to your ideas.** First, anticipate likely objections

and prepare possible responses. Second, take a positive attitude; look at the objection as an opportunity. Third, listen to the objection without interrupting. Fourth, show empathy for the client's concern. Fifth, evaluate it, determining its importance to the client and being sure that it is not a condition, which would block the sale. After these steps, you are ready to reply to the objection. Among the key techniques for offering your response are the "yes, but" method, asking questions, compensation, postponement, and direct denial.

5. **Apply the techniques discussed to the sales cycle.** The chapter presented specific techniques for presenting ideas and handling objections persuasively. These techniques are useful in many situations, but they are key in steps 5 and 6 of the sales cycle. The six guidelines we offered for presenting ideas persuasively, for example, should allow you to offer your recommendations in a clear and interesting way. Following the guidelines for handling objections should allow you to maintain your rapport with your client, clarify their needs, and move the sale along to closing.

New terms. The terms that follow were introduced in this chapter. If you do not recall their definitions, see the Glossary, which begins on page 237.

assumptive close
buying signal
choice close
closing the sale
complimentary close
conditions

cross-selling
direct close
selling-up
trial close
"yes, but" method

Review Exercises

Check-Up

Give yourself a quick test of your memory of a few basic points. Read each of the following statements and indicate whether it is true (T) or false (F). See the answers below the statements.

T   F   1. When the client offers obstacles, you have an opportunity to clarify your recommendation.

T   F   2. The motivating-to-action step is often called "closing the sale."

T   F   3. After the sale, customer satisfaction is no longer the salesperson's concern.

T   F   4. As you offer ideas, you should also ask questions that solicit an indication of the customer's reaction.

T   F   5. When you present your suggestions, you should begin by offering the customer a choice between two ideas.

T   F   6. Benefits are not universal; the benefit is in the eye of the customer.

T   F   7. When you sell to a group, you should target the presentation to the elite members of the group.

Answers: 1. T, 2. T, 3. F, 4. T, 5. F, 6. T, 7. F

Discussion Questions

1. **Feature/Benefit Analysis.** Here are some common features of travel products you might sell. Translate each of these features into benefits that would make a customer say, "Yes!" Remember, not all features appeal to all customers. Identify whether business or leisure travelers are likely to find each benefit appealing.

Feature	Benefit	Customer type
All taxes included	_____	_____
Three restaurants on hotel property	_____	_____
Indoor and outdoor pools	_____	_____
Theater tickets	_____	_____
Unlimited mileage on rental car	_____	_____
Admissions to theme park	_____	_____

Feature	Benefit	Customer type
Boat rentals available	_____	_____
Two phone lines in hotel rooms	_____	_____
Extra legroom between seats on plane	_____	_____
Fully equipped gymnasium	_____	_____
Round-trip transfers	_____	_____

2. **Presenting Recommendations.** If you completed the Tour Evaluation in Chapter 3, page 73, use the information you gathered to practice presenting a recommendation. Suppose that your client is Rose—a widowed, retired woman who taught French and German to high school students for many years. She has a lively interest in history, the arts of all kinds, and people-watching. As a young woman, she traveled widely in Europe, Africa, and South America; but she has not been out of the country in twenty years. Rose is healthy, eager to travel, and willing to spend up to $10,000 for a two-week vacation. Would one of the tours you researched suit her?

_____

a. Write a brief description of one of the tours to create a mental picture of it for Rose.

_____

_____

_____

_____

b. Select two features of the tour and describe them in terms of the benefits that they might offer Rose.

_____

_____

_____

_____

_____

3. **Dealing with Obstacles.** To practice dealing with obstacles, write a response to each of the following objections.

    a. "I didn't think a cruise would cost so much."

    _____

    _____

    _____

    _____

    _____

    b. "I'm not sure about Alaska. Isn't it too cold in May?"

    _____

    _____

    _____

    _____

    _____

    c. "Won't a hotel with a casino be too expensive?"

    _____

    _____

    _____

    _____

    _____

4. **Handling Other Objections.** For more practice in dealing with objections, write a possible response to each of these objections to the idea of taking a tour.

    a. "That's a lot of money!"

    _____

    _____

    _____

    _____

b. "I don't want to be stuck with a group all the time."

_____

_____

_____

_____

_____

c. "Aren't buses awfully uncomfortable?"

_____

_____

_____

_____

_____

d. "I don't want to spend all my time on the road getting from place to place."

_____

_____

_____

_____

_____

A Case in Question

1. Look again at "Calling Collect . . ." on page 119. What are some specific statements and questions that Susan might have offered during the sales cycle to avoid this problem?

_____

_____

_____

_____

_____

2. If you were Susan, what would you say to the Nortons to accept responsibility for solving the problem (problem-solving step 3)?

_____

_____

_____

_____

3. In the "Calling Collect . . ." case in this chapter, we considered problem-solving step 4: selecting a strategy to solve the problem. Look again at the "No Room at the Inn" case in Chapter 3 (page 51). What are three strategies for solving that problem?

_____

_____

_____

_____

4 Look again at "The Fish that Got Away" case in Chapter 4 (page 94). Even if Duncan had handled the situation better, the facts in this case do not suggest an easy solution. There simply isn't room for the schoolchildren. What would you suggest?

_____

_____

_____

_____

5. In the "Calling Collect . . ." case in this chapter, what should Susan do to carry out step 8 of the sales cycle, following up to ensure customer satisfaction?

_____

_____

_____

_____

Exercises in Selling

1. **Giving Information: Steps 6 and 7 of the Sales Cycle.**[*] To practice giving information in the sales cycle, let's return to the case of Hale & Company described in Chapter 4. First, break into groups of three and select roles. One member of the group should act as travel manager Alex Hernandez. A second member should act as the travel counselor, and the third as the observer.

   First, reread the description of Hale & Company's problems on page 97; then read the description of your role below. Do not read the descriptions of other roles until you have completed the exercise!

   - *Travel manager Hernandez*

     You make all the travel plans for Hale & Company and have been planning the three-day meeting requested by the acting chairman. To find a spot for the meeting, you have been working with a travel counselor at Cooper's Travel. You are intrigued by the latest recommendation: a resort in southwestern Arizona that offers spacious conference rooms, every support service imaginable, and luxurious accommodations. The resort also provides tennis, golf, Nautilus equipment, saunas, hiking trails, and exquisite scenery.

     You're almost convinced. But a lot rides on the outcome of this meeting. Everything must go right. You are seeing the travel counselor today and plan to bring up the following concerns:

     - The location is very remote. It will be difficult for your executives, who will probably fly in from various locations throughout the country, to get there easily.

     - The facility is untested. It opened a short time ago. Perhaps the management has not had a chance to work out the wrinkles.

     - Several of the executives will want to combine business with a family vacation. Will this location appeal to executives with children?

     - Cost is always an issue. Your company is accustomed to negotiating rates with major hotel chains. This is a small, independent resort. There appears to be little room for flexibility on the $275 room rates.

     Bring up these concerns with the travel counselor. Use your own concerns and needs to provide information or fill in the gaps. Don't hesitate to push for information. Don't be easily convinced. And make sure that your concerns are addressed.

   - *Travel counselor*

     You work for Cooper's Travel, a large agency, and have been the corporate travel counselor for Hale & Company for five years. You have been working with Alex Hernandez, the travel manager, to find the location for a three-day, high-level meeting. You think you have found the place that will provide the right mixture of tranquility, activity, and support systems to allow for productive and creative thought.

     You have proposed a new conference center in southwestern Arizona, an hour and a half west of Phoenix. It offers ample meeting space; executive boardrooms; secretarial services; fax, word processing, and copying facilities; as well as a variety of health services such as tennis courts, health club, hiking and jogging trails, and golf. Rates run about $275 a night.

---

[*]This exercise is adapted from *ICTA Sales Skills Development Program*, pp. 15–17. © ICTA.

You are about to meet with Hernandez at Hale's headquarters and hope to get approval to book the location. Take a few minutes to consider objections that your client might make to the recommendation. During the conversation, focus on handling objections and achieving an agreement.

After the role-play, the observer will discuss your performance. Before you begin, review Worksheet 5.1 on page 141 so that you are familiar with the criteria by which you will be evaluated.

■ *Observer*
Use Worksheet 5.1 on page 141 to evaluate the performance of the person playing the travel counselor. After the role-play, show the worksheet and discuss it with other members of the group.

2. **Succeeding through the Sales Cycle.** Now that we have completed our review of the sales cycle, do you think you could do a better selling job than Laurie did in the opening example of Chapter 4 (page 80)? To practice your selling skills, try it. Break into groups of three and select roles. One person should act as the travel counselor; a second person should act as Arlene, the client; the third member of the group will be the observer.

■ *Travel counselor: Laurie*
You have met the client, Arlene, only once, very briefly, when she picked up brochures about Scandinavia. You know only that she and her husband want to take a two-week trip to northern Europe at the end of the summer. Arlene has just entered the office. Begin with your greeting.

■ *The Client: Arlene*
Look back to the opening of Chapter 4 to determine your budget, schedule, and interests for the trip. But feel free to elaborate on the brief description of Arlene's needs that was given there. If you are enthusiastic about the trip and if it does not conflict with your husband's schedule, you know that he will agree with your decision. You have met the travel counselor only once, when you picked up brochures. Now you have just walked into the counselor's office.

■ *The Observer*
Use Worksheet 5.2 to evaluate the performance of the person playing the travel counselor. After the role-play, show the worksheet and discuss it with other members of the group.

Worksheet 5.1

Name _____ Date _____

Giving Information: Steps 6 and 7 of the Sales Cycle

As the observer for the "Giving Information" exercise described on pages 138–139, use this form to evaluate the performance of the "travel counselor." You may want to duplicate this form before writing on it.

Complete this worksheet in order to answer the first Discussion Question on page 133. You may want to duplicate this page before writing on it.

	Strengths	Recommendations for Improvement
Handling objections Listens to client without becoming defensive	_____ _____ _____	_____ _____ _____
Empathizes with client's concern	_____ _____ _____	_____ _____ _____
Clarifies source of objection by asking questions or restating it	_____ _____ _____	_____ _____ _____
Explains the advantage of recommendations	_____ _____ _____	_____ _____ _____

Motivating to action
Asks for the sale
at the appropriate time

    _____   _____

    _____   _____

    _____   _____

Asks for the sale appropriately

    _____   _____

    _____   _____

    _____   _____

Ends transaction on a positive note,
encouraging a continuing relationship

    _____   _____

    _____   _____

    _____   _____

Worksheet 5.2

Name _____   Date _____

Succeeding through the Sales Cycle

As the observer for the "Giving Information" exercise described on page 138, use this form to evaluate the performance of the "travel counselor." You may want to duplicate this form before writing on it.

Complete this worksheet in order to answer the first Discussion Question on page 133. You may want to duplicate this page before writing on it.

	Strengths	Recommendations for Improvement
Develops rapport	_____	_____
	_____	_____
	_____	_____
Determines needs	_____	_____
	_____	_____
	_____	_____
Matches product and client	_____	_____
	_____	_____
	_____	_____
Presents recommendations	_____	_____
	_____	_____
	_____	_____
Deals with obstacles	_____	_____
	_____	_____
	_____	_____

Motivates to action   _____   _____

_____   _____

_____   _____

Selling with Technology: Telephones, the Web, and Other Tools

Objectives

After reading this chapter, you should be able to

1. Describe how communicating by telephone differs from face-to-face communication.

2. Explain how you should adapt your voice and manner when selling on the telephone.

3. Identify some basic rules of telephone etiquette.

4. Discuss how travelers and travel sellers are using the Web.

5. Describe other technologies that can help you succeed in selling travel.

Preview

Today, face-to-face selling is just one of several ways of doing business. Not only is more business conducted over the telephone than ever before, but many clients expect to be able to communicate with sellers on the Web, through e-mail, or by fax. For salespeople who learn to use these technologies effectively, they are invaluable tools.

This chapter offers an overview of these technologies. We look first at the special characteristics of telephone communications and how to adapt to them; then we discuss how travel sellers are using CRSs, the Web, and other electronic tools.

Communicating by Telephone

In 1983 all of the goods and services sold over the telephone in the United States were worth only about $53 billion; today, telephone sales amount to hundreds of billions of dollars. Repeat customers are likely to conduct most of their business with you over the phone. Does it matter? Yes. Communicating by telephone and communicating face to face are different in some important ways. In particular,

- The telephone distorts the human voice.
- When you communicate by phone, you cannot use body language to help you understand the other person's message or to convey your own message.
- Because you cannot see the other person or his or her environment when you talk on the phone, you may find it more difficult to concentrate on what the other person is saying.
- Telephone communication has its own social norms, "rules of the road" that define good telephone manners.

How can you adapt to these characteristics so that you can communicate effectively on the phone? In this section we offer some guidelines.

Being Persuasive: Telephone Strategies

Telephones do several things to the human voice. They decrease its volume, make the voice drag, and raise the *pitch* (how high it sounds). To compensate for these distortions,

- Speak a little more loudly.
- Speak very clearly. Try not to slur your words, and check the proper pronunciation of unfamiliar words.
- If the pitch of your voice is normally high, lower it somewhat. Try to keep nasal, raspy, or throaty qualities out of your voice.

Perhaps the biggest challenge in communicating by telephone is the absence of body language. The communication depends completely on what is said and how it is said. Thus, your words and tone of voice take on far more importance than in face-to-face communication, as Figure 6.1 illustrates. You must make your message clear and interesting without the help of eye contact, nods, gestures, or other aids. And you need to find ways to "read between the lines" of the other person's comments in the absence of body language. Is he or she understanding you? Is he or she interested?

Here are some tips for dealing with the challenges of communicating without the help of body language:

- Smile. Try saying "Hello" while keeping a straight face, and then say "Hello" while smiling. The smile changes the tone and pitch of your voice, and a person can hear the difference over the phone. Many people who work on the phone all day keep a small mirror next to the phone; they look into it and smile before picking up a call.
- Match the rate of your speech to that of the other person. This will help your client feel comfortable. Most people speak at an average rate of 130–150 words per minute.
- Vary your pitch so you do not speak in a monotone.
- Raise your energy level.
- Let the other person know you are listening by using phrases like "Uh-huh," "Yes, go on," "Okay," or "I see." These acknowledgments encourage the other person to continue speaking.
- Pause and ask questions to be sure you are giving the other person a chance to talk.
- Don't forget the importance of the words you choose. Use correct grammar; avoid slang and jargon that the listener might not understand.

Because getting distracted is easier on the telephone than in face-to-face conversation, you should make a special effort to focus on the person you are talking with. Take notes; avoid distractions and interruptions.

You must also make a special effort to keep your listener's attention. In your office, you can

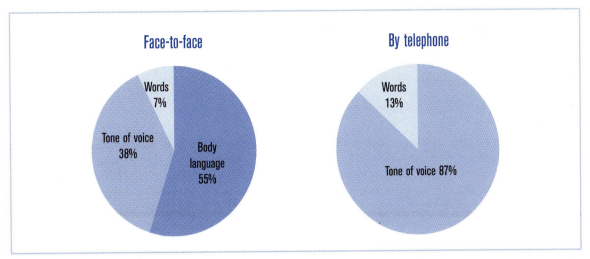

Figure 6.1 Communicating by Telephone
The words you use and how you say them become especially important in telephone communications because they must carry the entire message.
Source: Portion adapted from Albert Mehrabian, *Silent Messages* (Belmont, California: Wadsworth, 1971) © 1971 Wadsworth Publishing Company, Inc.

tune out distractions to help you focus on the client, but can your clients do the same in their environments? When clients call from home, they probably feel more comfortable than if they were in your office; but they may also face more distractions. Barking dogs, crying children, and ringing doorbells are just a few of the possibilities. Listen carefully in order to get a sense of whether your client is giving you his or her full attention. If your client seems distracted, asking "Is it a good time to talk now?" might save you the frustration of dealing with an unfocused customer.

Finally, get into the habit of analyzing your calls when they are completed. You may be able to identify ways to improve your performance.

Being Polite: Telephone Etiquette

According to Bob Kwortnick, Director of Training for CLIA, a survey by the Telephone Institute lists these as the top consumer complaints regarding the telephone:

1. You get a constant busy signal.
2. The phone rings too long before it is answered.

Tips
Selling on the Telephone

When you talk to clients on the phone, remember to

■ Raise the volume of your voice slightly.
■ Be especially careful to speak clearly.
■ Lower your pitch if your voice is normally high.
■ Raise your energy level and vary your tone.
■ Adjust your pace to match the client's.
■ Smile and let the client know you are listening by saying things like "I see."
■ Compensate for not being able to see your client's body language by asking feedback questions and being especially careful to listen closely.
■ Take notes and avoid distractions.

3. The salutation is abrupt.
4. The speaker mumbles.
5. You are placed on hold, without being asked for permission.
6. You are placed on hold, then get disconnected.
7. You are placed on hold, and left there indefinitely.
8. The speaker never uses your name after it has been given.
9. The speaker sounds distracted or impatient.
10. At the end of the call, you are not thanked for calling.

These complaints amount to a litany of rude behaviors that can drive customers away. To keep your customers, follow these rules of good telephone manners:

- Answer the phone by the third ring. Today most people hang up after the fourth or fifth ring.

- Greet the caller by speaking clearly. Use an unimportant phrase first (like "Good morning" or "Thank you for calling"); then identify your company, giving your name and the department, if applicable. It usually takes the caller two or three seconds to register and respond to what you have said.

- Ask the caller something like "How may I help you?"

- Find out the caller's name and use it during the conversation. You can use the fill-in-the-blank format: "And you are _____?" Try to use the caller's name at least twice during the conversation, but do not overuse it.

- If you must put the caller on hold, ask permission. Wait for the caller's response before hitting the hold button.

- Keep a caller on hold no longer than 30 to 45 seconds before you get back. Thank the caller for waiting. If there will be a lengthy hold, inform the caller and ask if he or she would like to continue to hold, to leave a message, or to call back later.

- If you must transfer a call, tell the caller why you are transferring and then ask permission. ("Debbie is handling that now. May I transfer you?")

- If you must take a message, use a message pad that has blanks to indicate the informa-

tion needed—such as the caller's name and company, phone number, time and date of the call, and your signature. Make sure you obtain the correct spelling and number and as complete a message as possible.

- When the call is complete, thank the caller.
- Let the caller be the first to disconnect.

The popularity of automated phone-answering systems—*voice mail*—has brought new complaints from customers. Some are victims of badly designed voice-mail systems that give callers an over-long menu of options to consider before they can reach a real human being. Some customers resent talking to machines instead of people. Some complain that they never receive a call back.

If you have a voice-mail system, you can minimize customer complaints by following these simple guidelines:

- Answer your own phone whenever possible.
- Check your voice-mail messages frequently.
- Return all messages promptly.

Telephone Tag

In the children's game of tag, one child is "It" and chases all the other children until catching someone; then that child is "It," chasing everyone else all over again. The modern, adult version is the seemingly never-ending game of telephone tag, and it can be very frustrating. Only one out of three phone calls is completed on the first try.

How do you cope with telephone tag? When you must leave a message for someone, be explicit about the best time to reach you ("I can be reached between 10:00 A.M. and noon Eastern Time"); then let anyone who might answer your phone know that you are expecting the call. Also, make your message as complete as possible.

Voice mail can shorten the game of telephone tag because it allows people to leave detailed messages and to feel certain the messages will be transmitted accurately. If you are leaving a message on voice mail, anticipate questions and answer them so that the other person does not have to restart the game of telephone tag. If you were calling to ask for information, let the other person know what information you are seeking in case that person must leave a message for you. Remember, however, that many voice-mail systems record a message for only one minute. Be concise.

Time Out

Check your understanding of the discussion so far by evaluating this conversation:

"Hi. Can I help you?"

"Is this Atlantic Tours?"

"Sure is. What can I do for you?"

"Well, I'm not sure. I'm looking for someone who can tell me more about a tour I saw advertised in *Travel and Leisure*. Can you do that? Do I have the right place?"

"Yes, you do."

"But do you know about the tour?"

"Oh, yes. It's a terrific bargain. Give me just a second to get this other phone and I'll be right back."

How would you rate the skills of the person who answered the phone? Try listing at least three ways you would improve on his performance:

_____

_____

_____

_____

_____

_____

_____

_____

Selling by Telephone

Adjusting your voice, compensating for the absence of body language, making special efforts to focus on the client, following the rules of telephone etiquette—these steps will help you communicate effectively on the phone. But are there any differences in how you go about making the sale? Let's look at how selling occurs on the phone.

Making Contact

How does the sales conversation begin? If it is an *incoming call,* you are not in control; you are acting in response to a ringing phone and must be prepared to deal with anything. Be ready to pick up the phone by the third ring. Even before you remember to smile when you answer, take a breath and focus your attention on the call. Stop whatever else you are doing. Be prepared with a pen or pencil and a pad to take notes or messages.

Outgoing calls put you in control. You pick the time and place for the call, and you know what you want to say or to find out. Consider preparing a checklist or even a script; that will help you avoid getting distracted. Before you dial, make sure you have the following information:

- What is the objective of the call? Why are you calling? Is it to make a reservation, get information, or give information?
- What questions do you need to ask? If you need to get information, make a list of your questions.
- What objections might the person you are calling have? Be prepared with answers.
- What time zone are you calling or calling from? (You are in your office bright and early one morning and need to call a tour operator to make a reservation, but there is no answer. Oh no, is this another company gone out of business? No, it is just too early for them to be open.) Keep the local time in mind when placing a call. Also, mention your time zone if you are leaving a message for someone in another zone.

The more prepared you are, the more successful your telephone interactions will be.

The Sales Cycle by Phone

Whether you are on the telephone or meeting face to face, the basic steps of the sales cycle do not change. To sell effectively on the phone, you just need to adapt your strategies, to pay extra attention to certain skills and pitfalls. Let's look again at some steps in the cycle.

For developing rapport (step 2), the first thirty seconds of the telephone interaction are magical. How quickly your phone is answered and the initial greeting tell customers a great deal. Getting and using the customer's name is as important over the telephone as it is in person. Asking "How may I help you?" and offering your concern and enthusiasm will make the customer feel comfortable about doing business with you.

As in face-to-face sales, step 3, identifying the needs of your customer, is at the heart of a successful sale. You must answer the five basic *W*s and discover other needs by probing and using open-ended questions. But on the telephone, you must rely more on the spoken word to identify these needs.

The feedback you present to your customer when trying to match the client with a product (step 4) will tell you if you are on the right track. You cannot read the customer's body language, so you must pay close attention to verbal cues. Asking feedback questions like "Is that what you're looking for?" becomes even more important than in face-to-face conversations.

Similarly, when you are selling by telephone, you cannot use brochures or other visual aids to help you present your recommendation (step 5). As a result, your skills in painting word pictures and stressing the appropriate benefits become more important than ever. It is also essential to ask for feedback throughout your presentation so you will know how your customer is reacting. Listen carefully in order to determine which benefits to emphasize. For example,

Travel counselor: At night, there's lots of special entertainment—not glitzy Las Vegas-like revues like some other ships you've been on. One night you might be entertained by an opera singer from San Francisco, another night by a chamber orchestra, and several evenings feature local folkloric groups that really give you a sense of the local culture. Does that sound like something you and Patty might enjoy?
Client: Definitely. But we're really going to see Alaska's flora and fauna. You know, whales, puffins, sea otters. I'm kind of an amateur photographer.
Travel counselor: Well, this cruise will give you a great opportunity to give your telephoto lens some action. Many of my clients come back with pictures of whales they saw right from the ship. And the ice show in Glacier Bay is spectacular.
Client: Sounds exciting.

Listening carefully and asking feedback questions are also especially important in order to know whether the client is ready to commit to the sale. When you are on the telephone, you cannot see your client nod or take out a checkbook—or grimace or push away from the desk. And many clients may be reluctant to voice their questions or objections. If your client has not presented any objections but has not expressed any buying signals either, you should probe by asking, "Have you any questions about what we've discussed?" If the client raises objections or concerns, deal with them as you would in a face-to-face sale (step 6). Listen carefully to the obstacle, empathize and restate it, and then offer a solution.

Even after the client has committed to the sale (step 7), remember that the sales cycle is not completed. Make sure you have all the information necessary to make the travel arrangements. Follow up after the sale to be certain that your customer is satisfied.

In short, the principles for selling in person apply to telephone sales as well. But you must compensate for the absence of body language. You must learn to "read" your customers just from their words and tone of voice.

Some Special Challenges

Telephone sales offer an advantage over face-to-face sales in at least one situation: when clients stump you with their questions. Then it's good that the caller cannot see your body language, especially that puzzled look on your face! You can simply offer the legitimate excuse that you need to do some research. For example,

Travel counselor: That's a great request. We have some information on that. Let me look it over and I'll call you back with the details.

Other situations are more challenging. Overtalkative callers, callers who are difficult to understand, and cold calls are among the problems you are most likely to encounter on the phone. Here is some advice about how to handle these situations.

Chatty Cathys. You know the type. They go on and on about everything and everybody, or they just want to hear what's available and cannot make a decision, or they have no intention of making a decision. You should take control of the conversation. Ask questions of your own—but ask specific questions, not indirect ones that would encourage them to talk more. Let them know you need to get off the phone to do some research for their trip. You might set a time frame at the beginning of the conversation; for example,

Travel counselor: I'm so glad you called. I have about five minutes now to get the information from you for your trip, and then I'll get back to you when everything's complete.

Be tactful, be brief, but be in control.

Difficult-to-Understand Callers. What do you do if a caller is not fluent in English or speaks too fast or mumbles or has a heavy accent (regional or foreign)? Let these callers know that you are having difficulty understanding them. For example,

Travel counselor: Mrs. Green, I'm having trouble following what you've said. Could you start again and speak more slowly?

Cold Calls. One of the most dreaded telephone tasks is the *cold call*—making contact with a prospect for the first time. Probably at the heart of the dread about cold calling is the fear of rejection.

Even if you never learn to like cold calling, you can ease the anxiety it brings. It helps if you understand the odds from the start: getting just 25 percent of your callers to agree to receive more information or to make an appointment or to buy would be a good record. In other words, understand that you should not take rejection personally; it comes with the territory. Put yourself in a positive state of mind by reminding yourself that the skills required for cold calling are really no different from those you use in other selling situations. Focus on the rewards that cold calls can bring.

Time Out

Check your understanding of the discussion so far by completing the following statements:

1. To sell over the telephone you need to emphasize certain skills and watch out for special pitfalls, but the steps of the sales cycle

   _____

   _____

   _____

   _____

   _____

   _____

   _____ .

2. Because you cannot use visual aids when selling on the phone, you should make a special effort to

   _____

   when you present a recommendation.

3. Because you cannot see your client's body language to help you learn how they are reacting to your recommendation or to pick up certain buying signals,

   _____

   carefully and asking

   _____

   become especially important when selling over the telephone.

Selling with Computers: CRSs and the Web

Selling by telephone may seem impersonal compared with face-to-face contact, but it still consists of one-on-one selling, and you can at least connect a voice with a name. By the end of the 1990s, though, many experts believe that travel products and services worth more than $4 billion will be sold without any personal contact; they will go through cyberspace, from one computer to another. The spreading use of computers is creating a revolution in the travel industry.

Many travel professionals see this revolution not as an opportunity, but as a threat. That is ironic, because travel professionals were at the forefront of the computer revolution through their use of computer reservations systems or, CRSs. Today, in order to give their clients the best possible service and remain competitive, successful travel professionals are staying on top of this revolution.

Computer Reservations Systems

Years before personal computers sat on desks in offices throughout the country, travel agencies were using CRSs not only to research airline schedules and fares but also to book flights. Unlike personal computers, the CRS hardware had a *dumb terminal*—which means that it could do nothing except send and receive data to and from the host computer—and using the CRS required training in many obscure codes. Only travel agents and reservationists knew how to unlock the secrets of the airline schedules and fares that were hidden away in the depths of CRSs. Much about CRSs has changed, but they remain key tools in travel sales.

An Outline of the System. How does a CRS work? The *host* or *vendor*—such as SABRE, Apollo, WORLDSPAN, or Amadeus—maintains the database and leases the necessary computer hardware and software to the travel agency. (Look again at Table 3.1, page 52, for more information on these hosts.) Suppliers—hotels, car rental companies, tour companies, and cruise lines, as well as airlines—pay the host to participate in the system.

The suppliers' level of participation and the amount they pay vary. At the lowest level of participation, only information about the suppliers' products is included in the CRS. At a higher level of participation, the supplier's product can be booked through the CRS, but the reservation cannot be confirmed immediately. Unless the supplier participates in the CRS at the highest level, the flow of data between the supplier's own computer system and the CRS is not sufficient to create what is called a **direct link,** or a *seamless* connection. Without a direct link, there is a gap between the information in the supplier's own computer system and the information offered to the CRS user.

For example, in 1997 more than 200 hotel chains participated in the SABRE CRS, but only 49 chains participated at the highest level, which allows the CRS user to obtain real-time rates and availability. Thus, the quality of information on a CRS varies, and whether you can reserve a particular room or other travel product via the CRS depends on the supplier's level of participation in a particular CRS. Sometimes, a telephone call is still the best way to get information or to make a reservation.

The CRS hosts have taken large steps to expand the products that can be booked on their systems. Today, you can even book many tours and cruises on CRSs. If you are selling a tour, for example, you might use a CRS in order to

- Ask for information about a tour.
- Request brochures.
- Check tour availability.
- Check tour prices.
- Book a tour.
- Confirm a booking.
- Modify a booking.
- Cancel a booking.

The CRS hosts have also worked to adapt to the exploding use of personal computers. Since the mid-1990s, they have made CRSs easier to use and developed products that allow those who lease the CRS hardware to switch easily between the CRS and other tasks such as word processing, so that the CRS can itself act more like a personal computer. And they have developed software packages that give travel agencies access to the CRS database from a personal computer. For example, SABRE offers Planet SABRE, a software package for personal computers that allows on-line booking and also gives access to the Web.

CRSs and the Web. Has the Web made the CRSs obsolete? For CRS hosts, the Web represents a potential threat because it gives suppliers another way to distribute their products on-line. But at least for now, the CRS hosts have turned the Web into an opportunity.

For CRS hosts, the Web is a source of business in at least three ways. First, other companies that sell travel over the Web use the databases of a CRS; for example, Microsoft's Expedia—which allows consumers to book flights and hotel rooms and cars for themselves over the Web—uses the WORLDSPAN CRS. Second, the CRSs sell Internet tools—such as Internet access, e-mail services, and tools for setting up and maintaining Web sites. And the CRS hosts themselves offer services on the Web. For example, if you get on the Web, search for SABRE, and select SABRE's Travel Information Network Home Page, you'll find links to several other sites including Planet SABRE, SABRE Web

Marketing (which provides tools for designing and managing a Web site), as well as Travelocity and easySABRE (which amount to on-line travel agencies for consumers, offering destination guides as well as airline, car, and hotel bookings).

Can the Web take over the role of CRSs in travel agencies? For most travel counselors, CRSs remain their most useful electronic tool. Using a CRS is likely to be easier than using the Web in at least two situations:

- If you want to book several types of travel products for a trip—such as a rental car and a hotel and a flight. Cross-segment booking like this is easy on a CRS.
- If you want information about a certain category of travel products from different companies. A CRS, for example, will display a listing of all hotels that have rooms available this weekend in Philadelphia. To obtain the same information on the Web, you would need to visit the Web site for each hotel brand and check whether that hotel had any rooms available. Similarly, you can usually compare rates from different companies more easily on a CRS than on the Web.

Furthermore, Web sites that handle bookings often provide only simplified versions of the information available on a CRS. To make traditional bookings of flights, rental cars, and hotels, most travel counselors find that a CRS—or the telephone—remains their tool of first choice.

But what if clients want to communicate with you by e-mail? Or suppose they want help researching a trip for themselves on the Web? Or what if you need to research discount fares available from consolidators? For these and other tasks, many travel professionals turn to the Web. In the rest of this section we examine what the Web has to offer, for both travel consumers and travel sellers.

Travel on the Web: The Consumer's View

By 1998 there were an estimated 16 million personal computers in American households that were connected to the Web. Others were using their computers at work to surf the Web. Many people go on-line just to use e-mail or to play games or to browse from site to site, but some are using the Web to shop and even to buy. And travel is one of the most popular topics on the Web. Among those buying on-line, about 20 percent are buying travel-related products.

What travel sites can the consumer find on the Web? Here are the major possibilities:

1. *Full-service supersites.* Examples include Microsoft's Expedia, the Internet Travel Network, Travelocity, and America Online's Travel channel, with Preview Travel. These sites are intended to allow consumers to plan and book their trips on-line from start to finish. Consumers can go to these sites to find information about destinations, transportation, accommodations, tours, and cruises; to obtain maps; to swap travel tips with other consumers; and to book their trips.

2. *Transaction sites.* These sites allow consumers to find information about a specific type of travel product and to book that product on-line. Sites of major airlines are one example. But even sites sponsored by some cruise lines, travel agencies, and visitors' bureaus now allow consumers to book on-line.

3. *Information-only sites.* Many travel sites do not allow purchases on-line. Instead, they give information about the product and tell the consumer how to contact the site's sponsor by phone, mail, e-mail, or fax in order to book, or they tell the consumer to contact a travel agency. There are sites for finding the lowest air fares, sites that will e-mail weekly bulletins about travel bargains, sites that will keep track of a consumer's frequent-flyer and frequent-guest accounts, and sites that will print personalized maps. There are information-only sites sponsored by travel agencies, hotels, restaurants, cruise lines, tour companies, tourist offices, and visitors' bureaus for cities, regions, and countries. If consumers have enough time, patience, and interest, they can find just about any travel information on the Web.

With so much available on-line, why aren't

more consumers making their travel purchases on the Web? In 1997, only about 1 to 2 percent of people visiting travel sites actually made a reservation on-line, and only 1 to 2 percent of total bookings in the United States were made on the Internet. Industry watchers offer many reasons for these slow sales. For example,

- Many people are wary of providing the credit card information necessary to purchase on-line because they fear someone will get hold of that information and charge other purchases to their cards.
- Some people may hesitate to sign on as "members" in order to use a booking site.
- Many consumers may find on-line booking inconvenient or boring because their connection to the Web is too slow or the booking forms they must fill out are too tedious or too complicated.
- The list of options offered by the sites may not include the particular destination or other travel product that they want.

Time may eliminate some of these barriers to on-line purchases, as Web technology and content continue to improve. (For predictions about the future of on-line travel, see Chapter 9.) Other drawbacks to on-line purchases, though, are not likely to change. As the vice president of one large travel agency told *Travel Counselor* magazine (December 1996, p. 24), "We can make the Internet a lot of things, but we can't make it personal." Some people simply do not like to use computers, or they want to be able to ask questions, or they do not want to "buy blind" from some name on a computer screen. The sheer abundance of information on the Web is likely to push many people to look for help in sorting through it all.

For all of these people, the travel agency represents a necessary service. As Clifton Cooke wrote,

> The secret to continued success for today's—and tomorrow's—travel agents is to let their present and potential customers understand that well-informed travel agents know the difference between a good travel deal and a flaky one! (JAX FAX *Travel Marketing Magazine,* June 1998, p. 21)

Selling on the Web

Unlike consumers, travel professionals sometimes go to the Web out of necessity rather than choice. Travel sellers use it

- To research information.
- To make or to receive bookings.
- To communicate with clients and others.
- To market themselves.

How you use the Web depends on your place in the travel distribution channel. The possibilities can look quite different to a supplier and to a travel agency.

Suppliers, Travel Agencies, and the Web. For travel suppliers, the Web may offer a way to slash the cost of distributing their product. For example, one industry consultant estimated that airlines can save $15 to $20 for each ticket that is booked on the Web instead of through a travel agency.

In fact, air tickets are probably the travel product best suited to on-line booking. They are an essential component of many trips; yet the questions required before booking a flight are few compared with those required for many other travel arrangements. And the value of a particular flight changes little from customer to customer or from airline to airline. When the value of a travel product depends on many subjective variables, travelers are less likely to be interested in purchasing it on-line; tours and cruises are examples.

Travel suppliers have an important decision to make about how they use the Web: Should they use it as part of an effort to bypass travel agencies and sell directly to consumers? The airlines seem to be taking this route. They have placed a cap on the commissions available to travel agencies for on-line bookings, and they offer incentives to consumers who book for themselves on-line. For example, some airlines give bonus frequent-flyer miles when consumers book on-line.

Many other suppliers are using their Web sites in ways that keep travel agencies in the loop. For example, many Web sites encourage consumers to book through a travel agency; some list a directory to help consumers find an agency. Some sites that offer only information to the general public provide "agent-only" areas—or *pages*—that allow travel counselors to book on-line and to receive a commission for the booking. Agent-only areas of a Web site may also feature chat rooms, e-mail capabilities, and special information designed for travel counselors.

Travel Agencies On-Line. Figure 6.2 shows how travel agencies are using the Web today. If you take the long view, the Web may be a threat to the future prosperity of travel agencies; that is a possibility we discuss in Chapter 9. In the immediate future, though, using the Web can greatly enhance the service that travel counselors give their clients. At the least, if you are a travel counselor connected to the Web, you can use that connection to communicate with clients more efficiently through e-mail and (as we discussed in Chapter 3) to enhance your ability to research information. In addition, the Web has made it easier to do more of the work of travel selling out of the home.

The existence of the Web has also created some difficult choices for travel agencies. Should a travel agency establish its own Web site? If so, what kind of site should it be? Should it just advertise the agency, or should it allow clients to book on-line? Figure 6.3 outlines some of the questions that go into the process of making these decisions.

If an agency does not want the burden of creating and maintaining its own site, it can hire consultants to do the job, or it can "piggyback" on the expertise of other travel organizations. In particular, an agency can arrange to be listed in the directories of travel agencies on Web sites maintained by other travel companies and travel associations, or it can buy a customized version of a generic travel site. For example, the Internet Travel Network (ITN) offers travel agencies the choice of participating as a member agency on ITN's public Web site. If a consumer goes to that site, makes a reservation, and selects a travel agency, that agency receives the booking. Or the agency might go a step further and pay ITN for a "private label" site—a version of ITN's system that is customized to suit the agency.

Travel agencies face many possible pitfalls in trying to sell travel via the Web. If you set up a Web site, will anyone find it? If they do, will they use it just to browse? Web surfers may play with your Web site, use it as if were a public library

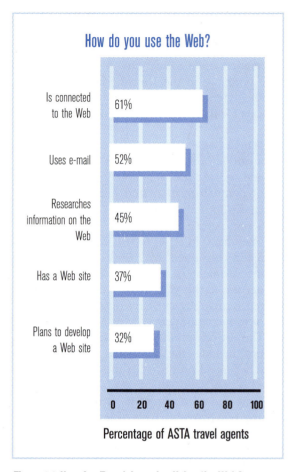

How do you use the Web?

Percentage of ASTA travel agents

Figure 6.2 How Are Travel Agencies Using the Web?
In 1996 only about 38 percent of travel counselors had Internet access; today, more than 60 percent do. For most, it is a tool for communicating and for gathering information.
Source: Data from the 1998 ASTA Automation Survey

in order to gain access to a CRS, send tons of e-mail requesting information, and then never buy anything. The travel agency that pioneered Internet-based booking—PCTravel of Raleigh, N.C.—shut down in 1997, squeezed out by airline commission caps on the one hand and CRS fees run up by the users of its site on the other. As of 1997, the full-service supersites were not yet making a profit. "Look-to-book" ratios were as low as 73 to 1. (In other words, for every 1 visitor to the site who made a purchase, 73 just browsed.) According to the 1998 ASTA Automation Survey, 87 percent of agents with a Web site say the site has not directly generated any on-line sales.

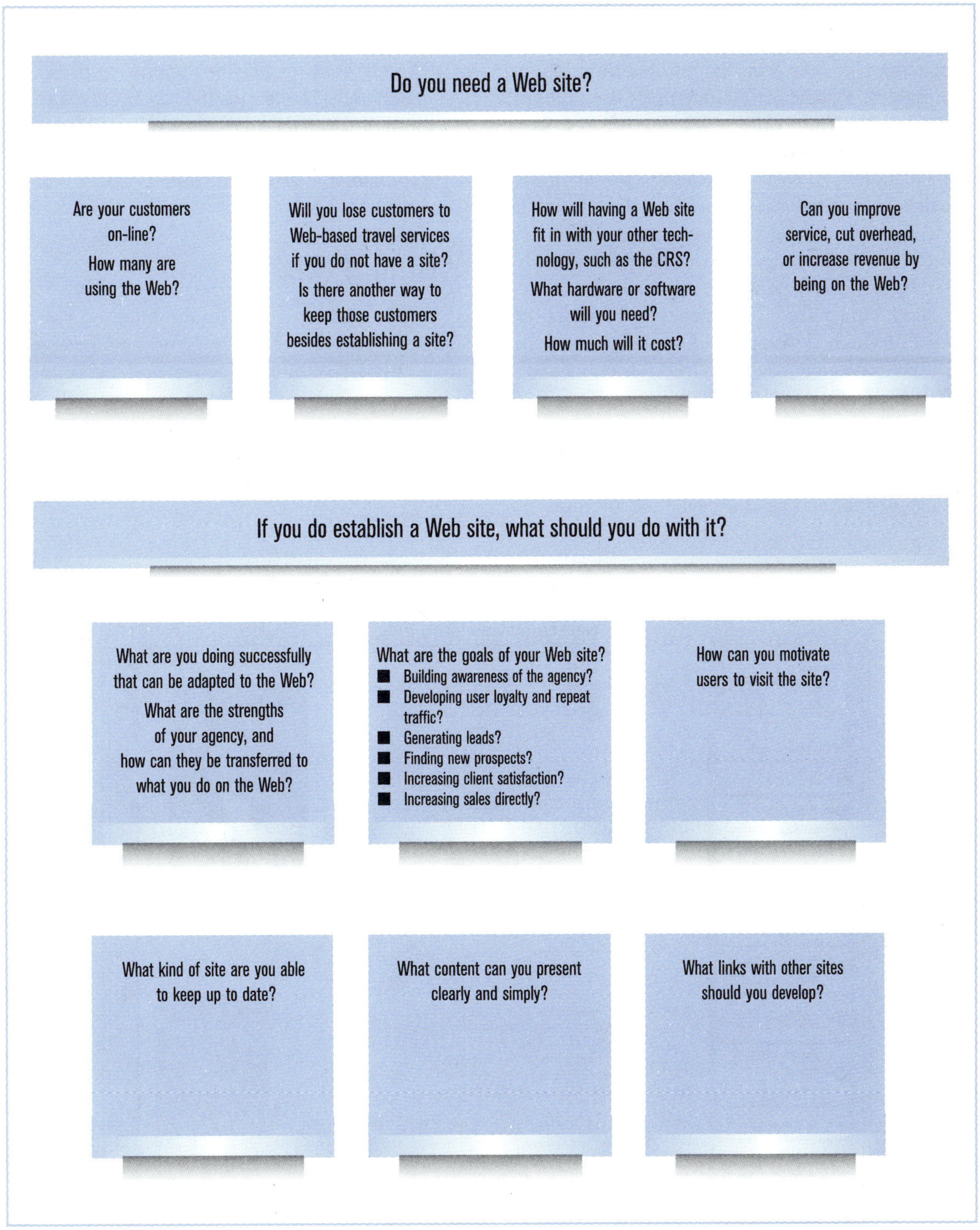

Do you need a Web site?

Are your customers on-line?

How many are using the Web?

Will you lose customers to Web-based travel services if you do not have a site?

Is there another way to keep those customers besides establishing a site?

How will having a Web site fit in with your other technology, such as the CRS?

What hardware or software will you need?

How much will it cost?

Can you improve service, cut overhead, or increase revenue by being on the Web?

If you do establish a Web site, what should you do with it?

What are you doing successfully that can be adapted to the Web?

What are the strengths of your agency, and how can they be transferred to what you do on the Web?

What are the goals of your Web site?
- Building awareness of the agency?
- Developing user loyalty and repeat traffic?
- Generating leads?
- Finding new prospects?
- Increasing client satisfaction?
- Increasing sales directly?

How can you motivate users to visit the site?

What kind of site are you able to keep up to date?

What content can you present clearly and simply?

What links with other sites should you develop?

Figure 6.3 Pondering the Web

Many factors influence whether a business should have its own Web site; a few are shown here. If a travel agency does create its own site, that does not mean it must take bookings over the site. In fact, few agencies report making sales on their sites. Many experts suggest that it is best to start slow: learn to walk before you run.

Source: Based on Elaine X. Elliott, "Be a Web Whiz," *Travel Agent,* November 10, 1997, pp. 28-32; Erik Hosek, "Could a Home Page Enhance Your Agency's Profit Potential?" *Travel Weekly,* December 25, 1997, p.16; Erik Hosek, "The Ten Commandments of Successful Marketing on the Net," *Travel Weekly,* January 5, 1998, p. 11.

If your competitors are on the Web, though, can you afford not to be? In 1998 there were more than 26,000 Web pages featuring travel companies. Even if an agency does not attempt to accept bookings on-line, having its own Web site may be a useful promotional tool, as Figure 6.4 illustrates. A Web site extends the agency's reach to potential clients around the world. It appeals to computer-savvy clients. It offers an effective, efficient way to communicate quickly with a great many people.

Scott Ahlsmith, CTC, general manager of TRAMS (which develops and supports software for retail travel agencies), offered this conclusion about Web sites for travel agencies in 1996:

It's a tremendous communication device. Broadcast things to a large group of people. Accept and send e-mail. Take informa-

tion you've been mailing and display it. I see the Internet right now as a communication device that rivals the phone and fax machine. . . . My suggestion to agents is to be there, to gain experience with as low as possible an initial investment. (*Travel Counselor,* December 1996, p. 28)

Writing E-Mail*

If you do nothing else with the Internet, you are likely to use it in order to send and receive e-mail. E-mail is both effective and economical. Long messages and short messages, delivered

---

*Special thanks to Scott Ahlsmith, CTC, for his contributions to this section.

Figure 6.4 A Travel Agency on the Web
Even if a Web site does not involve on-line booking, it can be an effective marketing tool for a travel agency.
Source: Traveling Inc.

next door or around the world, are all included in the cost of an Internet connection. E-mail messages are usually received within minutes of being transmitted, and each recipient receives his or her own copy. Recipients can retrieve messages when and where it is convenient. Messages can also be filed in electronic "folders" and retrieved when needed.

Personal computers today usually come with programs already installed to make sending and receiving e-mail as easy as preparing a memo on a word processor. In fact, sending e-mail is so fast and simple that you may need to be careful that you do not become too casual as you write it. Sending e-mail from your office calls for different standards than those people may follow when they visit chat rooms from their home computers. In particular,

- Use upper- and lower-case text as you would in a conventional letter. A message in which everything is capitalized is not only difficult to read but is considered the equivalent of shouting, which is rude.
- Adjust your tone and style to suit the purpose of the e-mail and its recipient. Travel counselors, for example, use e-mail to communicate with (1) other people in the agency, (2) colleagues in the travel industry, (3) travel suppliers, and (4) clients. An e-mail message suitable for someone in the office might be inappropriate for a supplier or client.
- Use the same rules regarding grammar, punctuation, and word choice as you would in a letter.

Remember, however, that e-mail in fact is *not* the same as a conventional letter. How is it different? Three characteristics are especially important.

First, many people read their e-mail messages directly on the computer screen, not in printed form. Long lines and long messages can be difficult to read on the screen. Furthermore, some people resist scrolling through screen after screen of text; as a result, parts of the message that extend beyond the first computer screen may never be read. Thus, to be sure your e-mail is easy to read, use short sentences and short paragraphs, and state your key points in the first paragraph of the message.

Second, what the recipient of your e-mail sees depends on the software the recipient is using. Some e-mail software does not handle changes in typeface or its size or other attributes (such as italics, boldface, underlining). Also, some recipients of your e-mail may not have software that can handle files that contain photographs or other graphics or files of text that was formatted by a word processor. As a result, to be sure your recipients can understand your e-mail, send plain text. Do not include formatting (such as boldface, font changes, size

Tips
Sending E-Mail

To communicate effectively with clients by e-mail, follow these easy guidelines.

- Use short sentences and short paragraphs.
- State your key points in the first paragraph of the message.
- Limit the content of the e-mail message to one topic.
- Within your message do not include changes in the typeface, its size, or other attributes (such as italics, boldface, or underlinings).
- Use upper- and lower-case text as you would in a conventional letter.
- Avoid attaching files that contain graphics or that include text that has been formatted by a word processor.
- Adjust your style and tone to match the purpose and recipient of the message.
- Use correct grammar, punctuation, and word choice.
- Obtain permission from recipients before you send them sales messages.

Source: Scott Ahlsmith, CTC

changes), graphics files, or attached files of formatted text unless you know that the recipients can receive and process this material. (You might attach small test files to e-mail in order to determine the type of material that the recipient can process.) Waiting to download a large e-mail containing a photograph that cannot be viewed is frustrating, to say the least!

Third, e-mail is often used as a substitute for a phone call, and it is meant to get a response. Limit the content of your e-mail message to one topic so that the recipient can respond easily.

One final caution is important: Obtain permission from recipients before you e-mail commercial messages to them. Unsolicited advertising is junk mail, whether it comes by conventional mail or e-mail. (When it comes by e-mail, junk mail is often called *spam*.) Although e-mail can be a very effective sales tool, unsolicited e-mail that does not interest customers can end up irritating them and tarnishing a company's image.

*T*he Electronic Office: Other Selling Tools

CRSs and the Web are the most glamorous of the electronic tools used in selling travel, but they are certainly not the only ones. To sell travel efficiently, you might use all of the following:

- *VCRs.* Many travel agencies place VCRs in their display windows to attract passersby, or they put them in reception areas so that clients can enjoy destination tapes while they wait to talk with a travel counselor. Travel agencies also use videos to enhance sales presentations and in-house training.
- *Computer software* for everyday tasks, from letters to financial recordkeeping. With word processing and desktop publishing programs, you can send professional-looking fliers or newsletters to clients. With spreadsheet programs you can simplify the tasks of financial recordkeeping and analysis and the preparation of financial statements.
- *Fax machines.* Sending or receiving a fax is often faster and cheaper than other methods of communicating with clients. During the early 1990s fax machines became an invaluable tool for sending clients their itineraries, confirmations, and other tangible proof of their travel plans. (Clients also find them useful, as the Selling through Service case on page 161 illustrates.) Travel sellers also discovered *broadcast faxing,* using the

fax machine to send updates on tour packages, group discounts, and so on to multiple sites. For some uses, however, e-mail is replacing faxes.

Compared with this familiar equipment, other selling tools require at least a little more training. There are many software packages created to help travel sellers. For example, Automated Travel Solutions' EasyFEE program processes service fees; SABRE Business Travel Solutions gives agencies tools to integrate travel booking, policy management, expense reporting, and other tasks involved in corporate travel.

Database programs can be especially useful. They allow you to store, organize, and retrieve mountains of information efficiently. A travel agency might use fairly simple, all-purpose database programs such as Claris Filemaker PRO or Microsoft Fox Pro, or it might hire a local computer service to set up a database system, or it might use a database program specifically designed for the travel industry.

For example, Third Party Solution's ClientBASE and TRAM's Marketing Advantage were created to be used by travel agencies and can be integrated with a CRS and an accounting system. With a database program like these, you can keep track of clients' likes, dislikes, special interests, and demographic characteristics. Once you have entered information into the database, it can organize and reorganize the information. You might use it, for example, to give you mailing lists for targeted promotional campaigns or reminders for birthday messages or follow-up calls. Suppose you make an entry in the database to note that client Alice Addams is interested in Pacific cruises and then forget about it. Six months later, when you are sending out information about a new Pacific cruise, Alice Addams will show up on the mailing list to receive that information.

Airline ticketing, however, remains the task most influenced by technology. Besides CRSs and the Web, electronic tools for ticketing include

- ***Satellite ticket printers (STPs),*** which use a telephone-line hookup to enable a travel agency to print tickets electronically in the offices of their corporate accounts.
- ***Automated ticketing machines (ATMs),*** which are owned and operated by airlines. By inserting a credit card into an ATM and responding to prompts on a video terminal, the consumer can access flight information, make a reservation, and receive a ticket and boarding pass, much like getting cash from an automated teller machine.
- ***E-tickets,*** also called *electronic ticketing* or *ticketless travel,* in which a computer record replaces the paper ticket. The passenger receives a confirmation number and

Selling through Service (continues on next page)

Smooth Sailing

Toby leaned back in the chair. It had been a tough morning. First the coffee maker went on the fritz, then came news of an impending airline strike, and now this. He stared down at the fax in his hand marked "Urgent." John and Jennie Hobart had missed the boat. Literally.

Fax Transmittal
Date: Sunday, 7/9/98
Time: 9:00 P.M.
Company: ABC Travel
Name: Toby Crandall
FAX #:   617/ 555-8379

Message: Stranded in Miami. Flight delayed in DC due to weather. Arrived late—no one at the airport to meet us. Pulled up at the pier just in time to wave goodbye and watch the ship sail. Castaway Cruises found us the last hotel room in the city for tonight, but claims it is not responsible for transportation to next port of call to meet the ship. Jenny's been on the phone to the

airlines, but no luck yet. And to top it off the airline lost our luggage. What a way to start our honeymoon! Call me first thing Monday morning. The number here is 800-555-5512; we're in room 719. Get us out of here!

Sender: John/Jennie Hobart

Toby checked his watch. It was 8:15 Monday morning. No time to waste. He started calling up information on his CRS.

A half hour later he placed the call to the Hobarts. "Room 719, please," he told the operator who answered.

"Hello."

"John, it's Toby Crandall at ABC Travel. I'm sorry you've had such a shaky start to your honeymoon, but I think I have a solution. How's Jennie doing?"

"She's not a happy camper, Toby. What's your plan?"

"Well, I've got you booked on a TransGlobal flight that leaves Miami at 2:00 P.M. That will put you into St. Thomas even before the ship

Selling through Service (continued)

arrives. Castaway will have a representative meet you at the airport and bring you and Jennie right to the dock. How does that sound?"

"Sounds great, but what about our luggage?"

"Oh yeah. It's a good thing you filed a report at the airport. The airline found your luggage, and I'm having it delivered to your hotel room this morning. It should be there by noon."

"Well, that's a relief." Toby listened as John relayed the information to Jennie. "Toby, I just saw my wife smile for the first time since we arrived in Miami. Thanks."

"You're welcome, pal. Oh, and John, I asked the hotel to deliver a champagne brunch to your room. Congratulations on your wedding. It should be smooth sailing from here."

Toby leaned back, smiling. "Good work," he thought to himself.

Is Toby's job done?

■ ■ ■

Toby still has some work ahead of him. Much as the sales cycle does not end with the sale, problem resolution is not over when you think you have found the solution. Once you have found a strategy and tested it, checking with the customer (as Toby did), two other steps remain: resolution and follow up.

The "resolution" step consists of taking the actions you promised and checking that the desired result has occurred. Toby should call the cruise line to inform them of John and Jennie's arrival in St. Thomas, including flight number and arrival time, and request that a representative meet them and transfer them to the ship. He should also call John and Jennie shortly after noon to confirm that their luggage arrived safely.

As his final step in resolving this problem, Toby's follow-up might include a call to Castaway Cruises to discuss the extent of the cruise line's responsibility for John and Jennie's air transportation to St. Thomas. If a refund is due (as may be the case if Toby booked the Hobarts on one of the cruise line's air/sea packages), Toby may be able to begin the refund process prior to the Hobarts' return. Once the Hobarts have returned, Toby might call to see how the rest of their vacation went.

What else should Toby do to follow up on his resolution of the problem?

sometimes a printed itinerary, but not a conventional ticket. By 1998 more than 18 percent of airline tickets sold by travel agencies were e-tickets. E-tickets may make STPs obsolete.

■ **Interactive Agent Reporting (IAR),** which is software that automates the process of reporting airline ticket sales to ARC (Airlines Reporting Corporation). Instead of sending masses of paper weekly to ARC, travel agencies can report their sales electronically with IAR.

Certainly, technology has increased efficiency. Gone are the days of handwriting tickets, consulting individual airline timetables for departure times, or using a manual typewriter to process paperwork. Savvy travel professionals realize the importance of technology and make an effort to learn how to put it to their advantage.

Chapter Wrap-Up

Chapter Highlights

The telephone is just the oldest of the technologies that travel sellers are using to communicate with clients. Successful travel professionals are mastering an array of electronic tools—CRSs, the Web, e-mail, fax machines, and many types of software. In this chapter we have outlined some of the ways you can use these technologies to sell more effectively. Here is a review of the objectives with which we began this chapter.

1. **Describe how communicating by telephone differs from face-to-face communication.** The voice itself is distorted over the phone, with the pitch raised and the volume dropped. Voices are disembodied, making it more difficult to focus. Without body language, the words and the tone of voice must carry the entire message. Finally, special rules define good manners on the telephone.

2. **Explain how you should adapt your voice and manner when selling on the telephone.** Extra attention to enunciation, volume, pitch, tone, and choice of words is needed when selling over the phone. In presenting recommendations, you must rely on your verbal skills alone to paint mental pictures and describe benefits. You should raise your energy level and volume; adjust your pace to that of the speaker. Vary your tone. Avoid distractions and take notes. Smile (it shows in your voice) and give feedback often in order to develop your link with the customer. Ask for feedback frequently and listen carefully in order to identify your client's needs and reactions. Extra probing for objections is needed because the customer's reactions cannot be seen.

3. **Identify some basic rules of telephone etiquette.** Answer the call by the third ring with a clear, friendly greeting. Find out and use the caller's name, and ask for permission before putting the call on hold or transferring it. Do not keep callers on hold for more than 30-45 seconds before getting back to them. To complete the call, thank the caller, but let the caller disconnect first. If you have a voice-mail system, be sure you check your messages frequently and return all calls.

4. **Discuss how travelers and travel sellers are using the Web.** So far, only a tiny percentage of travel sales occur on-line. Consumers who visit travel sites on the Web will find full-service supersites, transaction sites, and information-only sites. Travel sellers use the Web to research information, to communicate with clients and others, to promote themselves, and to make or receive bookings. Among travel agencies, the most important uses of the Web are for sending and receiving e-mail and for researching information. Even among travel agencies that have their own sites, the Web serves mostly as a tool for communications and promotion; actual on-line sales are few.

5. **Describe other technologies that can help you succeed in selling travel.** Despite the many benefits of using the Web, CRSs remain an important electronic tool for travel agencies. Meanwhile, e-ticketing and IAR are taking airline sales close to total automation. In addition, VCRs, fax machines, and a variety of software packages can help travel professionals run their offices more efficiently and communicate with clients more effectively. Database software is especially useful to travel sellers who are trying to improve customer service and marketing.

New Terms. The terms that follow were introduced in this chapter. If you do not recall their definitions, see the Glossary, which begins on page 237.

automated ticket machine (ATM)	Interactive Agent Reporting (IAR)
direct link	satellite ticket printer (STP)
e-ticket	

Review Exercises

Check-Up

Give yourself a quick test of your memory of a few basic points. Read each of the following statements and indicate whether it is true (T) or false (F). See the answers below the statements.

T   F   1. Telephones distort your voice by lowering the pitch and decreasing the volume.

T   F   2. If you smile while you're talking on the telephone, your voice changes.

T   F   3. You should talk more quickly on the telephone, about 200 words per minute, so that you do not bore your listeners.

T   F   4. For the best and most reliable information, you can always count on the Web.

T   F   5. Most travel agencies are using the Web to allow clients to book on-line.

Answers: 1. F 2. T 3. F 4. F 5. F

Discussion Questions

1. **How's Your Voice?** This self-assessment will give you a chance to rate your telephone voice. Tape-record yourself reading the following paragraph, using your usual telephone voice, and time how long it takes you to read the paragraph.

> I am now aware of the importance of my voice during a telephone conversation with my customer. I must keep in mind that the telephone instrument itself distorts my voice, so I must be conscious of speaking at a moderate pace, and with more energy and slightly more volume to overcome that distortion. I will make sure that I enunciate carefully and eliminate any slang or jargon from my conversations with customers. Variety in the pitch of my voice will make my message clear and keep my customer's attention. The tone of my voice also sends an important message to my customer, so I will strive for a sincere and upbeat tone. I know that my voice on the telephone represents my company and my professionalism, so I want to leave my customer with positive images of both. I will listen to this tape and try to hear myself as my customer hears me.

Now listen to the tape and assess the following characteristics of your voice:

a. Rate

_____ Fast (under 45 seconds)   _____ Slow (over 90 seconds)   _____ Good (1 minute)

b. Pitch

_____ High   _____ Nasal   _____ Raspy

_____ Low   _____ Natural   _____ Monotone

c. Tone

____ Sincere   ____ Friendly   ____ Confident

____ Pushy   ____ Nervous   ____ Bored

d. Volume

____ Too loud   ____ Too soft   ____ Moderate

e. Enunciation

____ Clear   ____ Mumbled   ____ Mechanical

2. **Reading Between the Lines.** After your next phone conversation, answer the following questions:

a. Were you interested in what the person was saying?

_____

Did you do anything to let the person know that?

_____

_____

_____

_____

b. Was the other person interested in your comments?

_____

How do you know?

_____

_____

_____

c. How did you know when the other person wanted the conversation to end?

_____

_____

_____

_____

3. **Using Technology.** Suppose you work in a small travel agency that has just established its own Web site, which does not take on-line bookings. Can you describe at least three ways in which having the site could benefit the agency?

_____

_____

_____

_____

_____

4. **Caught in the Web.*** The abundance of travel information on the Web can end up complicating some sales. Cindy Bertram, a cruise specialist in Indiana, had spent about an hour qualifying Mr. and Mrs. Goodwin and putting together sample itineraries and quotes for their first cruise. But before the cruise was booked, Mr. Goodwin went Web-surfing, discovered a site for a cruise agency, and found that it listed the cruise the Goodwins wanted for $800 less than Bertram's quote. The Goodwins were wary about giving their credit card number to this unknown cruise agency, so first they called Bertram and asked if she could match the rate they'd found on the Web. What should she do?

_____

_____

_____

_____

_____

_____

_____

_____

_____

*Based on Phyllis Fine, "Good Vibrations," *Travel Agent,* April 7, 1997, p. 24.

A Case in Question

Refer to "Smooth Sailing" on page 161 to answer the following questions.

1. How did Toby deal with the first four steps of the problem-resolution process?

_____

_____

_____

_____

2. If Toby's initial resolution steps do not solve the problem (for example, if the bags do not arrive), what should he do next?

_____

_____

_____

_____

3. How would Toby have handled this problem if he did not have a fax machine, telephone, or CRS?

_____

_____

_____

_____

Exercises in Selling

1. **The Sales Cycle by Telephone.** Break into teams of two and select one of the exercises at the end of Chapter 4, page 107, or Chapter 5, page 138. This time, conduct the exercise over the phone and tape the conversation. For both situations, have the client initiate the telephone call.

   Both members of the team should listen to the tape and fill out Worksheet 6.1. Compare and discuss your assessments.

2. **Using E-Mail.** Suppose that weeks ago, a travel counselor made a booking for a client from San Francisco to Seattle at a fare of $325. The flight departs on a Saturday morning at 9:00 A.M. and returns the following Saturday at 2:30 P.M. Yesterday, the airline published a special limited-time fare for this routing for $75 less; however, the client must depart Friday night at 8:00 P.M. instead of Saturday morning. Break into teams of two: one person represents a travel counselor and the other plays the client.

■ *Travel counselor.* Send an e-mail to the client advising him or her of this new development and asking whether you should change the client's reservation.

■ *Client.* Send an e-mail in response to the travel counselor's message.

Evaluate each other's e-mail by checking the guidelines in the Tips box on page 159.

Worksheet 6.1

Name _____   Date _____

Selling by Telephone

Use this form to evaluate the tape of the performance by the "travel counselor" in the "Sales Cycle by Telephone" exercise described on page 167. You may want to duplicate this form before writing on it.

	Good	Fair	Poor
1. Did the travel counselor sound energetic?	_____	_____	_____
2. Could you hear the travel counselor's voice easily?	_____	_____	_____
3. Did the travel counselor enunciate clearly and speak grammatically?	_____	_____	_____
4. Did the travel counselor avoid a monotone pitch?	_____	_____	_____
5. Did the travel counselor speak at a rate like that of the client?	_____	_____	_____
6. Overall, how would you evaluate the travel counselor's speaking voice?	_____	_____	_____
7. Did the travel counselor answer the call with an unimportant phrase and identify him- or herself?	_____	_____	_____
8. Did the travel counselor ask to help the client and find out his or her name?	_____	_____	_____
9. Did the travel counselor use the client's name?	_____	_____	_____
10. Did the travel counselor pause in order to avoid monopolizing the conversation and allow the client to speak?	_____	_____	_____
11. Did the travel counselor give feedback frequently to indicate that he or she was listening?	_____	_____	_____
12. Did the travel counselor ask for feedback frequently?	_____	_____	_____
13. Did the travel counselor make an effort to paint word pictures?	_____	_____	_____

If you are enacting a situation from Chapter 4, "Determining Customer Needs," complete the following:

	Good	Fair	Poor
14. Did the travel counselor obtain answers to the five basic *W*s?	_____	_____	_____
15. Did the travel counselor probe to identify the client's other needs?	_____	_____	_____
16. Did the travel counselor paraphrase what the client said and ask for confirmation?	_____	_____	_____

If you are enacting the situation from Chapter 5, "Giving Information," complete the following:

	Good	Fair	Poor
17. Did the travel counselor empathize with and clarify the client's objections?	_____	_____	_____
18. Did the travel counselor answer those objections?	_____	_____	_____
19. Did the travel counselor ask for the sale at the appropriate time?	_____	_____	_____

Comments:

_____

_____

_____

_____

_____

_____

_____

_____

_____

_____

_____

_____

_____

Strategies for Sales and Marketing Success

Focusing on Customer Service

Objectives

After reading this chapter, you should be able to

1. Describe what customer service is from the buyer's point of view.

2. Explain the importance of customer service from the seller's point of view.

3. Identify four ways of finding out how customers perceive your service.

4. Outline a program for developing a focus on customer service.

5. Describe the relationship between sales and service.

Preview

Gaining a competitive edge is the goal of most businesses. They struggle to analyze the market-place, define their customers, and plan strategies that will give them an advantage among their competitors. For many organizations, providing excellent service has become that competitive edge; it is the strategy that sets their company or product apart from the rest.

What is customer service, from the buyer's and from the seller's point of view? How can you evaluate customer service, and what can you do to provide it? This chapter will help you answer those questions and more.

Components of Service: The Buyer's View

Like Vegas without casinos or California without sun, selling without service disappoints. A missing travel document, a flight attendant who ignores you, a dirty carpet in the hotel room, a surly desk clerk—even such small failures in service can cast a shadow over a travel experience. Successful selling requires customer service that meets or exceeds the customer's expectations.

This requirement would be easier to satisfy if service were a simple commodity like the number of peanuts given as your "snack" on an airplane. But service, like travel itself, has an intangible aspect. **Customer service** refers both to the benefits provided clients and to how those benefits are provided. Moreover, the quality of customer service is defined by how it compares with the customer's expectations.

Table 7.1 gives examples of the variety of services offered by different parts of the travel industry. Some services are almost universal; others are rare and set one company apart from others. Our focus here, though, is not on what is delivered but on how it is delivered—on how salespeople treat their customers.

Clients, of course, have differing expectations about how they will be treated. But most expect five basic qualities to characterize their treatment:

- *Respect*. Customers want to be treated fairly, intelligently, and individually—in other words, with respect. To meet this requirement, you should use the customer's name often, listen to what the customer is saying, and demonstrate concern for his or her needs. Give clients your undivided attention, and show them that their well-being is important to you and your business.
- *Prompt service*. Customers want their time to be treated as valuable. Everyone has deadlines to meet, or appointments to keep, or other responsibilities. If you cannot wait on clients immediately, acknowledge their presence and indicate when you will be able to help them. Thank waiting clients for their patience and make them as comfortable as possible.
- *Efficient service*. Promptness without effi-

Table 7.1

Services in the Travel Industry: A Sampling

Supplier or Intermediary	Services
Hotels	In-room coffee, concierge, room service, turn-down service, in-room irons and ironing boards, in-room video, express check-in, non-smoking rooms and floors, room security systems, complimentary newspaper, free continental breakfast in lobby, business center, ice/vending machines, airport limo service
Airlines	Complimentary in-flight magazines, complimentary newspapers, in-flight food and beverage service, frequent-flyer programs, pillows and blankets, ticket counters in hotel lobbies
Cruise lines	Teen counselor on board, special "theme" cruises, captain's cocktail party, low-cal/low-fat menus, shore excursions, complimentary movies, sports programs, masseuse, fitness programs, duty-free shopping
Travel agencies	Bon voyage gifts, document/ticket delivery, complimentary flight bag to members of tour groups, assistance obtaining passports and visas, agency newsletter, welcome-home cards and gifts, after-hours emergency assistance, travelogues, personalized itinerary

ciency is like an appetizer without the main course. Take the time you need with each client in order to do things right the first time.

- *Product knowledge.* Customers expect you to know enough about your products to be helpful and to take responsibility to find the answers you do not have.

- *Enthusiasm.* Customers want to deal with people who appear to enjoy their work, and they want to feel good about themselves after the encounter. By showing enthusiasm you open the path to these goals.

More generally, clients expect *professional-*

ism—a commitment to high standards. (Chapter 8 examines professionalism in detail.) In other words, clients want competent, businesslike performance and an image of quality. They expect the place of business to be clean and attractive and telephone conversations to be pleasant. They count on salespeople to be on time, pleasant, patient, attentive, and neatly dressed. They want promises to be kept and things done right.

Respect, prompt and efficient service, product knowledge, enthusiasm, professionalism—these characteristics form the core of customer service. Whatever else customers look for, they expect salespeople to demonstrate these qualities.

Why Does Service Matter? The Seller's View

It is obvious why a customer would care about service, but why is it important to the seller? For the seller, quality service can differentiate the seller's product, avoid the consequences of customer dissatisfaction, establish a base of loyal clients, and lead to more business through word-of-mouth advertising.

Differentiating the Product

Consider the travel industry and its products. How many hotels, motels, and resorts are there across the United States? How many car rental companies? Cruise companies? Restaurants? To some extent, each company within any particular family of products offers a similar product. Hotels and motels offer sleeping accommodations for out-of-town guests. Car rental companies offer transportation. Restaurants offer food for hungry travelers.

If the products of competing companies are similar, how can one company position itself in the marketplace to attract buyers? Price, of course, is one way; another is the quality of the product itself. But if price and quality are similar, what causes one buyer to

purchase product A and another to purchase product B?

Often the answer lies in how a buyer perceives the service that accompanies the buying experience. Thus, service provides a strategy for differentiating one product from another. Today, it often holds a key place in marketing strategy.

For travel agencies, the challenge is to differentiate their "product" not just from that of other agencies but also from do-it-yourself travel arrangements. Many companies are trying to lure travelers to bypass travel agencies and book travel on the Web themselves. Service gives travelers a reason to go instead to the travel agency. For example, a travel agency can offer clients help when their flights are canceled. In addition, a travel agency might keep records of when passports expire and send reminders ahead of time to the client. Or it might provide clients who are traveling abroad with a list of ATMs at their destinations. Or the agency might have a fax waiting at the client's hotel asking how things went and suggesting that the client contact the agency if there are any problems. Robinson Travel, an agency in an affluent California community, arranges limos to the airport and confirms tee-times for its clients. By offering services like these, agencies give clients something that they cannot get if they book trips themselves directly with suppliers.

The service that differentiates an agency may also take the form of expertise in arranging special types of travel. For example, Great Trips agency in California focuses on trips for upscale, experienced travelers and has developed expertise in special-interest tours to Great Britain and France. It arranged one trip for a group to explore Victorian greenhouses, for example, and another for a group going on the Scotch Whisky Trail. Similarly, Churchill & Turen, an Illinois-based agency, created an eleven-day tour of parts of Italy with cooking demonstrations by local chefs. By offering expertise in arranging special types of trips, agencies can differentiate themselves and secure their own marketing niche.

Avoiding Customer Dissatisfaction

Customer service is important not only for attracting customers but also for keeping them. Think for a moment about the expectations you had the last time you ate dinner in a restaurant. Were your expectations met or exceeded? If your expectations were not met, did you let the owner or manager know? Did you tell anyone else about your experience with the restaurant? Will you go back to that restaurant?

A study prepared by the Technical Assistance Research Program found that 96 percent of customers who have complaints never make those complaints known to the business itself. Furthermore, according to other research, about 63 percent of unhappy customers who do not complain take their business elsewhere, quite often permanently. The owner or manager may be left wondering why the business is shrinking.

What bothers customers most? In a 1989 *Wall Street Journal* survey by Peter Hart, some of the complaints most frequently mentioned were

- Salespeople or delivery people who do not show up when they say they will (cited by 40 percent of respondents).
- Salespeople who are poorly informed (37 percent).

- Salespeople who say, "It is not my department" (25 percent).
- Salespeople who "talk down to you" (21 percent).

If you want to keep your present customers, service matters.

Winning Loyal Customers

Delivering service that exceeds customer expectations creates loyalty that keeps your customers coming back to you. But is it worth the trouble? Would your effort be better spent just advertising for different customers? Is loyalty cost-effective for the seller?

Over the years, many companies, in many types of industries, have conducted research in order to answer this question. The result is almost always the same: your present customers are almost always your best prospects for additional business, and present customers are almost always your most profitable customers.

In most businesses, it is very expensive to acquire a new customer. Advertising, direct mail, and other ways of soliciting clients are very expensive. By the time you add up all the costs of obtaining new clients, it is hard to make money from their business at the start. The costs involved in acquiring a new customer far exceed the costs of maintaining an existing customer, by about as much as three to five times. In fact, repeat business is often the difference between success and failure in the travel industry.

In dollars and cents alone, then, it makes sense to devote a significant portion of your time and money to maintaining your existing clients. And as we have seen, customer service is a key to keeping these customers. Service nurtures long-lasting relationships that might be profitable for years.

The good news for travel agencies is that leisure travelers tend to be very loyal to them. One recent survey found that on a scale of 1 to 10, travel counselors earned a satisfaction rating of 8.5 and that, on average, the leisure travelers surveyed had used their current travel agency for 6 years and 4 months (see Figure 7.1).

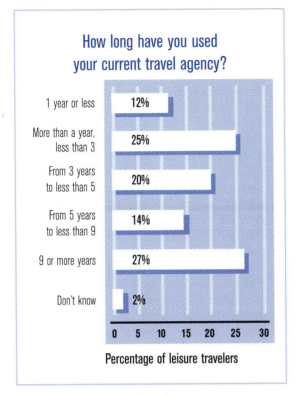

How long have you used your current travel agency?

1 year or less	12%
More than a year, less than 3	25%
From 3 years to less than 5	20%
From 5 years to less than 9	14%
9 or more years	27%
Don't know	2%

Percentage of leisure travelers

Figure 7.1 Loyalty to Travel Agencies
Travel agencies must be doing many things right. Leisure travelers who go to travel agencies on average have changed travel agencies less than three times in the last ten years.
Source: TTG's Path to Consumer Loyalty and Service Fees Study 1997, as reported in *Tour & Travel News/TTG North America,* December 15, 1997, p. P4.

Gaining and Losing from Word of Mouth

A satisfied customer not only returns to do business with you another day but may also tell three to five other people about your business. This word-of-mouth advertising is very effective.

But what about dissatisfied customers? They are more likely to tell friends about bad service they receive than about good service. In general, customers whose expectations are not met or who perceive their experience as poor will tell at least 8 other people about that experience; 20 percent will tell as many as 20 others. In other words, 1 unhappy customer could bias 8 to 20 other potential customers against you. In competitive businesses like travel, a successful business is a service-focused business.

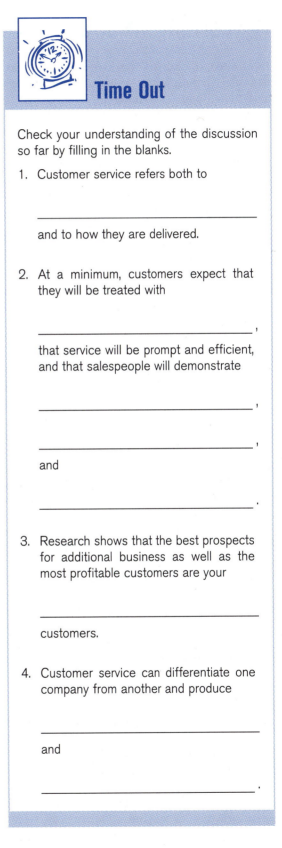

Time Out

Check your understanding of the discussion so far by filling in the blanks.

1. Customer service refers both to

   _____

   and to how they are delivered.

2. At a minimum, customers expect that they will be treated with

   _____ ,

   that service will be prompt and efficient, and that salespeople will demonstrate

   _____ ,

   _____ ,

   and

   _____ .

3. Research shows that the best prospects for additional business as well as the most profitable customers are your

   _____

   customers.

4. Customer service can differentiate one company from another and produce

   _____

   and

   _____ .

*L*earning from Clients

In essence, the key to providing quality service is understanding what your customers expect and then doing everything in your power to deliver it, and more. But what you think constitutes good service and what your customers think may be quite different. Furthermore, what you deliver and how your customers perceive what you deliver can also diverge. But it is the customer's perception of service that determines its value. If what you do is not perceived as valuable by the customer, then it isn't valuable.

As an example, look again at Figure 1.4 (page 11); it shows which of the many services offered by travel agencies appear to be most important to leisure travelers who use agencies. What about corporate travel buyers? If you managed a corporate travel agency, would you want your employees to devote their time to providing VIP service to clients or developing travel policies? According to one large 1997 survey of corporate travel buyers by Plog Research Inc. (reported in *Travel Counselor,* June 1998, p. 46), most corporate travel buyers would prefer to have their own departments—not the travel agency—develop policy. But most corporate buyers prefer to pay a travel agency to find the lowest possible fares, provide timely management reports, hire and train reservationists, and provide VIP service.

In short, to provide top-quality service, you need to see it from the client's point of view. Are your clients like those in these large-scale surveys? How do you learn the client's view?

Informal methods of obtaining feedback from clients should not be overlooked. You can learn a lot from informal chats. Call clients on the phone to inquire how a trip went or ask how you could improve service. ("What can we do to make booking your next trip more convenient?")

More structured, formal methods of obtaining customer feedback include the following:

- *Focus groups.* A ***focus group*** consists of about eight to ten participants and a trained moderator who meet to discuss a particular issue. Like informal conversations, focus groups offer the advantage of allowing people to talk about their concerns in an unstructured way. But comment cards and surveys offer easier ways of getting simple, quantifiable answers.

- *Comment cards.* These are used by many restaurants, hotels, travel agencies, and other businesses to elicit customer feedback. Figures 7.2 and 7.3 show examples. Many travel agencies package postage-paid comment cards with the travel documents sent to clients. Obviously, not all customers are willing to bother filling out the cards. To increase the response rate, some companies offer gifts to those who respond.

- *Other surveys.* You might, for example, send a trip evaluation form to all of your clients by conventional mail or e-mail, or you might administer a questionnaire over the phone. (In the Selling through Service case on page 161 we discuss some of the advantages of telephone surveys.)

What should you ask clients? Keep in mind who the clients are and ask about characteristics and benefits that are likely to be important to them. For most customers, this boils down to questions about timeliness, consistency, accuracy, and results. But tailor the questions to the type of travel involved. For example, if you are surveying clients involved with incentive travel, you would address different questions to the organizers and the participants. You might want to ask the organizers about whether the goals of the incentive program were achieved; you might ask the participants on the incentive trip about the choice of destination and the service given there.

Both open-ended and closed-ended questions can be useful. If you want quantifiable results, however, the survey should include very specific closed questions that are tied to performance standards. For example, you might ask, "Were you greeted within 10–20 seconds of your visit?" or "Did the receptionist ask your permission before placing you on hold?"

You can also obtain quantifiable results by using a rating scale. For example, you might give people a choice of five responses to a question about a specific aspect of service: very satisfied, satisfied, neutral, dissatisfied, and very dissatisfied. For each response, you might then

CHOICE HOTELS
I N T E R N A T I O N A L

Sleep   Comfort   Quality   *Clarion*

RODEWAY   Econo Lodge   MainStay Suites

PLEASE CHECK ONE BOX

Quality	Comfort	Clarion	Sleep	Rodeway	Econo	Mainstay
Inn ❑	Inn ❑	Inn ❑	Inn ❑	Inn ❑	Lodge ❑	Suites ❑
Hotel ❑	Suites ❑	Suites ❑				
Suites ❑	Resort ❑					
Resort ❑						

I am traveling for Business ❑   Pleasure ❑

I decided to stay at this hotel because:
- ❑ Prefer to stay with your chain
- ❑ Saw your highway signs
- ❑ Used Chain Directory
- ❑ Was referred by: _____
- ❑ Because of your toll free reservation system
- ❑ Previous experience with your chain
- ❑ Saw your magazine or television advertisement
- ❑ Saw your listing in the AAA directory
- ❑ Other: _____

PLEASE CHECK THE APPROPRIATE BOX

	Excellent	Good	Fair	Poor
Guest Room & General				
Cleanliness of your room	❑	❑	❑	❑
Decor of your room	❑	❑	❑	❑
Attitude of our personnel	❑	❑	❑	❑
Quality of service	❑	❑	❑	❑
Comfort of your room	❑	❑	❑	❑
Convenience of location	❑	❑	❑	❑
Restaurant/Lounge/				
Continental Breakfast	❑	❑	❑	❑
Restaurant/Lounge decor	❑	❑	❑	❑
Menu selection	❑	❑	❑	❑
Restaurant/Lounge personnel	❑	❑	❑	❑
Quality of food	❑	❑	❑	❑
Quality of service	❑	❑	❑	❑
Would you stay with us again?	❑ Yes		❑ No	

My room was reserved through a travel agent ❑
or through your 800 number reservations system ❑

How many days a year do you stay in a hotel? _____

Hotel: _____ Rm. #: _____

City: _____ State: _____

Date of your stay: _____ / _____
                CHECK IN   CHECK OUT

To receive requested information or a personal response to your comments, please fill in:

Your Name: _____

Address: _____

City: _____

State: _____ Zip: _____

Province: _____ Postal Code: _____

Comments & Suggestions

_____
_____
_____
_____
_____
_____

PLEASE LEAVE AT FRONT DESK
Thank You

Figure 7.2 Comment Cards: An Example from One Supplier
Many businesses in the travel industry use comment cards such as this one to find out what their customers think about the quality of their services.
Source: Reprinted by permission of Choice Hotels International

37784

Please use capital letters, e.g.: G R O U P

In an effort to continually improve our service, we need to know about your experience with us. Please answer all questions by checking the appropriate box, then drop in the mail or fax to (800) 824-1481. Thank you.

When you contacted your Carlson Wagonlit Travel agent, how satisfied were you with:

	Very Satisfied	Satisfied	Dissatisfied	Very Dissatisfied	No Opinion	Don't Know
1. Phone response time?	O	O	O	O	O	O
2. Courtesy/manner of agent?	O	O	O	O	O	O
3. Agent's response to your	O	O	O	O	O	O
questions?	O	O	O	O	O	O
4. Agent's proactive recommendations to improve your trip? (including saving money)	O	O	O	O	O	O

	Yes	No	Don't Know
5. Were your travel documents delivered when promised?	O	O	O
6. Were your travel documents			
Complete?	O	O	O
Accurate?	O	O	O

7. Did the supplier provide the services as indicated on your reservation?

	Yes	No	Don't Know
Airline	O	O	O
Frequent Traveler number	O	O	O
Boarding Pass/Seat Assignment	O	O	O
Special request (meal)	O	O	O
Hotel	O	O	O
Car	O	O	O

	Very Satisfied	Satisfied	Dissatisfied	Very Dissatisfied	No Opinion
8. Overall, how satisfied were you with Carlson Wagonlit Travel's service to you?	O	O	O	O	O

Last Name

First Name | Mid. Ini.

Company Name

Phone Number

Start Date of Travel: Month / Day / Year | Length of Trip: Days

Number trips traveler has per year:
O 1–5 O 6–10 O 11 or More

	Very Satisfied	Satisfied	Dissatisfied	Very Dissatisfied	No Opinion
9. If you used our emergency service center, how satisfied were you with our service?	O	O	O	O	O

10. Given your satisfaction with your travel arrangements will you . . .	Yes	No
Use Carlson for your personal travel?	O	O
Recommend Carlson services to a friend?	O	O

11. Are you answering as: O Traveler only O Travel arranger only O Traveler; own arrangements

Comments

Thank you for answering these questions. Your comments will be used to better serve you.

Figure 7.3 Comment Cards: From a Travel Agency
Carlson Wagonlit Travel agencies collect data on a regular basis. By doing this, they learn about trends in their service and clients' perceptions of their performance over time.
Source: Reprinted by permission of Carlson Wagonlit Travel

assign a point value, such as 5 for very satisfied, 4 for satisfied, and so on.

Keeping track of all the information you obtain from customer feedback is a challenge. Software companies have come to the rescue. As discussed in Chapter 6, you can choose from among numerous programs to create a database of your customers on your computer or CRS. Some programs will not only design the surveys but also allow you to input the responses and

Dialing for Data

"That's what we have to do first," declared Teresa Sores, owner and manager of Shearwater Travel, a very small but well-established agency. Teresa had been worried for a couple of months. Business had been slow. The reason, she concluded, was that some old clients were no longer coming back. But why? The time had come to take customer service seriously. Now Teresa was telling her employees that the first step was to survey their clients.

A quick check of several books had told her how. According to William A. Band, author of *Creating Value for Customers* (New York: Wiley, 1991), telephone surveys offer several advantages over other methods of surveying customers, such as interviews or mailed surveys. For one thing, it is easier to reach people by phone than to arrange interviews. It is also quicker to call than to use the mail. And the people who respond to a phone survey are more likely than those responding to a mailed interview to be representative of your customers as a whole. The people who take the trouble to fill out and return a mailed survey are likely to be those who feel strongly about your questions.

Some people become experts at the craft and science of creating unbiased, informative questionnaires that yield scientifically valid results. But for purposes like Teresa's, even relatively unsophisticated questionnaires, if carefully done, can be useful. Trying to figure out how she should conduct her telephone survey, Teresa had found the following suggested sample:

Hello, Mr. Smith? I'm Sally Thompson from Thunderbird Travel. As part of our commitment to customer service, we would like to conduct a two-minute follow-up with select customers. Do you have two minutes now for five short questions relating to your recent trip to New York? Thank you.

I'd like to ask you to rate the service Thunderbird Travel provided to you in the following areas as excellent, good, fair, or poor.

1. How would you rate the courtesy of the agent who handled your travel arrangements? (Read options).
2. How would you rate the efficiency or timeliness of the handling of our travel plans? (Read options.)
3. How would you rate the accuracy of your travel plans? (Read options.)
4. How would you rate the knowledge and professionalism of the agent who handled your travel arrangements? (Read options.)
5. Finally, how would you rate your overall satisfaction with the service provided by Thunderbird Travel on this particular trip? (Read options.)

Thank you, Mr. Smith, for taking the time to help us monitor our customer service. (Adapted from Robert W. Joselyn, CTC, "Don't Guess—Investigate," *ASTA Agency Management Magazine,* August 1991.)

Using this model to create a brief and simple questionnaire, Teresa and her employers were able to complete a survey within a week. A pattern in the results was apparent right away: question 3, accuracy, was bringing very negative responses. Apparently, someone was making a lot of mistakes in reservations. Were one or two travel counselors the source of the errors? What should Teresa do next?

■ ■ ■

Before doing anything, Teresa should tabulate and analyze the answers to each question of the survey. With a survey like this one, if you

Selling through Service (continued)

do not need sophisticated measures, you might simply assign a value to each response—for example, 10 for excellent, 7 for good, 3 for fair, and 0 for poor—and then calculate the average response to each question. (Of course, more precise statistical analysis is also possible, and very often desirable.) The average for each question and the variability will let Teresa know how her travel counselors are doing.

Suppose the average responses are "good" despite the inaccuracies in reservations. What could Teresa do next? In this case, because the agency and the survey are both small, she could comb through her records, finding out which travel counselors handled the customers who gave the low ratings for accuracy.

then produce statistical analyses of the responses.

Whatever tools and questions you use in order to obtain customer feedback, keep two general guidelines in mind:

- Make it easy for your customers to give you feedback. Keep in touch with them and invite their comments and suggestions whenever possible. Your technology-oriented clients may consider a Web site to be the easiest way to communicate with you. Have a survey built into your Web site. Ask for demographic and psychographic information first; then ask for specifics about your services, including the ease of using your Web site.
- Remember that measuring service is a very fallible effort to place a tangible value on an intangible experience.

Time Out

Check your understanding of the discussion so far by completing these statements.

1. The value of customer service depends on how

   _____

   perceives it.

2. Ways of gathering information about clients' perceptions of service include (a) informal conversations, (b) organizing a

   _____ ,

   (c) using

   _____ ,

and (d) conducting a

_____ .

3. To obtain quantifiable results, you should use

   _____

   questions in a survey or use a

   _____ .

*I*mplementing a Focus on Customer Service

Memory can be treacherous. If you have five good experiences followed by one or two bad experiences, it is the bad experience that might stick in your mind. Even though you give good service most of the time, clients are likely to remember the rare failures. If a business is to be successful, service must be consistently good.

No one person can guarantee this consistency. Achieving it requires a deliberate program that teaches everyone in the organization—from the frontline clerk to the owner or manager—to focus on service. The program should create throughout the organization a single vision of (1) what quality service is, (2) how it can be delivered, and (3) how it can be monitored. To take the first step, defining what quality service is, the organization needs to look to its customers.

Surveying Customers

An obvious way to find out what your customers think is to ask them. For example, when Marriott Hotels wanted to find out what room services were most important to its budget-conscious guests, they invited consumers to examine prototype rooms designed for a limited-service hotel. Most of the room's features were tagged with a price. The participants were given $49 in "Monopoly money" and asked which features they were willing to buy with those dollars. Marriott quickly found out that in-room coffee and security systems had more appeal to the budget-conscious than an indoor pool or a second restaurant. Hence the birth of Courtyard by Marriott.

In fact, asking for the client's viewpoint serves three purposes:

1. It can give you information about what clients want and expect.
2. It can tell you how clients perceive what you are doing.
3. It can make your clients feel that they are important to you. Feeling valued as a customer is a powerful link in the chain of loyalty to your business.

Setting Standards

Once you have a clear understanding of your clients' expectations, the real work begins. With this information on expectations, you can define the standards for service. The standards can be as simple as answering the telephone within three rings. They can also be complex, such as following a seven-step process to resolve complaints.

The standards set may require new procedures, new policies, or even new technology. For example, to ensure that standards for accuracy are met, a travel agency might begin using quality-check software that monitors documents and catches problems before the documents are released.

Whatever standards are established, they should meet four criteria:

1. The standards should have the commitment of everyone in the organization.
2. The standards should be clear.
3. They should be concise.
4. They should be achievable.

If these criteria are not met, the standards themselves are likely to create problems. Suppose, for example, that a proposed standard is to answer the telephone within three rings. If in practice this standard would require people to leap over their desks to answer a colleague's phone or to interrupt a sales encounter of their own, then the standard is not achievable and can only lead to frustration. Every member of the team should be able to meet a standard, and in many cases exceed it, without unduly disrupting others. The more open the standards are to interpretation and the more difficult they are to achieve, the greater the opportunity for conflict.

Monitoring Service

Suppose you have surveyed customers to determine their expectations about service and have established standards in order to meet those expectations. What next? You need to monitor services.

Customer feedback provides the information necessary not only to set standards for service but also to keep service on track. Soliciting feedback from clients in the ways we described earlier in this chapter should be an ongoing effort.

Measures of customer satisfaction provide the most meaningful data on how service is perceived, but they are not the only way of monitoring service. You might also use ***process measurements,*** which look at how service was created. For example, you might measure how long a client must wait before speaking with a customer service representative. Or you might use ***product measurements,*** which assess the results of service. For example, a quality control agent might recheck documents before they are sent and measure accuracy rates.

Once information about service has been collected, the results must be tabulated and analyzed. This feedback may just tell you about isolated complaints, or it may pinpoint recurring problems; for example, perhaps travel documents are being delivered late. The feedback may also include suggestions that you can implement.

Whatever the results of efforts to monitor customer service, everyone in the organization should be aware of the purpose, process, and results of the monitoring. This should help ensure that everyone is committed to implementing the plan to resolve any problems that are uncovered.

Handling Problems

If customer feedback does indicate that a problem exists, the organization should implement a plan to reduce or eliminate it. The results of this new strategy, in turn, should be monitored to ensure that it is effective.

Of course, all too often, problems will simply come to you as a salesperson. Perhaps a client is thrown out of a hotel, or the hotel loses a reservation. Any effective campaign to keep clients satisfied includes a plan for resolving such problems. In earlier chapters we've described one such plan. Recall the seven steps outlined in Figure 1.5 (page 15) and described in earlier Selling through Service cases: (1) acknowledge the problem, (2) collect the facts, (3) take responsibility, (4) select a strategy,

(5) test the strategy, (6) solve the problem, and (7) follow up.

Managing for Service

Rosenbluth Travel is one agency that emphasizes service. Its operations are described in *The Customer Comes Second* (New York: Morrow, 1992) by CEO Hal Rosenbluth and Diane McFerrin Peters. At Rosenbluth Travel, travelers can expect the company to locate lost baggage and set up golf-tee hours. Clients who take a coast-to-coast flight after an overseas trip can even have their mail delivered so they can read it during the flight home. Even more impressive, though, is the company's accuracy rate. Rosenbluth writes that his research indicated that the company's accuracy rate is "consistently over 99 percent."

What is behind this success? Are Rosenbluth's employees unusual? Perhaps, but employees alone do not make a customer ser-

Tips
A Program for Customer Service

To ensure consistent delivery of customer service, an organization should plan to

1. Determine what services customers expect to receive and how they expect to receive them.
2. Set standards for service that are known to everyone and are clear, concise, and achievable.
3. Continue to obtain customer feedback about the service provided.
4. Analyze the results of customer feedback.
5. Establish a plan for handling problems.
6. Follow through on the results.

vice program. It is up to managers to ensure that employees have the tools they need in order to give service and that they are motivated to do so. "Companies that are serious about service," writes Rosenbluth, "should put their money where their mouth is." In other words, a plan for customer service should include rewards for employees who give good service.

At Rosenbluth Travel, the rewards take the form of extra money, and the plan is called "Pay for Quality." It helps ensure that Rosenbluth's employees share his zeal for customer service, and for accuracy in particular. It allows reservationists to earn bonuses based on three criteria: accuracy, professionalism, and productivity. The plan works as follows:

- Accuracy comes first: bonuses cannot be earned on reservations containing any errors.
- For all error-free reservations, employees can earn points toward bonuses by displaying professionalism. Referring to the caller by name, using elegant language, and offering additional services, for example, are all counted as signs of professionalism.
- The more error-free, professionally handled reservations an employee makes, the more points he or she earns toward a bonus. Thus, once the criteria of accuracy and professionalism are met, productivity becomes a standard for earning a bonus.

In one stroke, the Pay for Quality plan hits two important targets: it brings employees into a shared vision of the service they will give, and it sets a specific standard for that service. The results? After the Pay for Quality plan was implemented, quality improved, productivity rose, and employees enjoyed a 32 percent average gain in compensation. At the same time, the company's costs actually went down because, says Rosenbluth, "we were doing things right the first time," thus saving the costs of correcting errors and dealing with complaints from customers. With the improved service, everyone won—the company, the employees, and the clients.

The Sales/Service Connection

Do any of our comments about service sound familiar? They should, because many of the principles for delivering quality service also apply to selling. For example, much as the sales cycle of success calls for the salesperson to determine customer needs, a program for effective customer service requires that you first find out what services are important to the customer. For both service and sales, the customer's perception is the key.

Another very close link between sales and service occurs in the last step of the sales cycle of success—the follow-up to ensure satisfaction. Recall that during this step, you keep in touch with customers in case they have questions or problems, and you seek feedback from them, among other things. Thus, when you follow the sales cycle, you are also implementing aspects of a customer service program.

Sales and service overlap, too, in the characteristics needed for success. To succeed in delivering high-quality service or in selling, you need to be polite, informative, friendly, professional, enthusiastic, concerned about customer needs, respectful, responsible, a good listener, and knowledgeable.

In short, sales and service are so linked that it is difficult to say where one ends and the other begins. When you deliver service and customers are satisfied, the result is repeat business, customer loyalty, and referrals—in other words, more sales. And when you sell, you create opportunities for providing additional service.

Chapter Wrap-Up

Chapter Highlights

In this chapter we have looked at reasons and methods for creating a focus on customer service. Successful strategies are those that look at service from the client's perspective. Here is a review of the objectives with which we began this chapter.

1. **Describe what customer service is, from the buyer's point of view.** Both the services provided by a business and the way they are provided shape the buyer's perception of customer service. At the least, customers expect that they will be served with respect and enthusiasm and that the service will be knowledgeable, prompt, efficient, and professional. In other ways, however, customers' wants and expectations regarding service vary.

2. **Explain the importance of customer service from the seller's point of view.** To the seller, delivering a high quality of service provides a strategy for gaining an edge on competitors and attracting a solid base of customers. It can differentiate the seller's product and avoid customer dissatisfaction while developing loyal customers who will refer the seller's services to others.

3. **Identify four ways of finding out how customers perceive your service.** Informal, follow-up conversations are one important way of understanding your customers' perceptions of service. In addition, focus groups, comment cards, surveys (by phone, mail, or interactive Web sites) offer other ways of gathering information about their perceptions.

4. **Outline a program for developing a focus on customer service.** Finding out what is important to customers is the first step in creating a focus on customer service. Based on the customers' wants and expectations, the organization can then develop standards of service. These standards should be shared by every member of the organization and should be clear, concise, and achievable. Next, actual service must be monitored regularly. If the feedback from customers reveals problems, they should be dealt with. Finally, managers must ensure that everyone in the organization understands the program and is motivated to work for its success.

5. **Describe the relationship between sales and service.** Successful selling provides customer service, and service brings sales. Both the sales cycle and a focus on customer service require attention to the customers' perceptions and efforts to obtain customer feedback. Furthermore, many of the qualities of successful salespeople are also the qualities of successful service people.

New terms. The terms that follow were introduced in this chapter. If you do not recall their definitions, see the Glossary, which begins on page 237.

customer service	process measurement
focus group	product measurement

Review Exercises

Check-Up

Give yourself a quick test of your memory of a few basic points. Read each of the following statements and indicate whether it is true (T) or false (F). See the answers below the statements.

T   F   1. Whether a service is valuable depends on whether the customer views it as valuable.

T   F   2. Customers are more likely to tell their friends about good service than about bad service.

T   F   3. The standards for service should be ideals for people to strive toward, even if they cannot be met.

T   F   4. Customer feedback should be solicited regularly.

T   F   5. Customer feedback is confidential information and so should usually be known only by owners and managers.

Answers: 1. T, 2. F, 3. F, 4. T, 5. F

Discussion Questions

1. **Components of Service: The Mystery Shopper.** Visit two or three retail stores in your community. Interact with at least one member of the sales or service staff at each store and observe his or her service skills. Use Worksheet 7.1 on page 191 to assess the service of each store after the visit. Discuss the results of your findings.

2. **Learning from Clients.** Assume that you are a regional sales manager for Exotique Cruise Line, a luxury cruise line characterized by small, intimate ships, unique itineraries, and superior service. You have noticed a drop in bookings in your region during the past year and a significant increase in the number of complaint letters from travel agencies. You decide to run a focus group to get to the bottom of this. In particular, you want to find out what you can do to increase sales in your region and to make the job of selling an Exotique cruise easier for travel counselors.

    a. Whom will you invite?

    _____

    b. What questions will you ask?

    _____

    _____

    _____

c. How will you record and measure the results?

_____

_____

_____

_____

3. **Monitoring Service: An Exercise.** Assume that you are a travel counselor for a very small but busy agency specializing in leisure travel. The agency has well-developed standards of service but no system for monitoring its delivery. The manager does not want to talk about, much less institute, any monitoring system for at least the next few months. But you want to monitor your own clients' reactions to service. How will you do it? In particular,

a. What methods will you use for obtaining feedback?

_____

_____

_____

_____

b. What questions will you ask?

_____

_____

_____

c. How will you record and measure the results?

_____

_____

_____

_____

4. **Managing for Service.** Apart from offering bonuses or other monetary rewards, what can managers do to ensure that employees focus on customer service?

_____

_____

_____

_____

A Case in Question

1. Look again at the "Dialing for Data" case (page 181). What additional questions, if any, could Teresa have included in her telephone survey to clarify the problem with accuracy?

_____

_____

_____

_____

2. What additional questions, if any, could Teresa have used to find out why "old clients were no longer coming back" to Shearwater Travel?

_____

_____

_____

_____

Exercises in Selling

1. **Handling Problems: Dealing with Irma.** Irma Grump is a perpetual complainer. She takes at least six extended trips a year and grumbles about every one of them. However, she continues to travel and continues to book her tours with Such a Deal Travel Agency. On a busy Monday morning she has just entered the office, which is full of clients and short of staff due to vacations. Irma demands to see the manager immediately. She is already muttering to other clients about her terrible trip.

   Break into groups of three and use this situation to practice your skill at handling problems. One person will act as Irma; a second person as the travel counselor who talks to her; and a third person as an observer. Here is a description of your roles.

- *Irma.* Remember, you are a grumbler. You have ideas about how everything should be done, notice every detail, and never fail to speak your mind. You have just declared, to no one in particular, that you want to talk to the manager. It is up to you to determine your complaints about your latest experience with Such a Deal Travel Agency. Unpleasant though you are, remember that you like to travel and you like dealing with this agency. Give the travel counselor a chance.

- *Travel counselor.* Everyone else in the office is busy with clients, so it is your job to talk with Irma. You want to keep her from disturbing the other clients and counselors. The manager is not available, and you need to persuade Irma to discuss her problem with you instead. Follow the first five steps of the problem-resolution process that was introduced in Chapter 1 and reviewed in this chapter.

- *Observer.* Watch the interaction between "Irma" and the "travel counselor" carefully and use Worksheet 7.2 to evaluate the performance of the person acting as the travel counselor. Then share your evaluation with other members of the group.

2. **More Problems: Dealing with the Disappointed.** For additional practice in handling problems, suppose that Mr. and Mrs. Sargent have just returned from a cherry blossom tour of Washington, D.C. They walk into the travel agency with itineraries and sales brochures in hand, ready for battle. The brochures say that they will "see such historical monuments as the Washington, Lincoln, and Jefferson Memorials." But they simply rode by the monuments. Their request to get off the bus so they could visit monuments was refused. Now they are very angry. Break into groups of three—with one person acting as Mr. or Mrs. Sargent, a second playing the role of the travel counselor, and the third acting as an observer.

- *Mr. or Mrs. Sargent.* You are so angry you demand a refund, at least a partial one.

- *Travel counselor.* Assume that the itinerary and brochures do not mention actually stopping or visiting the monuments and that you remember going over the itinerary and brochures with the Sargents. Assume, too, that your agency has a policy against giving a refund in circumstances like this.

- *Observer.* Use Worksheet 7.2 (page 193) to evaluate how well the "travel counselor" handles this problem. Discuss your evaluation with other members of the group.

Worksheet 7.1

Name _____ Date _____

Mystery Shoppers: A Checklist

Fill out this checklist to complete the "Components of Service" exercise described on page 187. You may want to duplicate this page before writing on it so that you can complete several checklists.

Name of Store (optional) _____

Type of Store _____

Date of Visit _____ Length of Visit _____

	Yes	No	N/A
1. I was greeted pleasantly.	_____	_____	_____
2. The store was clean and well organized.	_____	_____	_____
3. The products were displayed attractively.	_____	_____	_____
4. I did not have to wait an unreasonable length of time for assistance.	_____	_____	_____
5. The salesperson apologized for any wait.	_____	_____	_____
6. The salesperson was neatly and professionally dressed.	_____	_____	_____
7. The salesperson introduced her/himself.	_____	_____	_____
8. The salesperson asked for my name and used it.	_____	_____	_____
9. The salesperson gave me his/her full attention.	_____	_____	_____
10. The salesperson apologized for interruptions.	_____	_____	_____
11. The salesperson was friendly and helpful.	_____	_____	_____
12. The salesperson asked questions to clarify my needs.	_____	_____	_____
13. The salesperson listened carefully to what I said.	_____	_____	_____
14. The salesperson demonstrated knowledge of the products he or she sold.	_____	_____	_____

	Yes	No	N/A
15. The salesperson offered me informational literature on the store or product.	_____	_____	_____
16. The salesperson used language that was easy to understand when explaining the product features.	_____	_____	_____
17. The salesperson pointed out how the product could benefit me.	_____	_____	_____
18. The salesperson concluded the interaction politely.	_____	_____	_____
19. The salesperson thanked me for my business.	_____	_____	_____
20. The salesperson offered me his or her business card.	_____	_____	_____
Total	_____	_____	_____

Comments:

_____

_____

_____

_____

_____

_____

_____

_____

_____

_____

_____

_____

_____

Worksheet 7.2

Name _____   Date _____

Handling Problems

As the observer for the Exercises in Selling (page 189), your job is to evaluate how well the "travel counselor" handled the problem. Circle the response that best describes the counselor's performance for each step of the problem-solving process. Be ready to discuss the reasons for your evaluation. You may want to duplicate this page before writing on it so that you can evaluate several role-playing exercises.

	Good	Fair	Poor
Step 1: Acknowledging the problem	3	2	1
Step 2: Collecting the facts	3	2	1
Step 3: Taking responsibility	3	2	1
Step 4: Selecting a strategy	3	2	1
Step 5: Testing the strategy	3	2	1

Comments:

_____

_____

_____

_____

_____

_____

_____

_____

_____

_____

_____

Maintaining Professional Standards

Objectives

After reading this chapter, you should be able to

1. Identify key characteristics of professionalism.

2. Discuss how to make ethical choices as a travel professional.

3. Describe some simple ways of relieving stress.

4. Explain some tools and methods for managing your time more effectively.

5. Outline ways to control the flow of paper.

Preview

Professionalism, as we noted in the last chapter, is one characteristic of good service. What does professionalism require, and why is it difficult to maintain? When you have a headache and you're a week behind schedule on a major project and you have a mountain of paperwork on your desk, do you still look calm and neat and businesslike when a customer comes in? Do you still listen patiently while that customer is angrily complaining about a perfectly correct and reasonable bill? Do you treat clients fairly even if you're pressured to take advantage of them? These are all challenges to professionalism. In this chapter, after discussing what professionalism is, we examine ways of coping with such challenges.

Understanding Professionalism

If you want to succeed in selling travel, we noted in Chapter 7, you must meet or exceed your clients' expectations for service, and one of those expectations is that you will demonstrate professionalism. Thus, for those selling travel, professionalism is not a goal, but a requirement.

What is professionalism? A *professional* is a person who engages in an occupation that requires a specialized body of knowledge, but *professionalism* connotes something more. **Professionalism** requires not only that you master a specific body of knowledge, but also that you demonstrate a commitment to the standards of the occupation and to the interests of the client. Professionalism requires a willingness to give those standards and the client's interests priority over personal considerations.

What does this mean in practice? A professional must, first of all, have the knowledge and skills necessary to carry out the responsibilities of the job. On the job, a professional acts ethically. And at the least, a professional presents an image that reflects well on the occupation and on the employer. Let's take a closer look at each of these requirements, beginning with the last.

A Professional Image

Basically, a professional image is an image of competence. Dress, grooming, and manners create the image.

Dress and Grooming. Food-stained clothing. Unpolished shoes. Fly-away hair. Socks that don't match each other. An unraveled hem. Frayed cuffs. Wrinkled clothing. An unzipped fly. A missing button. Too much make-up. Too much jewelry. Obviously, these are all grooming gaffes that would make you look unprofessional.

To make a professional appearance, your clothing and hairstyle should be neat and clean. Skin, teeth, and nails must be clean. Your shoes should be scuff-free and well-heeled.

Are there other standards? When you visit your doctor's office, chances are your doctor will be wearing a white lab coat. If you go to court, the judge will be wearing a black gown and the lawyers will be dressed in business suits. What is the professional dress for travel offices today?

It depends. It depends on where the office is located: city, suburbs, rural, northeast, southwest, and so on. It depends on the type of travel sold in the office. It depends on the clients who come to the office: businesspeople in suits, or parents coming from the gym with kids in tow. Each office has its own style and customs. Some travel agencies, for example, require suits and ties; others may allow casual clothing like chinos and polo shirts with sneakers; still others require uniforms.

Even if the dress standards in your office are casual, though, more formal clothing is best for certain situations. In particular, dressing up is likely to be appropriate for meetings with clients and for industry functions such as trade shows. On fam trips, too, you should put yourself and your employer in the best light by avoiding outlandish or sloppy clothing and dressing appropriately.

Manners. Image is more than a matter of dress; how you act also shapes the impression you make. To appear professional, you should use a moderate tone of voice and good grammar and diction. Avoid street colloquialisms and profanities.

More generally, be courteous. People are tired of rude, insensitive, and aggressive behavior. *Etiquette*—the set of practices prescribed by social convention—is making a comeback. For professionals, it never really went out of style.

Being on time is one mark of courtesy. If you are running late, let the person know that fact and estimate how late you will be. You may have to reschedule. Always apologize for the delay. Try to allow for overruns of time when scheduling appointments. It is better to be early than to be late.

Introductions can be awkward. Here are a few guidelines on how to handle them:

- When a client comes into your office, you are in charge of the introduction.
- Always introduce the person with the position of greatest authority first.
- Say the names of both people, not just the

person being introduced. It sometimes helps to add a little information about the people being introduced. For example, "Mr. Stevens, I'd like you to meet Danny Banks, our new sales rep for Wonderful Cruises."

- If you find you do not remember a name, admit it. Say "I'm sorry, but I've forgotten your name."
- If someone forgets to introduce you, don't just stand there—introduce yourself! Say, "Hi, I don't believe we've met. I'm Diane Baker."
- As a sign of respect, always use the person's last name and title unless he or she tells you otherwise.

In most cultures today, the handshake is recognized as the standard greeting; so your handshake becomes the first message you send about yourself. Your handshake should be firm, but not bone-crushing. Stand up, extend your right hand and arm and aim for the web between thumb and forefinger. Make eye contact, smile, and shake hands firmly.

Ethical Requirements

Beyond the courteous behavior that is part of a professional image, professionalism also requires *ethical behavior,* which means following principles of proper conduct. Sometimes, the ethical choice is difficult to determine. (See the Selling through Service case on page 198.) No law prohibits many unethical behaviors. It is not illegal, for example, to tell a neighbor about a client's travel plans, but it is usually unethical.

One aid in determining the ethical course of action comes from the codes of ethics published by professional associations. Figure 8.1 shows two examples. Many professional associations ask their members to adhere to such published codes.

Basically, these codes assert that travel professionals should fulfill all legal, contractual, and moral obligations to all of those with whom they conduct business. These codes hold, for example, that it is unethical

- To use false or deceptive advertising practices.
- To undermine the integrity or public image of any member of the organization.

- To provide information that is factually inaccurate or to misrepresent services provided or to fail to advise clients of cancellation policies or service charges.

Often, though, no rule defines what should be done in a particular situation. Managers can help by establishing policies and giving advice that encourage ethical behavior, but some employers look instead for the shortcut to the quick buck. In a survey by *Travel Counselor* magazine of selected readers (*Travel Counselor,* October 1997, p. 16), 48 percent of the respondents said they had experienced a situation in which their personal code of ethics clashed with the practices or procedures of their agency employer.

For a great many situations, you can determine what is ethical only by thinking hard about a situation and consulting your own conscience. Ask yourself, To whom in the situation do you have legal, moral, or contractual obligations? In a particular case you might have such obligations to your employer, to a colleague, to a supplier, and above all to the client. Is the action you are considering fair? Is it just? Will it harm anyone?

There are ethical standards and ethical dilemmas in every aspect of business life. For example,

- Managers might be tempted to cheat an employee and the government by claiming that the person is an "independent contractor" rather than an employee—and thus avoid paying the company's share of the employee's Social Security taxes. (We describe the difference between independent contractors and employees in Chapter 9.)
- Travel counselors might be tempted to book reservations they have no intention of using so that they can cancel them at the last moment and make the space available to a client who wants an upgrade.
- Travel professionals of all stripes might be tempted to breach the confidentiality they owe clients or to allow friends to use their credentials to obtain discounts that are supposed to be available only to travel professionals.

Selling through Service

*Lure of the Laptop**

Matt stared at the phone. Where was everyone? He got up and walked to the coffeemaker, took a cup of coffee back to his desk, and sat down with a sigh. "Maybe I should catch up on some paperwork," he decided unhappily.

What he really wanted was for a client to call; in particular, someone who would need a rental car. The company Matt frequently recommended—call it Winning Car—was offering a laptop computer to travel agents who booked 75 clients in a month. Matt needs only one more booking to qualify, but it's almost 4:00 P.M. on the last day of the month.

When the phone finally rings, Matt is more than ready. At first, he thinks he's home free: the caller, Sheila Kelly, a frequent customer, does indeed need a rental car. Unfortunately, she wants to use a different rental company, not Winning Car. What should Matt say to her?

■ ■ ■

Matt might

1. Find some reason to tell Sheila that he can get her a car only through Winning Car.
2. Tell Sheila that the agency has always found Winning Car to be very dependable and helpful and that he believes she would be better off staying with them.
3. Do what Sheila wants and hope that another client asks for a car in the next hour.

---

*Based on Rebecca F. Sox, "Questions of Ethics," *Travel Life*, May/June 1989, p. 14.

4. Explain his situation to Sheila and ask if she really prefers a different company or would be willing to use Winning Car to help him out.

The first option is obviously unethical, but what about the others? Many suppliers offer prizes so that agents will notice their products. Is there any reason to resist the lure of these contests?

If you aim to be a professional, there just might be. A travel agency consultant from Round Rock, Texas, mentioned one possible problem to *Travel Life* magazine: giving bookings to one supplier in response to a contest might end up hindering your agency's efforts to meet the terms of an agreement with a different, preferred supplier. If that is the case, going for the prize could violate your implicit obligations to your employer or a supplier.

Even more obviously, the sponsor of a contest might be offering a good deal for you, but not good service for your client. In that case, your interest in the prize and your obligations to your client conflict.

Even when you can earn perks without doing anything unethical, contests and prizes may lead to unprofessional behavior. A thirty-year veteran with Continental Travel in Lexington, Kentucky, takes a strong view of these incentives. She told *Travel Life* magazine: "The majority of the time, the people taking advantage of [prizes] are new travel agents who don't know any better.... I sell the best rate for the client, not a book that will get me a prize. What client wants to work with an agent who wants his business so she can win a prize?" Do you agree?

Let's take a closer look at a few of the situations that very often create ethical problems for travel professionals and particularly for travel counselors.

Misrepresentation and Disclosure. Deceptive advertising is clearly unethical. Avoiding blatant lies is only a first step in creating ethical advertising. The facts in an advertisement should be

ASTA Code of Ethics

1. Accuracy. ASTA members will be factual and accurate when providing information about their services and the services of any firm they represent. They will not use deceptive practices.

2. Disclosure. ASTA members will provide in writing, upon written request, complete details about the cost, restrictions, and other terms and conditions of any travel service sold, including cancellation and service fee policies. Full details of the time, place, duration, and nature of any sales or promotional presentation the consumer will be required to attend in connection with his/her travel arrangements shall be disclosed in writing before any payment is accepted.

3. Responsiveness. ASTA members will promptly respond to their clients' complaints.

4. Refunds. ASTA members will remit any undisputed funds under their control within the specified time limit. Reasons for delay in providing funds will be given to the claimant promptly.

5. Cooperation. ASTA members will cooperate with any inquiry conducted by ASTA to resolve any dispute involving consumers or another member.

6. Confidences. ASTA members will not use improperly obtained client lists or other confidential information obtained from an employee's former employer.

7. Confidentiality. ASTA members will treat every client transaction confidentially and not disclose any information without permission of the client, unless required by law.

8. Affiliation. ASTA members will not falsely represent a person's affiliation with their firm.

9. Conflict of Interest. ASTA members will not allow any preferred relationship with a supplier to interfere with the interests of their clients.

10. Compliance. ASTA members shall abide by all federal, state and local laws and regulations.

11. Notice. ASTA members operating tours will promptly advise the agent or client who reserved the space of any change in itinerary, services, features or price. If substantial changes are made that are within the control of the operator, the client will be allowed to cancel without penalty.

12. Delivery. ASTA members operating tours will provide all components as stated in their brochure or written confirmation, or provide alternate services of equal or greater value, or provide appropriate compensation.

13. Credentials. An ASTA member shall not, in exchange for money or otherwise, provide travel agent credentials to any person as to whom there is no reasonable expectation that the person will engage in a bona fide effort to sell or manage the sale of travel services to the general public on behalf of the member through the period of validity of such credentials. This principle applies to the ASTA member and all affiliated or commonly controlled enterprises.

USTOA: Principles of Professional Conduct and Ethics

1. It is the responsibility of Active and Affiliated Active Tour Operator Members of the United States Tour Operators Association (USTOA) to conduct their business affairs forthrightly, with professional competence and factual accuracy.

2. Representations to the public and retailers shall be truthful, explicit, intelligible and avoid deception, and concealment or obscuring of material facts, conditions or requirements.

3. In advertising and quoting of prices for tours, the total deliverable price, including service charges and special charges, shall be stated or clearly and readily determinable; and the pendency of any known condition or contingency, such as fares subject to Conference and/or Government approval, shall be openly and noticeably disclosed.

4. Advertising and explanation of tour features shall clearly state and identify the facilities, accommodations and services included; any substitutions of features or deviation from the advertised tour shall be communicated expeditiously and the cause thereof be explained to agents and/or clients involved.

5. Each Active and Affiliate Active Tour Operator Member of USTOA shall so arrange and conduct its business as to instill retailer, consumer and public confidence in such Member's financial stability, reliability and integrity, and shall avoid any conduct or action conducive to discrediting membership in USTOA as signifying allegiance to professional and financial "Integrity in Tourism."

Figure 8.1 Codes of Ethics for Travel Professionals
Many travel organizations ask their members to adhere to a professional code of conduct. Here are two examples.
Source: Reprinted by permission of the American Society of Travel Agents and the United States Tour Operators Association.

clear and complete. And ethical companies do not "bait and switch"—they do not advertise services that are not available or that are so limited very few can obtain them.

Similarly, it is unethical for salespeople to misrepresent a product. The offense can come from what you do not say as well as from what you do: salespeople have a duty to disclose facts that the customer needs in order to make an informed decision. For example,

- Customers who are considering code-shared flights should be told if the airline operating a flight is different from the airline noted on the ticket.
- A client who is planning a trip to a resort that was recently plagued with violent crimes against tourists should be warned of that fact.
- A rental-car client who is contemplating the purchase of insurance that the client's credit card company already provides should be told that the purchase is unnecessary.

The fact that a client does not know enough to ask the right questions does not alter your responsibility to disclose vital information.

Selecting Suppliers.

More and more in recent years, travel agencies have established preferred supplier relationships; they depend on the overrides earned from preferred suppliers. As employees, travel counselors have a duty to try to sell the products of these preferred suppliers. But they also have a duty to meet the needs of their clients. Thus the stage is set for a conflict of interest.

Disclosure helps. Travel agencies should make lists of their preferred suppliers available to clients. This practice, however, does not eliminate the possibility of conflicting interests.

Ideally, the agency selects as preferred suppliers only companies that provide excellent value and service. Thus, in theory, by recommending preferred suppliers to their clients, travel counselors advance the interests of both their agency and their clients. In practice, however, selecting a preferred supplier might not be in the client's best interest in a particular situation. In that case, the travel counselor has an obligation to help the client select the supplier best suited to the client's needs.

Booking and Ticketing.

Sometimes the pressure to act unethically comes from clients themselves. To get the best deal for themselves, they ask salespeople to break the rules set by an airline or hotel or other supplier. For travel counselors, the most frequent examples include back-to-back ticketing, hidden-city ticketing, and doublebooking, which are explained in Table 8.1.

Suppose you are a travel counselor faced with a client who is asking you to engage in one of these unethical practices. If your obligation is to serve the client, why not do what the client asks? In fact, you also have an obligation to suppliers. As a travel counselor, you are contracted to sell suppliers' services according to their rules and regulations, and you must try to follow and enforce those rules. Certainly, you should not tell clients how to get around the regulations. If you do not agree with the suppliers' policies, you can steer clients elsewhere so long as it does not harm their interests. Clients who insist you act unethically are clients you do not want.

Professionalism through Education

In addition to a professional image and ethical behavior, professionalism requires a commitment to ongoing education and training. This commitment is also a keystone to success. Only if you keep up with changes and trends in the travel industry will you be able to provide knowledgeable and valuable service to your customers.

Many travel industry organizations—including CLIA, ASTA, NTA, and numerous tourist boards—offer educational opportunities for travel professionals. ICTA offers a certification program with two levels of recognition. The first level, Certified Travel Associate (CTA), is designed for those at an early stage in their travel careers; it focuses on core knowledge and practical skills. The second level, Certified Travel Counselor (CTC), represents the pinnacle of industry professionalism; it focuses on a broad range of business topics and personal skills. In Chapter 9 we further describe these and other opportunities for enhancing your skills in selling travel.

Table 8.1

Some Forbidden Practices in Ticketing and Reservations

Practice	Explanation	Example
Hidden-city ticketing	Booking a ticket with a connection when the traveler will actually end the trip at the connecting city	A traveler wants to go from City X to City Y but buys a ticket for a flight from City X to City Z with a connection at City Y—because the fare for a flight from X to Y is more than the fare for the flight from X to Z. The traveler actually ends the flight at Y.
Back-to-back ticketing	Booking two round-trip discount tickets and rearranging the departures and arrivals rather than buying one round-trip ticket at full fare	A client who wants to go from City X to City Y on Saturday morning and return on Sunday afternoon finds that no discount ticket is available for that schedule. So the client buys two discount round-trip tickets—which are cheaper than one round trip at full fare—and rearranges the arrivals and departures.
Doublebooking	Booking two reservations for an individual at the same time	A client who wants to fly to Boulder next weekend if it has fresh snow but otherwise wants to fly to New York asks for reservations for flights to both cities.

Time Out

Check your understanding of the discussion so far by completing the following statements.

1. Professionalism requires a willingness to give priority over personal considerations to both the standards of the profession and

   _____ .

2. Three marks of professionalism are a professional image,

   _____ ,

   and a commitment to continuing education.

3. Three of the behaviors prohibited by codes of ethics in the travel industry are

   (a) _____ ,

   (b) _____ ,

   and

   (c) _____ .

Dealing with Stress

Are any of these experiences familiar to you?

- Your body tenses and tightens up.
- You clench your jaw.
- Your pulse or blood pressure rises.
- Your eye twitches, or you suddenly realize that you're tapping the table or swinging your knee or making some other nervous gesture.
- Your breathing rate increases.
- You "see red."
- Your voice gets louder.
- Your thoughts become less coherent.
- You're queasy.

Chances are, you have experienced some, if not all, of these reactions when you start to feel "stressed out." Different people respond to stress in different ways, but this list indicates some of the most common reactions. Stress is not only in your mind; it brings definite physiological changes, which are summarized in Figure 8.2.

It is inevitable and even beneficial that people experience some stress. Stress can push people to work harder or to change how they work or how they live. But stress also pushes people into making mistakes, into losing their tempers, into worrying and wasting time, even into illness. It can be a major obstacle to your efforts to maintain professional standards. Thus, understanding both the causes of stress and ways to relieve it can help you stay on the path to professionalism.

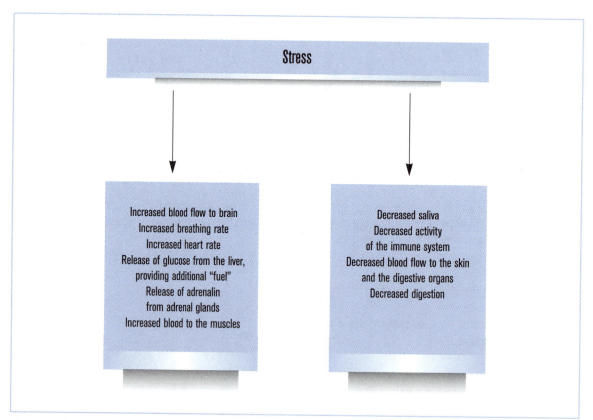

Figure 8.2 Physical Changes Associated with Stress
Experiencing stress on the job has physical and emotional implications.

What Causes Stress?

Sometimes stress results from uncomfortable physical conditions, such as poor working conditions. A crowded office, noise, smoke, poor ventilation—all of these can lead to feelings of stress. Sitting in front of a computer screen for seven or eight hours can strain both the body and the eyes. Cradling a telephone on your shoulder can create a pain in the neck, literally. Add these up, and at the end of the day you might be ready to scream.

In addition to physical conditions like these, conflicts or frustrations may also bring on stress. Disputes with fellow workers or supervisors, angry customers, and just daily hassles can all be stressful. Little frustrations—if the computer is down, or there is no room at the hotel for your best customer, or reservations are lost—all add up.

Probably the most frequent cause of workplace stress is lack of time. While you are talking to one customer, other customers walk in and you must see to their needs; then the phone rings, or a colleague comes by with a question.

Tips
Steps for Managing Stress

Stress is as inevitable as taxes, and it can bring benefits if you control its effects. To manage stress,

1. Watch for early warnings that you are experiencing stress.
2. Try to determine the cause of the stress.
3. Eliminate the source of the stress if that is desirable and possible.
4. If the source of the stress is not eliminated, try to relieve its consequences by applying relaxation techniques, exercising regularly, and applying time-management techniques.

By the end of the day, you wonder where all the time has gone as you look at your desk piled high with unfinished work.

Can You Eliminate Stress?

So how do you manage stress? How do you take control of it, rather than letting stress control you?

First, be aware of early signs that you are becoming stressed (like the symptoms on page 202). Second, analyze the source of the stress. Is it something you can change, or should you instead try to change your reaction to it?

Sometimes, you may be able to root out the source of stress. Perhaps a frank conversation can smooth out a personality conflict. Perhaps you can negotiate a change in your workload. If long hours on the computer are creating tension in your body, try to have ergonomically designed chairs, handrests, and footrests, as well as glare reducers on your computer screen. If you spend lots of time on the telephone, try working with a headset rather than a handset; the headset will free up your hands as well as straighten out your neck.

Often, you cannot eliminate the source of stress, but you can alter your response to it, reducing the physical and psychological consequences. One key method is relaxation. For example, if you usually clench your jaw as you begin to feel stress, take a deep breath or yawn whenever you feel yourself tighten up. Leave your office during your lunch break or take short breaks while you are working just to flex and stretch. Deep breathing, neck rolls, stretches, and isometric exercises can all help you cope with daily stress.

Techniques for mental relaxation can help, too. Close your eyes, relax your body, picture your ideal vacation spot, and see yourself there. Placing pictures of favorite people or places on your desk or wall can also help you relax.

Also, make time in your life for regular exercise. Whether it is a workout at a health club or a twenty-minute walk several times a week, a regular schedule of exercise can help you prevent or at least allay feelings of stress.

Finally, one of the most important ways of reducing workplace stress is by developing good techniques of time management. These are worth a closer look.

Managing Your Time

No matter who you are, the president of a large corporation or the person who delivers tickets for a travel agency, you have the same amount of time per day—24 hours. And you have seven 24-hour days per week. No one can grant you any more time than those 168 hours per week. So why does it seem that some people complete all their tasks and have time to spare, and others do not have time to breathe?

The secret is the ability to manage the time you have. If you learn to manage your time well, you can decrease stress, increase your productivity, and raise your feeling of competency. Let's look at a few basic tools and habits that can help you gain greater control over your time.

Time Logs

Do you know where your time goes? Most people say they don't know, that all they know is that there is never enough time. The first step in successful time management is to know how your time is spent each day. Try keeping a **time log,** a record of what you do and how long it takes you to do it. Figure 8.3 shows an example.

Keep a time log for a one- to two-week period. Every fifteen minutes, put down in your log what you are doing at that moment. At the end of the logging period you will be able to identify what your habits are and where your time is being wasted.

A time log can also help you identify your most productive times of the day. Are you a morning, afternoon, or evening person? Your time log should indicate when you get most of your work done.

Try keeping a time log at least twice a year. That should keep you on track and on top of your "time wasters."

"To Do" Lists and Calendars

Most successful people keep daily "to do" lists. Set aside five minutes at the end of your day to list the things you should do the next day. Write them down, and then arrange them by priority. A good system is the *A-B-C method:*

- Anything labeled "A" is something that needs your "*a*ttention now." This must get done today.
- "B" items are those that can "*be* done later, if need be." They can be postponed, but not for long.
- Tasks that fall into the "C" category are those that "*c*an wait." They may eventually become "B" or even "A" tasks.

Within each category of A-B-C, arrange each task according to its priority.

Often you will find that the "A" tasks are the most difficult and time-consuming. These are the tasks that you might tend to put off doing, thereby perpetuating the cycle of wasted time and procrastination. Do not be tempted to do your "C" items first because they are easy and quick. Complete the "A"s, then the "B"s, and finally the "C"s. Those "B" and "C" items that you do not get to do today will eventually become "A"s or drop off your list completely.

If you use this method to plan your day, you will be able to do those things that must get done during your most productive hours. You will be able to accomplish much more in a day, thereby giving you better control of your time.

As another aid in time management, try keeping a daily calendar. Make a note of project-due dates, important meetings, and the like.

Many people like to use a Day-Timer, Day-Runner, or Filo-Fax (on computer or paper) to keep everything in one central location. These "organizers" have calendars, daily to-do lists, telephone and address books, expense and mileage logs, and many other features that help you manage your time more effectively.

Other Time Savers

Yet another time-management tool is named

Your Time Log: Week of _____

Time	Mon	Tues	Wed	Thurs	Fri	Sat	Sun	Activity	Total hours
6:00 – 6:15 A.M.								**Business:**	
6:15 – 6:30								1. Commuting	
6:30 – 6:45								2. Air travel	
6:45 – 7:00								3. Car travel	
7:00 – 7:15								4. Miscellaneous travel	
7:15 – 7:30								5. Telephone/outgoing	
7:30 – 7:45								6. Telephone/incoming	
7:45 – 8:00								7. Staff meetings	
8:00 – 8:15								8. Training	
8:15 – 8:30								9. Meetings with subordinates	
8:30 – 8:45								10. Meetings with supervisor	
8:45 – 9:00								11. Meetings with colleagues	
9:00 – 9:15								12. Meetings with outsiders	
9:15 – 9:30								13. Reading/analysis	
9:30 – 9:45								14. Writing memos, letters	
9:45 – 10:00								15. Preparing documents	
10:00 – 10:15								16. Planning/analysis	
10:15 – 10:30								17. Visiting clients	
10:30 – 10:45								18. Lunch	
10:45 – 11:00								19. Dinner	
11:00 – 11:15								20. Accounting	
11:15 – 11:30								21. Filing/organizing	
11:30 – 11:45								22. Miscellaneous	
11:45 – 12:00									
Noon – 12:15								**Personal:**	
12:15 – 12:30								23. Sleeping	
12:30 – 12:45								24. Meals	
12:45 – 1:00								25. Grooming	
1:00 – 1:15								26. Exercise	
1:15 – 1:30								27. Errands	
1:30 – 1:45								28. Accounting	
1:45 – 2:00								29. Cooking	
2:00 – 2:15								30. Cleaning	
2:15 – 2:30								31. Laundry	
2:30 – 2:45								32. Family	
2:45 – 3:00								33. Child care	
3:00 – 3:15								34. Outings	
3:15 – 3:30								35. TV, VCR	
3:30 – 3:45								36. Reading	
3:45 – 4:00								37. Socializing	
4:00 – 4:15								38. Study	
4:15 – 4:30								39. Events	
4:30 – 4:45								40. Church	
4:45 – 5:00								41. Hobbies	
5:00 – 5:15								42. Miscellaneous	
5:15 – 5:30									
5:30 – 5:45									
5:45 – 6:00									

Figure 8.3 A Time Log
Using a time log such as this one can help you identify how you spend your time during the day.
Source: Reprinted from Marc Mancini, Time Management (New York: Irwin, 1994). (c) Richard D. Irwin, Inc., 1994.

after an old method of keeping people awake during church services. If someone was nodding off during the service, an elder would come around with a large feather and "tickle" the person awake. ***Tickler files*** are files that remind you to do something; they help you to stay awake and on top of things.

Tickler files can take several forms, from file cards set up in a monthly and daily file drawer; to a yearly calendar with room to note all appointments, events, payments, and projects; to a special file on your computer. The queue system on CRSs, which reminds you of ticketing dates, is another form of a tickler file.

Here are some other time-saving tips:

- If you procrastinate when you are faced with a large project, divide it into a series of smaller tasks. For example, thinking about researching, preparing, and presenting a complicated plan for a custom-designed tour

can be intimidating. But if you look at the plan as a series of smaller jobs and tackle each part of it individually, then the job becomes manageable.

- When you are reading or talking on the telephone, stand up. Both activities will take less time if you are standing.

- Whenever possible, plan your errands in advance and group them together. For example, go to the cleaners, the bank, and the post office in one trip rather than three.

- Make use of the time you spend standing in line or waiting for an appointment. Bring your own reading to the doctor's office rather than reading the magazines in the waiting room.

Finally, most people waste time because they are overwhelmed by the flow of paper. In the next section we look at some advice for handling paper, and hence your time, more efficiently.

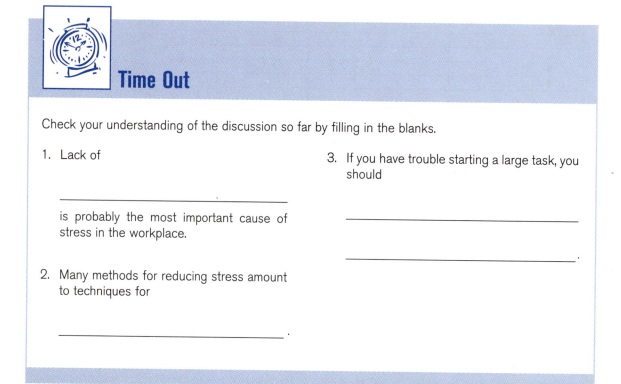

Time Out

Check your understanding of the discussion so far by filling in the blanks.

1. Lack of

   _____

   is probably the most important cause of stress in the workplace.

2. Many methods for reducing stress amount to techniques for

   _____ .

3. If you have trouble starting a large task, you should

   _____

   _____ .

Controlling the Flow of Paper

When computerized systems entered the workplace, many predicted that the office of the future would be a paperless workplace. But reality tells a different story. In many offices, there is more paper today than ever before. These mountains of paper are likely to be a major obstacle to your efforts to manage your time.

Is there a solution? According to one popular maxim, you should never handle a piece of paper more than once. That is easier said than done, but here are some ways to reduce the time spent shuffling papers.

- When you receive mail or a memo, determine immediately which of three things you will do with it: (1) read the paper and then toss it out; (2) read the paper and act on it immediately; or (3) read the paper and file it for future reference.
- If you feel uncomfortable about throwing out certain papers, create a "maybe" file for papers to be looked at later.
- Try answering routine correspondence and memos on the original; then make a copy for

yourself and send the original back to the sender.

No matter how ruthlessly you throw things out, you still need an efficient method of keeping some documents. You need to file them so they are readily accessible when you want them. Thus, different types of documents are best filed by different systems. In a travel agency, for example,

- Destination information is usually filed geographically.
- Brochures may be filed geographically or by subject. Cruises, tour packages, and hotels may be grouped by subject and then further classified by region.
- Accountable documents such as tickets, invoices, and checks may be filed numerically.
- Customer records are usually filed alphabetically, although they may also be filed chronologically by date of departure.
- Completed ARC (Airlines Reporting Corporation) reports are filed chronologically.

Chapter Wrap-Up

Chapter Highlights

In today's very competitive travel industry, professionalism may be the characteristic that differentiates one company from another. In this chapter we have examined both what professionalism is and how to deal with common obstacles to maintaining your professionalism on the job. Here is a review of the objectives with which we began.

1. **Identify key characteristics of professionalism.** A professional is someone who engages in an occupation that requires a

specialized body of knowledge, but professionalism also implies a commitment to the standards of the occupation and to the interests of the client. Thus, in addition to knowledge and skill, professionalism requires (a) a professional image, which is projected through dress, grooming, and manners; (b) adherence to a code of ethics, and (c) a commitment to continuing education and training.

2. **Discuss how to make ethical choices as a travel professional.** One step toward acting ethically is to be familiar with and follow

the ethical codes of professional travel associations such as ASTA. Owners and managers sometimes help employees by establishing policies that encourage ethical behavior, but not all companies favor ethical conduct. In any event, neither these policies nor published codes of behavior are likely to cover every situation a travel professional encounters. To make ethical choices, travel professionals also need to understand their legal, moral, and contractual obligations to those they do business with—their employers, colleagues, suppliers, and clients. Travel professionals need to evaluate the situation with these obligations in mind and to examine their consciences to decide whether the proposed action is just, fair, or likely to hurt someone. Basic ethical obligations include maintaining confidentiality and providing complete and accurate information about services provided.

3. **Describe some simple ways of relieving stress.** Sometimes the source of stress can be eliminated; for example, changes in furniture or other equipment may end certain causes of physical stress. When the source of stress cannot be eliminated, its effects can be reduced by taking "mental vacations," by practicing other relaxation techniques, by exercising regularly, and by managing time more effectively.

4. **Explain some tools and methods for managing your time more effectively.** Keeping a time log is a first step in time management. Time logs are especially helpful for identifying both time wasters and productive periods. Using "to do" lists organized by the A-B-C method helps ensure that the most important tasks are performed. Calendars and tickler files make it easy to keep track of what needs to be done. To overcome procrastination, breaking large jobs into a series of smaller tasks is a tried-and-true method.

5. **Outline ways to control the flow of paper.** Papers should be categorized as soon as they are received into those that should be tossed out, acted on, or filed. Answers to some correspondence can be given on the original. Papers that are kept should be filed according to a system that takes into account how they are used and makes their retrieval easy.

New terms. The terms that follow were introduced in this chapter. If you do not recall their definitions, see the Glossary, which begins on page 237.

professionalism   time log
tickler files

Review Exercises

Check-Up

Give yourself a quick test of your memory of a few basic points. Read each of the following statements and indicate whether it is true (T) or false (F). See the answers below the statements.

T   F   1. A commitment to success is the hallmark of professionals.

T   F   2. Physiological changes accompany stress.

T   F   3. To save time, you should tackle the easiest tasks first.

T   F   4. Depending on the type of material they contain, filing systems arranged geographically, by subject, alphabetically, numerically, or chronologically may be appropriate.

T   F   5. Failing to tell clients that they will face a service charge is unethical.

Answers: 1. F, 2. T, 3. F, 4. T, 5. T

Discussion Questions

1. **Assessing Your Professionalism.** Complete Worksheet 8.1 to determine your self-image as a travel industry professional.

2. **The A-B-C Method of Time Management: A Practice Exercise.** Here is a sample "to do" list for a travel counselor.

   Today is: Monday, January 17, 1999

   _____ File tour brochures that arrived last week.

   _____ Order hotel brochure for clients departing 1/31.

   _____ Order special meal for Mike M. departing AA # 450 on 1/21.

   _____ Check lowest available airfare for M/M Johansson's trip to PR in March.

   _____ Send Dana P.'s passport for Vietnam entry visa (August departure).

   _____ Order bon voyage gift for M/M Offenbach's Carib. cruise (dep. 1/30 MIA).

   _____ Send documents to P. Christopher for June honeymoon.

   _____ Write Pleasure Inn to complain of filthy accommodations. (M/M Cushing checked out 1/10.)

   _____ Submit weekly time sheet (due last Friday).

   _____ Submit FAM trip report (3-day Bahamas cruise, Jan. 7-9).

   _____ Submit expense report for same FAM.

   _____ Request vacation time to attend Gina's wedding next month.

a. Use the A-B-C method and assign priorities by labeling each item A, B, or C. (Remember, anything labeled "A" needs your "attention now." "B" items can "be done later, if need be." Tasks that fall into the "C" category "can wait" without creating too much adversity.)

b. List and number all "A" items in priority of what needs to be done first, second, third, etc.

_____

_____

_____

_____

_____

c. List and number all "B" items in priority of what needs to be done first, second, third, etc.

_____

_____

_____

_____

_____

d. List and number all "C" items in priority of what needs to be done first, second, third, etc.

_____

_____

_____

_____

_____

3. **Evaluating Ethical Choices.** Recall a situation in which you faced an ethical challenge.

   a. What was the issue, what were your options, and how did you resolve the situation?

   _____

   _____

   _____

   _____

   _____

   b. Were there any consequences to your solution?

   _____

   _____

   _____

   c. Faced with a similar situation in the future, would you try to respond differently?

   _____

      Why or why not?

   _____

   _____

   _____

   _____

   _____

4. **An Ethical Challenge.** What would you say to a friend who wanted to use your professional credentials in order to obtain a special fare?

   _____

   _____

   _____

   _____

A Case in Question

1. Look again at the "Lure of the Laptop" case (page 198). Suppose that Winning Car is a winner, a good supplier for Matt's client and agency. What would you tell him to say?

_____

_____

_____

_____

2. What points in the professional codes of ethics in Figure 8.1 relate to Matt's situation in this case?

_____

_____

_____

Exercises in Selling

1. **Clients, Suppliers, and Ethical Choices.** Marty Howard, a long-time client of ABC Travel, is sitting across from you at your desk. She needs a ticket for midweek travel from Washington, D.C., to Dallas and back next week. The fare you quoted sent her into semishock. "That's ridiculous!" she tells you, "Last month Sybil got me a great deal. I just bought a ticket from D.C. to Albuquerque and got off the plane when it stopped in Dallas."

   What Marty is implying is that you should issue her a ticket that takes advantage of "hidden city" price breaks. The airline charges less for a flight from D.C. to Albuquerque that makes a stop at Dallas than for a flight from D.C. to Dallas. Issuing the D.C.–Albuquerque ticket to a passenger headed to Dallas amounts to deception of the airline. That is unethical and may even be illegal. But Marty is a loyal client. How do you respond?

   Form teams of two persons and assign one person to play the travel counselor and one to play the role of Marty. Role-play the situation for 5-10 minutes. The remainder of the class should then critique it.

2. **More Ethical Choices.** Form teams of two persons and assign one person to play the travel counselor and one to play the client, Brian Elliot, who is making a trip on which his flight departs during a peak travel time. Role-play the following situation for 5–10 minutes and then discuss it.

   - *Brian Elliot.* You have a meeting just an hour and a half before your departing flight, and you're not sure you can get to the airport on time. You ask the travel counselor to arrange a second reservation on the next flight just in case.

   - *Travel counselor.* Mr. Elliot is an important client to you and your company, but doing what he wants would be a case of doublebooking. What do you say to him?

Worksheet 8.1

Assessing Your Professionalism

To assess your professionalism, read each statement and circle the response that best describes your attitude and behavior. You may want to duplicate this form before writing on it and then assess yourself again in the future.

	Always	Sometimes	Never
1. I dress appropriately for my work environment.	5	3	1
2. I am well-groomed every day.	5	3	1
3. I speak in a pleasant tone of voice.	5	3	1
4. I am careful about the words I use when speaking with customers.	5	3	1
5. I focus on the customer's needs and wants before my own.	5	3	1
6. I would not push a product on a customer just to make a sale.	5	3	1
7. I do whatever my customer asks me to do, even if it is unethical.	5	3	1
8. I attend as many educational events as I can to increase my professionalism.	5	3	1

Total Points _____

Scoring Guide

- If your score is 30–40, you possess a professional attitude.

- If your score is 20–29, you have some professional qualities but could improve in some areas.

- If your score is 19 or less, you have lots of room for improvement.

Identify your weak areas and begin to work on them.

Building Sales and Marketing Skills for the Future

Objectives

After reading this chapter, you should be able to

1. Describe some of the forces and trends that are reshaping the travel industry.

2. Identify at least four ways in which travel agencies are adapting to changes in the travel market.

3. Outline a plan for enhancing your skills and staying current with changes in the travel industry.

Preview

A century ago, who would have thought that people would be able to fly from city to city, let alone to the moon? Fifty years ago, who would have thought that people would be sitting in their living rooms watching movies and sports events beamed in via satellite and cable? And twenty years ago, who would have predicted that Las Vegas would become a family attraction or that millions would flock to sleepy Branson, Missouri? Change is inevitable. If you are prepared to deal with it, you can transform it into an exciting opportunity.

What will travel look like in the future? We don't know. But recognizing the changes that are underway now can help prepare you to adapt to whatever the future brings. What trends seem to be shaping the travel market? How do they affect travel sellers, and what can you do to prepare for a changing workplace? These are some of the questions we address in this chapter.

*T*he Travel Market in the Twenty-First Century

No matter how you look at it—by total dollars spent on travel, numbers of people employed in the industry, or volume of travelers worldwide—travel and tourism is a growing industry (see Figure 9.1). In 1996

- The world's scheduled airlines carried 1.34 billion passengers.
- International arrivals in the United States exceeded 46 million.
- Total expenditures for tourism in the United States rose to $447.7 billion.
- The U.S. travel and tourism industry generated more than 11 percent of U.S. employment.
- Worldwide, travel and tourism provided jobs for more than 230 million people.

What determines whether and how the travel market will continue to grow? Where can you look to understand how the travel market might change?

Some Driving Forces

A multitude of social and political forces influences the travel industry. Improvements in transportation or other technology may open up new travel possibilities. Political unrest, outbreaks of disease, strikes, or natural disasters may halt travel and tourism in a particular area. A local tourism business may be jolted both by global forces (such as a worldwide recession) or by very local ones (such as a hurricane). Fashion makes the future even more unpredictable. Popularity may come and go for certain destinations, activities, and types of accommodations.

Changes in the economy can have a very direct effect on the amount of travel. Business growth brings increased corporate travel; rising incomes bring more leisure travel. Changes in rates of inflation, currency exchange rates, or energy prices may push travel up or down.

Current indicators point to continued growth in travel. Worldwide, travel is expected to triple over the coming decade, and the number of people traveling for pleasure each year is expected to exceed one *billion*. All of this is

good news for anyone interested in pursuing a career in travel and tourism.

Forecasts, however, are chancy. In 1998 economic crises were unsettling much of the world, but the United States was experiencing its best economic times in years. Most predictions call for continued economic growth in the United States over the next decade, but there are no guarantees. A falling stock market or rising energy prices could produce economic shock waves that would also reverse the outlook for the travel industry.

Trends among Travelers

The picture of the coming travel market looks a little clearer if we narrow the focus and examine travelers themselves. Who is it that is likely to have the time, money, and inclination to travel? Demographic trends in the overall population suggest part of the answer.

Demographic Characteristics. If you could take a snapshot of everyone in the American market,

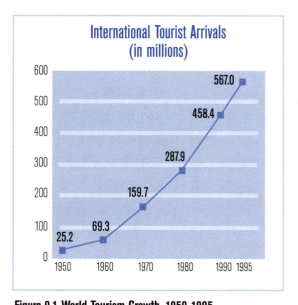

Figure 9.1 World Tourism Growth, 1950-1995
Around the world, travel and tourism has soared. It has become the fastest growing sector of the global economy.
Source: Data from World Tourism Organization (WTO)

what would it look like? For several years, two characteristics have dominated any portrait of the American population: the average age was rising, and a disproportionate number were born between 1946 and 1964, a generation known as the *babyboomers*.

These demographic characteristics helped shape the travel market in the past decade. Because of the growing number of travelers who were over 65, demand picked up for tour packages and for features that promised safety and security. As the babyboomers reached adulthood and acquired the money for travel in the 1980s and 1990s, the travel industry appealed to them with spa vacations, adventure travel, and sports-oriented programs.

In the coming decades, improved health habits and medical care should help Americans stay active longer; at the same time, as a group, people over 65 are relatively wealthy. In short, many older Americans are likely to have the money and health that will allow them to travel. Meanwhile, babyboomers will reach their 40s, 50s, and early 60s during the next decade. These are traditionally the years when people make their highest earnings; they are also prime travel years.

Thus, older Americans and babyboomers are likely to continue to shape the marketplace. Their ability to travel and their interest in doing so should help fuel continued growth for the industry, and their tastes will play a large role in determining which travel products succeed.

One Forecast. Beyond their demographic characteristics, is there anything else we can say about the people who are likely to make up the travel market in the near future? Two current trends suggest some likely answers.

First, if the economy continues to grow, the number of people traveling on business and attending meetings is likely to grow. Instead of decreasing the need for travel, e-mail and the Web may stimulate it, as businesspeople want to meet face to face with the ever-growing number of people they encounter in cyberspace.

Second, if economic gains continue to be distributed as they were in the mid-1990s, then growth in leisure travel is likely to come mostly among upper-income Americans. This trend shows up in extensive data collected by Plog Research on what people are buying from trav-

el agencies: international bookings are rising, and leisure travelers are moving a bit upscale in their choice of accommodations.

Consultant Harry S. Dent, Jr., suggests this picture of what the traveling population will be like in coming years:

> Conventions and meetings are only going to increase. . . . and so is high-end travel. The rich are getting richer. The top 20 percent of people in this country are running away with almost all the wealth. . . . For people worth millions of dollars . . . like me, time is very critical. . . . And we're not price sensitive. . . . You have to select which markets are going to add more value, and be a part of that. (*Travel Counselor,* December 1997, pp. 27-28.)

Time Out

Check your understanding of the discussion so far by filling in the blanks.

1. Among the forces that shape the prosperity of the travel industry are

   _____.

2. _____

   and

   _____,

   are two age groups that are likely to dominate the travel market.

3. Senior citizens are likely to be especially concerned with the

   _____

   of their travel arrangements.

Travel Marketing and Tomorrow's Workplace

More striking than trends in the travel market are the changes going on in how travel is marketed and sold. No trend has generated more excitement or more fear than the automation of travel selling, but the job of travel sellers is being reshaped by other forces as well.

The Outlook for On-Line Travel Sales

Is face-to-face selling about to become obsolete? Will commerce in cyberspace take over? That seems unlikely. But on-line sales are headed upward. Travel sellers who do not stay on the cutting edge of new technologies risk being left behind in the dust of the past.

There are many reasons to expect that on-line sales will rise. In April 1998 the Commerce Department reported that traffic on the Internet was doubling every hundred days. By 2002, the number of on-line PC users is expected to quadruple. As time goes on, a larger percentage of American travelers will have little resistance to using computers for all sorts of tasks.

Of course, predictions vary regarding just how high on-line sales will go. One respected market research firm, Jupiter Communications, predicts that by 2002 a little more than 8 percent of airline sales will occur on-line, along with 5 to 8 percent of the sales of hotels, rental cars, and cruises. After that, the move to on-line sales may accelerate. New technologies often move into the marketplace slowly at first, but once a new way of doing things is adopted by many people, the pace of acceptance usually picks up rapidly. Thus, one research firm predicts that, ultimately, 20 to 40 percent of travel sales will move on-line.

The Four *Ps* and the Changing Travel Agency

On-line sales are only one of the challenges travel agencies have faced in recent years.

Stanley Plog observes, "Consumers now can buy travel at . . . discount stores, at banks and S&Ls, through offers they receive by mail, by calling toll-free telephone numbers advertised on radio or TV, or through hundreds of sites on the Web" (*ASTA Agency Management,* October 1997, pp. 12-13). On top of all of this new competition, travel agencies have also faced new airline policies that reduced commissions on airline sales.

As one way of responding to these economic pressures, some agencies have joined forces. The number of traditional one-location agencies is declining. More agencies have become part of chains. Many have joined *cooperatives* (such as GIANTS), *consortia* (such as GEM), or *franchises* (such as UNIGLOBE); these are all associations of travel agencies in which the agencies pool their resources for purposes such as marketing and training.

More generally, responding to changes in the marketplace is the job of marketing. Recall from Chapter 1 that marketing begins with market research and continues with a marketing plan that formulates decisions about the marketing mix. The four *Ps*—decisions about product, place, price, and promotion—form the core of the marketing mix. (To review these concepts, look again at Figure 1.2, page 5.) For each of the four *Ps*, travel agencies have been making changes to adjust to today's marketplace. Let's look briefly at trends in how travel agencies are handling each of them.

Product and Price. Increasingly, travel agencies have heeded the call of specialization. Agencies may specialize in a particular niche market (family vacations, mature travelers, adventure travel, ecotourism, and so on) or in an area like meeting planning or incentive travel.

Agencies also appear to be changing which products they emphasize in their product mix. In a 1997 study by Plog Research, sales of airline tickets and of budget and economy hotel rooms were down as a percentage of total agency sales; meanwhile, car rentals, packaged tours, international travel, and midpriced hotels were up. These trends suggest a broader pattern: travel agencies were selling more of those products on which they can make money. As the airlines drop the commissions they pay on airline tickets sold by travel agencies, agencies seem to be emphasizing products on which they can make better commissions.

Travel agencies are also trying another response to dwindling commissions: they are looking to fees as an alternative source of revenue. They might, for example, charge a fee for each transaction, such as a fee for each ticket issued, or a fee for the time they spend consulting with a client. Travel agencies long feared that leisure travelers would not be willing to pay for their services. But clients' reactions to fees are likely to depend on what they get for their money, as Figure 9.2 suggests.

Place: Home-Based Agents and the Web. The challenges of today's travel market are even affecting where travel sellers work. These days, travel agencies rely less on the conventional "brick and mortar" agency. A few depend on sales over the Web rather than walk-in traffic to storefront locations; more rely on a mix of walk-in, telephone, and Web-based sales. And many agencies now recruit home-based independent contractors.

Is this a path you'd like to take? Becoming an independent contractor offers the promise of greater freedom and the satisfaction of working for yourself. But there are also many possible pitfalls (the Selling through Service case on page 220 describes one example). Starting up your own business, however small, requires an investment of time and money. You will need to check the laws in your state regarding the sale of travel. You must make sure that your contracts are clear. You should be prepared to lose the motivational and emotional support, as well as the economic security, that good colleagues and a position with a secure company can bring. Instead of learning about changes in the industry through daily chats with your co-workers, you will have to make an extra effort to stay in touch.

For businesses, hiring independent contractors offers a way of saving money. Depending on their arrangements with the contractors, businesses may escape a host of expenses—for office space, desks, phones, electricity, and so on, as well as for insurance, pensions, vacation time,

and other benefits. Depending on state and local laws, they might be spared the cost of contributing to workers' compensation and unemployment funds. And they will save the expense of contributing the employer's share of Social Security taxes for independent contractors.

In fact, these tax savings have motivated employers in many industries to turn to independent contractors. Some businesses have tried

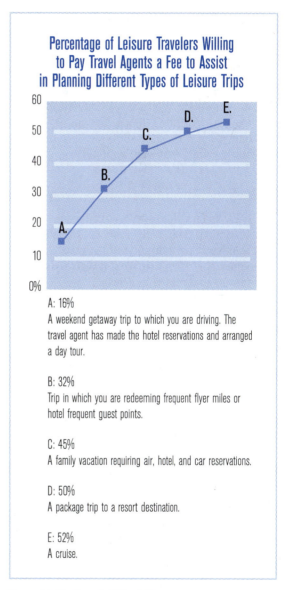

A: 16%
A weekend getaway trip to which you are driving. The travel agent has made the hotel reservations and arranged a day tour.

B: 32%
Trip in which you are redeeming frequent flyer miles or hotel frequent guest points.

C: 45%
A family vacation requiring air, hotel, and car reservations.

D: 50%
A package trip to a resort destination.

E: 52%
A cruise.

Figure 9.2 The Acceptability of Fees
Are leisure travelers willing to pay travel counselors a fee for help in planning trips? The answer depends in part on the type of trip involved, as the survey results shown here indicate.
Source: TTG's Path to Consumer Loyalty & Service Fees Study, 1997

The Hole in the Net

Fran Goodrich is in trouble. Four months ago, she opened her own home-based, cruise-only shop with a site on the Web. She spent $2,800 for her computer and printer and paid a consultant $800 to create her five-page Web site, complete with photos. She also pays the consultant a $10 monthly "maintenance fee," and she owes $20 a month for her access fee to an Internet service provider.

What does she have to show for her investment? So far, she has had 300 e-mail inquiries, and answering them has amounted to a full-time job. But she's made just four sales, for commissions of just $800. At this rate, she can't survive. What went wrong?

■ ■ ■

By itself, a Web site is not a business, and a site doesn't sell itself. Fran concluded that a business could not survive if it could get customers only from the Web; it would also need referrals and repeat business.

Contrast Fran's experience with the story of a cruise agency in Charlotte. It opened in 1991, and in the spring of 1997 it set up a Web site.

Within months it hired a dozen new employees to handle the increased business. Its owner told *Travel Agent* magazine (December 8, 1997, p. 46):

> The key to the Internet is putting salesmanship first. . . . The Internet is really just a way of generating leads, but you still have to have the skills to close the sale. You've got to have the staff to do it, and the staff has to give the client that warm and fuzzy feeling. . . . Our company was growing significantly before the Internet, but at a much slower rate. What the Internet did is put us into overdrive.

Perhaps Fran counted too much on the wonders of the Web. As Matthew Upchurch, CTC, the managing principal of API Travel Consultants, noted, "In many segments of travel sales, technology combined with the human touch can be far more powerful than technology alone. Those travel consultants who strike the balance between the two will be successful in the future" (personal communication).

to pass employees off as independent contractors, only to be caught as tax cheats by the IRS. What's the difference? For tax and other legal purposes, the distinction between employees and independent contractors can get complicated. Basically, though, you are an independent contractor only if you, not the company, decides when, where, and how you work, and if you are free to work for whomever you choose.

Promotion. So far, we have seen how travel agencies have responded to a challenging market by changes in three elements of the marketing mix—product, price, and place. What about the fourth *P*—promotion?

Many travel counselors, especially in smaller agencies, help plan and execute promotional campaigns. They may help organize cruise nights, write press releases, or place ads in local media. Table 9.1 gives examples of low-cost ways of getting an agency's name and message in front of the public.

New technology and financial pressures, however, have raised the bar for promotional campaigns. Consumers are accustomed to a flood of attractive, sophisticated advertising coming at them from everywhere—the mailbox, the television, the computer screen. To get their message through, many travel agencies are using the help available from associations such

Table 9.1
Low-Cost Promotion

Method	Example
Booklets	Publish your own "How to Save Money on Your Next Vacation" booklet.
Bouncebacks— repeat-business incentives	Coupons,. special offers, or announcements of events or programs can be produced on the back of receipts, enclosed in ticket jackets, or sent with brochures.
Cross-promotions with noncompeting companies	Ask the owners of bridal shops, sporting goods stores, dive shops, luggage stores, bookstores, etc., if they would be willing to distribute coupons for your travel agency if you do the same for them.
Clubs	Start a "getaway-of-the-month" club, offering your customers a new tour or weekend resort package each month.
Endorsements	Ask a local radio personality or entertainer to serve as your spokesperson.
Sponsorships	Offer a modest underwriting fee or goods or services to help defray the expenses for sporting events, charitable events, tournaments, fairs, or other public events.
Stuffers	Enclose promotional material in everything you send out.

Source: Based on Martha Fink, CTC, "Five Simple Steps to Developing a Marketing Plan," *Travel Counselor,* September 1993, p. 42.

as ASTA and consortia. For example, agencies can distribute newsletters produced by these groups, perhaps adding their own customized content. Agencies themselves are also putting the new technology to work in their promotional campaigns. For example, some agencies produce their own professional-looking newsletters and other mailings with desktop publishing software. And they are using the database software described in Chapter 6 to target their campaigns.

Web sites, of course, represent the key new tool for promoting agencies. But agencies have learned that a Web site by itself does not sell an agency. You need to be sure the Web site is listed with search engines, and you need to advertise the site as part of a total promotional campaign. For example, you might ask sponsors of other Web sites, especially your suppliers, to place a link from their site to yours. Lynn Hoban, vice president of the advertising agency Earle Palmer Brown, suggests promoting a Web site by

- Putting the Web site address on everything you can think of—envelopes, mailers, business cards, letterhead, Yellow Pages ads, and so on.
- Sending out postcards announcing the Web site and its address.
- Advertising the Web site in the agency's newsletter.

The Role of the Salesperson. Person-to-person selling is also a part of the promotional mix. But if people can go on-line for information about travel and can even book themselves on-line, does personal selling have a future in the travel industry? What is the role of travel counselors to be?

Many travelers will still want and need the advice of professional travel counselors. Few consumers are willing to spend thousands of dollars on travel without consulting a professional to answer their questions or interpret the fine print. For many, even a trip that costs hundreds of dollars warrants advice from an expert.

Furthermore, time is a precious commodity for a great many people, and they will look to travel counselors in order to save time. As one travel seller told *Travel Agent* magazine (January 5, 1998, pp. 2, 131):

> People are going to try to learn as much as they can on the Internet. But do you want to book a $6,000 honeymoon without talking to anyone? . . . If you want to book a $299 weekend to Cancun and research your brains out, go for it. Or you can sit down and talk to a travel agent, and they'll tell you what they know from experience.

Ironically, the Web itself can create a demand for the travel counselor's help in dealing with the flood of information it provides. If a consumer searches the Web for "ski resort," he or she will be shown thousands of matches. Even a request for the combination of "Scotland" and "golf" will produce more than a hundred possibilities. How will typical consumers know what to make of all these choices? How will they know whether information found on the Web is outdated or biased, or whether sales on the Web are actually scams? Travel counselors will be needed, in Scott Ahlsmith's words, to give travelers help in "culling, valuing, and organizing mounds of data."

In short, tomorrow's travel counselors cannot just take orders or distribute tickets or look up information. They will prosper by providing clients with services that computers alone cannot offer: personal attention and the ability to filter mountains of data, to convert data into useful knowledge, and to interpret the value of products. In part, travel counselors will be returning to the roots of their profession. As Geof Cahoon, a travel-industry technology consultant, observed:

> The Internet has forever broken exclusive access for travel agents to airline rate, schedule and availability information. . . . What's left is the real business that travel agents have always had: getting the whole package put together with insider expertise, at the best price, faster, at a reasonable margin, and backing it as a local busi-

ness. (*ASTA Agency Management*, December 1997, p. 54)

Time Out

Check your understanding of the discussion so far by filling in the blanks.

1. To adjust to a changing marketplace, many travel agencies are joining chains or

   _____

   and changing the components of their marketing mix.

2. To adjust the product and price components of the marketing mix, many travel agencies are

   _____

   in what they sell, and some are testing whether clients are willing to pay

   _____.

3. Even though travelers can book many travel arrangements on-line for themselves, travel counselors will be needed in order to save travelers time, to filter the data available on-line, as well as to

   _____

   _____.

*E*nhancing Your Skills for the Future

Sometime in the not-too-distant future, the technologies of television, personal computers, and the Web might be brought together into one home appliance. Sitting in your living room, remote control in hand, you might be able to switch from watching a movie to paying a bill electronically to surfing the Web for a vacation package as easily as you now switch television channels. What will those vacation packages be like? Will Black Sea resorts and tours of Buddhist shrines be as popular tomorrow as the Caribbean and wine-tasting trips were yesterday? The world will not stand still.

Will you be ready for changes? Sue Shapiro, CTC, president of GIANTS, a travel agency cooperative, predicts that those travel sellers who "will be winners in this marketplace will have the education necessary to differentiate themselves from the rest of the pack." The need for training and education does not end once you obtain a job selling travel. How can you update and refine your skills in order to keep pace with the constantly changing world of travel?

The sources of information described in Chapter 3 and the Appendix on page 235 provide key aids for keeping up to date. Clip important articles from the travel periodicals listed in Table 3.2 (page 54) to keep on file or to share with clients. Make the best of every travel opportunity you have. Keep tuned for information from as many media sources as possible—from trade periodicals and travel books to specials on public television and travel chat rooms on the Web.

The most successful sales professionals go further: they pursue excellence by also enrolling in workshops and seminars, attending conferences and training programs, and seeking other chances to learn more. Let's take a brief look at some of the ways you can extend your professional education.

Continuing Education and Professional Development

The opportunities for continued education are boundless. You can find useful courses and workshops sponsored by colleges and universities, adult education programs, trade schools, and professional associations.

What should you learn? Strong sales skills form the foundation for professional success. A good understanding of geography is a plus. Additional expertise in computer skills, marketing, communications, accounting, and public relations will give you a competitive edge. These subjects are part of most college curricula. If you are unable to attend regular daytime classes, consider an evening or extension program. Also, to develop your computer skills, check adult education programs and workshops or seminars sponsored by the Small Business Association or independent computer organizations.

For more specialized education in travel, you can turn to professional travel associations. As mentioned in Chapter 8, the Institute of Certified Travel Agents (ICTA) offers a certification process with two steps. The Certified Travel Associate (CTA) designation is designed for those at an early stage in their careers. The CTA course of study focuses on core knowledge and practical skills; skill areas include geography, the travel industry, sales and service, and communication and technology. After completing the CTA program, many travel professionals continue the certification process by earning the Certified Travel Counselor (CTC) designation. Skill areas in the CTC program include business development, professional development, and global trends.

Many other professional organizations also offer training and education for members of the travel industry at all stages of their careers. Here are just a few.

- AH&MA (American Hotel & Motel Association) conducts an educational institute that offers training in all facets of the hotel industry.
- ASTA (American Society of Travel Agents) offers educational programs including courses on niche marketing strategies, mature adult travel, family travel, and special-interest travel. You can earn a Certified Specialist certificate by completing these courses and submitting a comprehensive marketing and advertising plan.

- CLIA (Cruise Lines International Association) has a two-step certification program: the Accredited Cruise Counselor (ACC) and the Master Cruise Counselor (MCC). Courses are offered aboard ships and in cities around the country. In addition to classroom training, the certificate programs include sales and marketing seminars, cruise conferences, ship inspections, and cruises.
- The Council on Hotel, Restaurant, and Institutional Education (CHRIE) offers education and training programs for the hospitality and tourism industry.
- The Convention Liaison Council (CLC) offers a certificate program—the Certified Meeting Professional (CMP) certificate. Criteria for earning a CMP include three years of experience and the ability to pass CLC's examination.
- Members of the National Tour Association (NTA) sponsor seminars, and the association awards a Certified Tour Professional (CTP) certificate to those who attain the required credits in courses and seminars and have five years of experience in the tour industry.
- The Society of Incentive Travel Associates (SITE) certifies members who pass requirements as Certified Incentive Travel Executives (CITE).

Finally, to become an expert on a particular country or region, consider destination education programs. Many destinations offer their own programs; Table 9.2 gives a sampling. These programs often include seminars, workshops, and even educational tours of the destination. For those who complete the program, the sponsor may offer consumer referrals, access to a help desk, a special listing on the destination's Web site, mailings of information about new products, and other advantages.

Table 9.2
Destination Training Programs

Program	Description	Contact
The Netherlands: Holland Travel Professional Program (HTP)	Home-study course with video and an optional trip to Holland	(888) 4-HOLLAND
Switzerland: Switzerland Network	Home-study course with video and an optional trip to Switzerland	(212) 757-5944
Germany: Destination Germany	Seminars, lectures, and a trade show in Germany	(212) 661-7200
Austria: Austrian Certified Travel Specialist (ACTS)	A nine-day program featuring travel through Austria	(914) 271-6941
Ireland: Shamrock Club	Home-study course with an optional trip to Ireland	(800) 223-6470
Wales: Wise Wales	Home-study program and study tour	(800) GO 2 BRIT
Australia: Aussie Specialist	Home-study program including a video	(800) 433-AUSSIE
Mexico: Magic of Mexico	Home-study program including a trip to Mexico	(800) 599-8633
Scandinavia: Scandinavia Travel Agents Registry (STAR)	Seminar with video	(212) 949-2333

ICTA also offers Destination Specialist (DS) courses that provide travel professionals with the knowledge they need to build sales to destinations throughout the world. The course materials help participants to master world geography and to develop the ability to use their knowledge effectively in selling travel. DS courses focus on specific regions of the world or specialized types of travel, including Africa, the Caribbean, China, corporate travel geography, Eastern Europe, Hawaii, Latin America, North America, the Pacific Rim, Western Europe, and special-interest travel.

A Plan for Action

In order to succeed in a career as a travel professional, you should map a strategy for enhancing your skills from year to year. First decide what skills you need to develop, what knowledge you need to acquire, and what time and money you can devote to this effort. Then you can investigate how to accomplish your goals.

We suggest that you use Worksheet 9.1 (page 231) to assess yourself and to identify five skills that you want to improve. List those skills in the space provided on Worksheet 9.2. Identify the steps you need to take to improve each skill and dates for completing these steps. Once you have improved those five skills, identify five more that need improvement and prepare another action plan.

Return to the self-assessment in Worksheet 9.1 periodically throughout your career to rate your skills. If you complete an action plan whenever your self-assessment score warrants, you will have a master plan for ongoing improvement throughout your career.

*C*hapter Wrap-Up

Chapter Highlights

The ever-changing nature of the world of travel adds to the challenges of the job of selling travel, but also to its fascination. In this chapter we have looked at some of the trends that are reshaping travel markets and the travel workplace, and we have suggested ways you can stay up to date and enhance your skills. Here is a review of the objectives with which we began this chapter.

1. **Describe some of the forces and trends that are reshaping the travel industry.** Economics, technology, political changes, natural disasters, and fashion may all have long- or short-term effects on the travel industry. Predictions about its future are thus hazardous. Continued growth has been forecast for the U.S. travel industry; but whether that forecast proves accurate depends to a great extent on whether the economy stays healthy and expands as predicted. In any event, babyboomers as well as travelers over the age of 65 are expected to remain the dominant demographic groups in the American travel market. If current economic trends continue, upscale travel, international travel, and meeting travel should be especially strong. Meanwhile, an increasing percentage of sales are likely to occur over the Web. But for the immediate future, on-line bookings will account for only a minority of sales.

2. **Identify at least four ways in which travel agencies are adapting to changes in the travel market.** In response to economic pressures, many agencies have either become part of a chain or joined a consortium, cooperative, or franchise. Many have turned to specialization as the path to survival. Travel agencies also appear to be alter-

ing their product mix, giving less emphasis to airline tickets and budget and economy hotels and more emphasis to sales that promise better commissions—such as car rentals, package tours, foreign travel, and midpriced hotels. Some have also begun charging fees for their services. Agencies are also adjusting the "place" component of the marketing mix by making sales through the Web and home-based agents. And even among agencies that do not sell on-line, the Web is becoming an important medium for promoting the agency.

Still, personal selling remains an essential component of the promotional mix. Although many travelers will use the Web to research travel information for themselves and even to buy products on-line, travel counselors will continue to provide invaluable services. For some travelers, that will mean saving them the time of doing research; for others, it will mean serving as a guide to Web-based information. For both groups, travel counselors can provide interpretations of the value of travel products and the benefit of their experience.

3. **Outline a plan for enhancing your skills and staying current with changes in the travel industry.** The first step is to decide what skills to enhance or what knowledge to acquire. Courses, seminars, and conferences offered by colleges, universities, adult education programs, trade groups, and professional associations all provide opportunities for continuing education and professional development. You can also learn a tremendous amount on your own through reading and experience. For ongoing improvement, assess your skills periodically, select skills to improve, and then prepare a plan for improving them.

Review Exercises

Check-Up

Give yourself a quick test of your memory of a few basic points. Read each of the following statements and indicate whether it is true (T) or false (F). See the answers below the statements.

T   F   1. Two demographic groups that dominate the travel marketplace are baby-boomers and senior citizens.

T   F   2. Within five years most travel sales are likely to occur over the Web.

T   F   3. Travelers are not willing to pay fees for a travel agency's services.

T   F   4. To enhance your skills and expand your knowledge of travel, postgraduate education at a university is essential.

Answers: 1. T, 2. F, 3. F, 4. F

Discussion Questions

1. **Preparing for Change.** What people buy reflects social, political, economic, and technological changes. Using the Sunday edition of your local newspaper, select a story relating to each of those four categories of change.

   a. What are the changes you selected?

   _____

   _____

   _____

   _____

   b. How might the changes described influence travel patterns?

   _____

   _____

   _____

   _____

   _____

c. What marketing strategy would you recommend in response to these changes?

_____

_____

_____

_____

_____

2. **On Your Own.** A friend tells you he is thinking of becoming an independent contractor. What characteristics do you think he'll need in order to succeed?

_____

_____

_____

_____

_____

3. **Web Wise.** You are a travel counselor at a leisure travel agency, and you've just handed your business card to an acquaintance who was telling you that she wants to take a vacation abroad in a few months. She says, "Oh, I've just gotten connected to the Web, so I don't need a travel agency any more." How would you respond?

_____

_____

_____

_____

_____

A Case in Question

Refer to the case on page 220 to answer the following questions.

1. What could Fran do if she wanted to attract more visitors to her site?

2. Do you think that would solve her problem?

Why or why not?

3. If Fran wanted a presence on the Web without the expense of establishing her own site, what could she do?

Worksheet 9.1

Self-Assessment

Take this self-test to determine your sales and service skills. Read each statement and circle the response that best describes your current attitude and behavior. You might want to duplicate this form before writing on it.

		Always	Sometimes	Never
1.	I use the 7-step method for solving problems.	5	3	1
2.	I try to understand my clients' technical and psychological needs when buying travel products.	5	3	1
3.	I am aware of where I am in the sales cycle of success and what I have to do to move forward.	5	3	1
4.	I use a variety of sources to gather information on destinations, accommodations, and tour products.	5	3	1
5.	I use the three-step process for developing rapport with my customers.	5	3	1
6	When recommending travel products to my clients, I focus on how their features will benefit them.	5	3	1
7.	I paint mental pictures for my clients when describing product recommendations.	5	3	1
8.	I use the five basic *W*s to determine the needs of my clients.	5	3	1
9.	I use both open- and closed-ended questions during a sales interview to understand my customers' needs.	5	3	1
10.	I paraphrase my customers' needs to check that I have correctly understood them.	5	3	1
11.	I deal with my customers' legitimate concerns in order to clarify information and move the sale along.	5	3	1
12.	I use CARE to listen effectively to my clients.	5	3	1
13.	I pay attention to body language when dealing with my clients.	5	3	1
14.	I use my client's communication style during a sales interview.	5	3	1
15.	I eliminate jargon when presenting product recommendations to my clients.	5	3	1

	Always	Sometimes	Never
16. I look for buying signals from my clients before asking for their business.	5	3	1
17. I make intangible products tangible for my clients by describing their benefits and using brochures or other visual aids.	5	3	1
18. When dealing with clients over the telephone, I adapt my voice and style.	5	3	1
19. Before placing a customer on hold, I ask permission.	5	3	1
20. I strive for consistent delivery of quality service.	5	3	1
21. I try to find out what services are important to my customers and how they feel about the quality of service I provide through formal or informal feedback methods.	5	3	1
22. I project a professional image.	5	3	1
23. I practice the ethical standards of the travel industry.	5	3	1
24. I manage my feelings of stress appropriately.	5	3	1
25. I practice the A-B-C method to manage my time.	5	3	1
26. I take advantage of opportunities to enhance my professional skills.	5	3	1
27. I look for trends in travel in order to maintain a competitive advantage.	5	3	1
28. I use primary and secondary marketing information to maintain an understanding of my customers and my products.	5	3	1
29. I follow a continuing education plan in order to stay current with the travel industry.	5	3	1
30. I am satisfied with my career path.	5	3	1

Total Points _____

Scoring Guide

- If your points total 150-100, you already practice effective sales and service techniques.

- If your points total 99-50, you use many sales and service techniques well, but you could improve your skills in some areas.

- If your points total less than 50, you have lots of room for improvement. Identify your weak areas and begin to work on them.

Worksheet 9.2

Action Plan

Use this form as described in "A Plan for Action," page 225, in order to build your skills. You may want to duplicate this form before writing on it.

Date prepared: _____

Skill	Start Date	End Date	Action Needed	Results
1. _____	_____	_____	_____	_____
_____	_____	_____	_____	_____
_____	_____	_____	_____	_____
2. _____	_____	_____	_____	_____
_____	_____	_____	_____	_____
_____	_____	_____	_____	_____
3. _____	_____	_____	_____	_____
_____	_____	_____	_____	_____
_____	_____	_____	_____	_____
4. _____	_____	_____	_____	_____
_____	_____	_____	_____	_____
_____	_____	_____	_____	_____
5. _____	_____	_____	_____	_____
_____	_____	_____	_____	_____
_____	_____	_____	_____	_____

Appendix

Travel-Related
Organizations and Associations

Airlines Reporting Corporation (ARC)
1530 Wilson Boulevard, Suite 800
Arlington, VA 22209-2448
telephone 703 816-8000
fax 703 816-8039
web site http://www.arccorp.com

American Hotel and Motel Association
(AH&MA)
1201 New York Avenue NW, Suite 600
Washington, DC 20005-3931
telephone 202 289-3100
fax 202 289-3199
web site http://www.ahma.com

American Society of Travel Agents (ASTA)
1101 King Street, Suite 200
Alexandria, VA 22314-2944
telephone 703 739-2782
fax 703 684-8319
web site http://www.astanet.com

Amtrak
60 Massachusetts Avenue NE
Washington, DC 20002
telephone 800 USA-RAIL
fax 215 349-3935
web site http://www.amtrak.com

Council on Hotel, Restaurant and Institutional
Education (CHRIE)
1200 17th Street
Washington, DC 20036-3097
telephone 202 331-5990
fax 202 785-2511
web site http://chrie.org

Cruise Lines International Association (CLIA)
500 Fifth Avenue, Suite 1407
New York, NY 10110
telephone 212 921-0066
fax 212 921-0549
web site http://www.cruising.org

Federal Aviation Administration (FAA)
800 Independence Avenue, SW
Washington, DC 20591
telephone 202 267-3484
web site http://www.faa.gov

Forsyth Travel Library, Inc.
226 Westchester Avenue
White Plains, NY 10604
telephone 914 681-7235
fax 914 681-7251
web site http://www.forsyth.com

Institute of Certified Travel Agents (ICTA)
148 Linden Street
Wellesley, MA 02482-0012
telephone 781 237-0280
fax 781 237-3860
web site http://www.icta.com

Jupiter Communications
627 Broadway
New York, NY 10012
telephone 212 780-6060
fax 212 780-6075
web site http://www.jup.com

National Association of Commissioned Travel
Agents (NACTA)
P.O. Box 2398
Valley Center, CA 92082-2398
telephone 760 751-1197
fax 760 751-1309
web site http://www.nacta.com

National Tour Association (NTA)
546 East Main Street
Lexington, KY 40508
telephone 800 682-8886
fax 606 226-4414
web site http://www.ntaonline.com

Plog Research
18631 Sherman Way
Reseda, CA 91335
telephone 818 345-7363
fax 818 345-9265
web site http://www.plogresearch.com

Society for the Advancement of Travel for the
Handicapped (SATH)
347 Fifth Avenue, 610
New York, NY 10016
telephone 212 447-0027
fax 212 725-8253
web site http://www.sath.org

Society of Incentive & Travel Executives (SITE)
21 W. 38th Street, 10th Floor
New York, NY 10018-5584
telephone 212 575-0910
fax 212 575-1838
web site http://www.site-intl.org

United States Tour Operators Association
 (USTOA)
342 Madison Avenue, Suite 1522
New York, NY 10173
telephone 212 599-6599
fax 212 599-6744
web site http://www.ustoa.com

U.S. Department of Transportation (DOT)
400 Seventh Street SW, Room 10413
Washington, DC 20590
telephone 202 366-5571
fax 202 366-5583
web site http://www.dot.gov

The U.S. State Department
2201 C. Street, NW
Washington, DC 20520
telephone 202 647-6575
fax 202 736-7720
web site http://www.state.gov

Glossary

American Society of Travel Agents (ASTA). A trade association that lobbies governments, presents educational programs, and speaks to the public on behalf of its members.

Assumptive close. Assuming a sale has been made because of customer buying signals.

Automated ticketing machines (ATMs). Machines that allow consumers to use a credit card to access flight information, make a reservation, and receive a ticket.

Benefits. The consequences of characteristics that are positively evaluated by the client.

Body language. Nonverbal communication consisting of eye contact, facial expressions, posture, gestures, and personal space.

Business travel. A category of travel that consists of travel services provided to a business. The travelers are conducting the business of the firm.

Buying signal. A sign that your customer is ready to make a commitment to buy the product.

Centrics. Those whose characteristics fall between those of venturers and dependables.

Choice close. A form of the assumptive close in which the salesperson offers the client a choice based on the assumption that the sale is made.

Close-ended questions. Questions that can usually be answered with a yes or no or with simple facts.

Closing the sale. The step in the sales cycle in which the salesperson motivates the client to action.

Communications style. The manner in which people communicate. The words people use and their eye movements define their communications style.

Complimentary close. Complimenting the client in a way that assumes that the client has decided to make the purchase.

Computer reservations systems (CRSs). Electronic systems set up to handle reservations and link distributers and suppliers to a centralized, computerized storehouse of information.

Conditions. Obstacles in the sales process that cannot be overcome.

Consolidators. Companies who buy unsold travel products in bulk from suppliers to be sold at a discount to travel agencies or directly to the public.

Corporate travel. See *business travel*.

Cross-selling. Offering additional products or service to a client.

Cruise Lines International Association (CLIA). The association that promotes cruising through public relations and advertising as well as by training travel counselors.

Customer service. Providing customers with what they need. The quality of customer service is defined by how it compares with the customer's expectations.

Database. An organized collection of data.

Demographics. A method of measuring characteristics of a population such as age, income, sex, and so on.

Dependables. People who focus on everyday problems and value familiarity and comfort; they are inhibited and unadventurous.

Direct close. Asking for a commitment to buy directly.

Direct link. A direct flow of information between a user and a computer reservation system.

Distribution channels. The ways in which travel products reach consumers. Travelers can buy directly from suppliers, or indirectly from intermediaries.

E-tickets. Flight information stored in a computer but not printed on a conventional ticket. Also known as electronic ticketing or ticketless travel.

Familiarization trips (fam trips). Trips offered to travel professionals at a reduced rate so that they can inspect hotels and restaurants, sample attractions, and experience the local culture.

Features. The objective and inherent characteristics of a product.

Feedback questions. Questions that seek the confirmation of details that have come up in conversation.

Five basic *Ws*. The essential bits of information you need to know about your clients' needs —who, when, where, why, and what.

Focus group. A group of about eight to ten participants and a trained moderator who meet to discuss a particular issue.

Four *Ps*. Four basic characteristics of a business: product, place, price, and promotion.

Hierarchy of needs. A theory that states that certain needs motivate people only if other, more fundamental needs have been largely satisfied.

Incentive travel. Travel that is offered by an organization as a reward; usually the reward is offered to employees for reaching certain specified goals.

Independent contractors. People who are self-employed and work under contract to a travel agency.

Institute of Certified Travel Agents (ICTA). The premier educational resource for members of the travel industry at all stages of their careers.

Interactive Agent Reporting (IAR). Software that automates the process of reporting airline ticket sales to ARC.

Intermediaries. Businesses that act as links between suppliers and travelers, such as tour operators and travel agencies.

Internet. The worldwide network of computer networks and computer services.

Leisure travel. Travel bought by individuals or groups for pleasure.

Marketing. A series of decisions and actions aimed at shaping consumers' preferences in order to make a match between a product or service and consumers' choices.

Marketing mix. The combination of variables selected to meet the needs of consumers.

Market research. The collection, analysis, and reporting of data relevant to a specific marketing situation.

Market segments. Clusters of individuals with similar characteristics.

Meeting travel. Travel that is undertaken to attend an organized gathering.

Mirroring. Body language between individuals in which they assume each other's position.

National Tour Association (NTA). An association made up of tour operators, suppliers, and destination marketing organizations.

Need for achievement. A need to excel, master tasks, and to set and achieve goals.

Need for affiliation. The need for positive relationships with others; people, not tasks, are the focus of your attention.

Need for power. The need to influence and control others.

On-line. Using a computer to connect with distant computers.

Open-ended questions. Questions that cannot be answered by a simple yes or no or with simple facts.

Outside sales agent. A person responsible for bringing new clients to a travel agency.

Override. Extra payments made by a supplier for a high volume of sales.

Personal selling. Making a sale through person-to-person contact.

Preferred supplier relationship. An arrangement in which a travel agency commits itself to maximize its use of particular suppliers; the supplier in turn may offer the agency an override.

Primary data. Information collected for the specific purpose at hand.

Process measurement. Measuring customer satisfaction by looking at how service was created.

Product measurement. Measuring customer satisfaction by assessing the results of service.

Professionalism. Mastering a specific body of knowledge and demonstrating a commitment to the standards of the occupation and to the interests of the client.

Prospecting. A preliminary stage of the sales cycle; finding new potential customers.

Psychographics. Grouping people according to their psychological characteristics such as values, beliefs, and lifestyle.

Psychological needs. The motives that influence a purchase.

Qualifying. A preliminary stage of the sales cycle; identifying potential qualified clients who have a need for your product, the means to purchase it, and the ability to make the buying decision.

Sales cycle of success. The eight steps of the selling process.

Salesperson. A person whose job is to identify the needs of clients and to meet those needs.

Satellite ticket printers (STPs). Machines that use a telephone-line hookup to enable a travel agency to print tickets electronically in the offices of their corporate accounts.

Secondary data. Information that already exists or has been collected for some other purpose.

Selling-up. Suggesting a more expensive, inclusive, or upgraded version of a product.

Suppliers. Businesses that own and control the product they are selling, such as airlines or hotels.

Target markets. Specific groups that sellers are trying to reach.

Technical needs. Specific features of a product required by the buyer, such as its quantity, date of deliver, and price.

Tickler files. Files that remind you to do something.

Time log. A record of what you do and how long it takes you to do it.

Tour operators. Companies who package several travel products together allowing them to offer discount packages.

Travel agent. The individual who sells travel arrangements to the public. Also known as travel counselor or travel consultant.

Travel consultant. The individual who sells travel arrangements to the public. Also known as travel counselor or travel agent.

Travel counselor. The individual who sells travel arrangements to the public. Also known as travel consultant or travel agent.

Trial close. The technique in the sales cycle of asking questions in order to gain the client's agreement and to move the client closer to purchase.

United States Tour Operators Association (USTOA). A professional association for tour operators who conduct business in the United States.

Value. The difference between the benefits of a product and the perceived costs.

Venturers. People who center their lives on varied interests; they are outgoing, confident, and curious.

VFR travel. Travel undertaken to visit friends or relatives.

World Wide Web. The system that makes it easy to present, link, and receive information on the Internet.

"Yes, but" method. A method for responding to an objection in which the salesperson first agrees that the objection is worthy of concern and then shows how it can be handled.

Sources and Further Readings

This selected bibliography is intended, not to list all works consulted, but to acknowledge writings used in the creations of this book and to aid those who would like to pursue these topics.

Part I
Getting Ready for the Sale

Travel Career Development, 6th ed., by Patricia J. Gagnon and Bruno Ociepka (Wellesley, MA: Institute of Certified Travel Agents, 1998) provides a more complete discussion of the topics examined in Part I. *Travel Agent* and *ASTA Agency Management* offer information on current conditions and events in the travel industry, and *Travel Industry World Yearbook, The Big Picture,* by Somerset R. Waters (New York: Child & Waters, 1997) gives updates on the status of all segments of the travel and tourism industry each year. More specific information on trends among consumers and travel sellers comes from studies by Plog Research; TTG's Path to Consumer Loyalty & Service Fees; and Yesawich, Pepperdine & Brown (YP&B) and Yankelovich Partners, 1997 National Business Travel Monitor survey; and the U.S. Travel Data Center. In-depth information and advice regarding travel products and the needs of various types of travel buyers are given in *Selling Hotels* (1996) and *Selling Tours and Vacation Packages* (1994) from the Institute of Certified Travel Agents (Wellesley, MA) and in *How to Sell Hawaii* and *How to Sell to First-Time Cruise Clients,* which are special supplements to *Travel Counselor* magazine.

Ahlsmith, Scott. "The Internet," *How to Sell Hawaii: Educational Sales Manual; A Supplement to Travel Counselor,* October 1997, pp. 50–52.

Forum Corporation. *Motivational Selling: Exceptional Performance.* Boston: Forum Corporation, 1986.

Gee, Chuck Y., James C. Makens, and Dexter J. L. Choy. *The Travel Industry,* 2d ed. New York: Van Nostrand Reinhold, 1989.

Jedziewski, David R. *The Complete Guide for the Meeting Planner.* Albany, NY: Delmar, 1991.

Jenkins, Darryl. *Managing Business Travel.* Homewood, IL: Business One Irwin, 1993.

———. *Savvy Business Travel.* Homewood, IL: Business One Irwin, 1993.

Mancini, Marc. *Selling Destinations: Geography for the Travel Professional.* Albany, NY: Delmar, 1995.

Plog, Stanley C. *Leisure Travel: Making It a Growth Market . . . Again!* New York: John Wiley, 1991.

Reiff, Annette. *Introduction to Corporate Travel.* Albany, NY: Delmar, 1994.

Rice, Kate. "Spending Trends in Travel," *ASTA Agency Management,* December 30, 1996, p. 10.

TTG. "Path to Consumer Loyalty & Service Fees Study," A Special Supplement to *Tour and Travel News/TTG North America,* December 15, 1997.

Part II
The Selling Process

Advice on how to deal with specific situations and problems in selling is given regularly in *Travel Counselor* magazine as well as in "Sales Clinic" columns by Marc Mancini and Arnold Sanow in *TravelAge/West.* Particularly useful information on the current use of technology by the travel industry is given in special supplements to *Travel Weekly* (September 8, 1997) and *Travel Agent* (July 28, 1998) magazines, as well as in the coverage of the 1998 ASTA Automation Survey in *ASTA Agency Management* (July 1998).

Becker, Dennis and Paula Borkum Becker. *Customer Service and the Telephone.* Burr Ridge, IL: Irwin Professional Publishing/ Mirror Press, 1994.

Cooke, Clif. "Publisher's Page," *JAX FAX Travel Marketing Magazine,* June 1998, pp. 2, 21.

deSouto, Martha Sarbey. *Group Travel,* 2d ed. Albany, NY: Delmar, 1983.

Edelson, Harriet. "Agents Are Riding the First Wave of Web-based Commerce," *Travel Agent,* June 1, 1998, p. 6.

Elliott, Elaine X. "Be a Web Whiz," *Travel Agent,* November 10, 1997, p. 28, 30–32.

———. "Working the Web," *Travel Agent,* April 7, 1997, pp. 26, 28.

———. "Online Outlook," *Travel Agent,* June 2, 1997, pp. 28 29.

———. "Low Fares Online," *Travel Agent,* March 31, 1997, pp. 22, 24.

Fairlie, Rik. "The Future of Cybersales," *Travel Weekly,* September 8, 1997, pp. 6–7.

Fine, Phyllis. "Good Vibrations," *Travel Agent,* April 7, 1997, p. 20.

Fisher, Judith E. *Telephone Skills at Work.* Burr Ridge, IL: Irwin Professional Publishing/ Mirror Press, 1994.

Hosek, Eric. "Could a Home Page Enhance Your Agency's Profit Potential?" *Travel Weekly,* December 25, 1997, p. 16.

———. "The Ten Commandments of Successful Marketing on the Net," *Travel Weekly,* January 5, 1998, p. 11.

Institute of Certified Travel Agents. *Sales Skills Development Program.* Videocassette. Wellesley, MA: Institute of Certified Travel Agents, 1992.

———. *Selling Hotels.* Participant Guide. Wellesley, MA: Institute of Certified Travel Agents, 1996.

———. *Selling Tours and Vacation Packages.* Participant guide and videocassette. Wellesley, MA: Institute of Certified Travel Agents, 1994.

———. *Understanding Client Needs: Travel Industry Core Course.* Wellesley, MA: Institute of Certified Travel Agents, 1998.

James, Art and Dennis Kratz. *Effective Listening Skills.* Burr Ridge, IL: Irwin Professional Publishing/Mirror Press, 1994.

Juliano, Suzanne. "Could Your Agency Use a Web Site?" *Tour & Travel News/TTG North America,* December 15, 1997, p. 20.

Langer, Gary. "Real-Life Stories," *Travel Counselor,* December 1996, pp. 22–28, 50.

O'Dowd, Sally. "Agents Get Wired," *Travel Agent,* July 27, 1998, pp. 20, 22.

Quinlan, Michael. "Building Your Dream Site," *Travel Agent,* July 27, 1998, pp. 24–25.

Saben, Tim. *Practical Business Communication.* Burr Ridge, IL: Irwin Professional Publishing/ Mirror Press, 1994.

Part III
Strategies for Sales and Marketing Success

Abbey, James R. *Hospitality Sales and Advertising,* 2d ed. East Lansing, MI: Educational Institute, 1993.

Aguilar, Leslie and Linda Stokes. *Multicultural Customer Service.* Burr Ridge, IL: Irwin Professional Publishing/Mirror Press, 1994.

Albrecht, Karl and Lawrence Bradford. *The Service Advantage.* Homewood, IL: Down Jones/Irwin, 1990.

Band, William A. *Creating Value for Customers.* New York: John J. Wiley, 1991.

Brody, Marjorie and Barbara Pachter. *Business Etiquette.* Burr Ridge, IL: Irwin Professional Publishing/Mirror Press, 1994.

Butters, John and Roberta A. Lew, editors. *Travel Industry Marketing.* Wellesley, MA: Institute of Certified Travel Agents, 1990.

Cahoon, Geoff. "The Future of the Travel Agency on the Internet," *ASTA Agency Management,* December 1997, p. 54.

Desatnick, Robert. *Managing to Keep the Customer.* San Francisco: Jossey-Bass, 1987.

Dobbs, Edwin. "Where the Good Begins: Notes on the Art of Modern Travel," *Harper's Magazine,* July 1998, pp. 59–64.

Edelson, Harriet. "Agents Are Riding the First Wave of Web-based Commerce," *Travel Agent,* June 1, 1998, p. 6.

Elliott, Elaine X. "Online Outlook," *Travel Agent,* June 2, 1997, pp. 28–29.

————. "Will the Web Turn Leisure Agents' Bread and Butter into Toast," *Travel Agent,* January 5, 1998, pp. 2, 131.

————. "What's Up on the Web," *Travel Agent,* November 3, 1997, p. 32.

Fine, Phyllis. "Surviving in Diversity," *Travel Agent,* December 2, 1996, pp. 74–76.

Glanz, Barbara A. *Building Customer Loyalty.* Burr Ridge, IL: Irwin Professional Publishing/Mirror Press, 1994.

Hill, Ruth. "The Net: Ally or Antagonist," *ASTA Agency Management,* June 15, 1998, pp. 12–14.

Joselyn, Robert W. "Don't Guess—Investigate," *ASTA Agency Management,* August 1991.

Langer, Gary. "Real-Life Stories," *Travel Counselor,* December 1996, pp. 22–28, 50.

————. "Leading Indicators," *Travel Counselor,* December 1997, p. 12.

Levine, Julie M. "Masters of the Web," *Travel Agent,* December 8, 1997, p. 46.

McGee, William J. "TC Interview: The Economy, The Future and Your Job," *Travel Counselor,* December 1997, pp. 26–29.

MacNeill, Debra J. *Customer Service Excellence.* Burr Ridge, IL.: Irwin Professional Publishing/Mirror Press, 1994.

Mancini, Marc. *Time Management.* Burr Ridge, IL: Irwin Professional Publishing/Mirror Press, 1994.

Merlino, Diane. "The Forum," *Travel Counselor,* October 1997, p. 16.

————. "Business Travel Trends," *Travel Counselor,* June 1998, p. 46.

Plog, Stanley S. "The Changing Landscape of Travel," *ASTA Agency Management,* October 1997, pp. 12–13.

Reilly, Robert T. *Travel and Tourism Marketing Techniques,* 2d ed. Albany, NY: Delmar, 1988.

Rosci, Frank. "Travel Purchasing: The Future Is Now," *ASTA Agency Management,* June 15, 1998, pp. 20–23.

Rosenbluth, Hal and Diane McFerrin Peters. *The Customer Comes Second.* New York: Morrow, 1992.

Sewell, Carl and Paul Brown. *Customers for Life.* New York: Doubleday, 1990.

Shapiro, Sue. Personal communication with Roberta Schwartz.

Sox, Rebecca F. "Questions of Ethics," *Travel Life,* May/June 1989, p. 14.

Tice, Kerry. "Consulting Fees Are the Way to Go," *Tour and Travel News/TTG North America,* December 17, 1997, p. 16.

Waters, Somerset R. *Travel Industry World Yearbook, The Big Picture, 1996–97.* New York: Child & Waters, 1997.

Whitely, Richard C. *The Customer Driven Company.* Boston: The Forum Corporation, 1991.

Zemke, Ron and Dick Schaaf. *The Service Edge.* New York: The New American Library, 1989.

Index